'Your Secret Language'

Classical Diaspora
Series Editor: Sarah Annes Brown

Classics and South African Identities
Michael Lambert
Russia and the Classics: Poetry's Foreign Muse
Zara Martirosova Torlone
'Your Secret Language': Classics in the British Colonies of West Africa
Barbara Goff

'Your Secret Language'

Classics in the British Colonies of West Africa

Barbara Goff

BLOOMSBURY
LONDON • NEW DELHI • NEW YORK • SYDNEY

Bloomsbury Academic
An imprint of Bloomsbury Publishing Plc

50 Bedford Square
London
WC1B 3DP
UK

1385 Broadway
New York
NY 10018
USA

www.bloomsbury.com

Bloomsbury is a registered trade mark of Bloomsbury Publishing Plc

First published 2013
Paperback edition first published 2014

British Library Cataloguing-in-Publication Data
A catalogue record for this book is available from the British Library.

ISBN: HB: 978-1-7809-3205-7
PB: 978-1-4725-8409-0

Library of Congress Cataloging-in-Publication Data
Goff, Barbara E.
'Your secret language' : classics in the British colonies of West Africa / Barbara Goff.
pages cm
ISBN 978-1-78093-205-7 (hardback) – ISBN 978-1-78093-467-9 (ebook (epdf)) – ISBN 978-1-78093-466-2 (ebook (epub)) 1. Classical education–Africa, West. 2. Education–Africa, West–Colonial influence. 3. Africa, West–Civilization– Foreign influences. 4. Africa, West–Civilization–19th century. 5. Africa, West–Civilization–20th century. 6. Great Britain–Colonies–Africa. I. Title.
LC1024.A37G64 2013
370.96603–dc23
2012045462

Typeset by Newgen Imaging Systems Pvt Ltd, Chennai, India

Contents

Introduction

In 1945, a young child in Africa acquired an anomalous form of immortality. His words were recorded by the *Report* of the Elliot Commission on Higher Education in West Africa, which was investigating, among other matters, the role of Latin in the West African colonies. The *Report* claims that:

> A small boy in another part of Africa, discussing the question of classical education, said to a member of another educational commission, years ago, 'We desire to learn Latin because it is your secret language, from which you derive your power.' (Elliot 1945: 16)

Without assuming too much about the historicity of this encounter with an unspecified commission, we can nonetheless acknowledge the force of the small boy's analysis.[1] He offered a trenchantly clear view of the colonial relationship, seeing it as structured around an unequal distribution of power between Africans and Europeans, and fuelled by quasi-mystical apparatuses of superiority. Within this relationship, the dynamics of education might well appear compromised, and so the boy represented Latin as a counter in a conflict rather than as a neutral, or even positive, piece of educational equipment. The boy's account wins its place in the Elliot Report because it so eloquently sums up one aspect of the struggle over cultural resources that did in fact characterize many interactions in British colonies. Yet by the time he entered the imperial archive of British government publications, the small boy's words would have to be put in the context of the many other roles that Latin, and the classics more generally, had been called upon to play within West African colonial culture. He formulates his response at an earlier stage – but arguably, by 1945, the small boy's view was wrong.

This study attempts to reconstruct a cultural history of classics in the British colonies of West Africa. By 'classics' I understand not only the languages of ancient Greece and Rome, but also the texts and artefacts; and I focus on West Africa because, as I shall show in more detail, the British colonies there developed a unique relationship with classical education that was not paralleled in other African colonies. My aim is both to shed light on the history of a discipline and to enable further understanding of the roles of education and culture within colonial and postcolonial formations. My inquiry seeks answers to the following questions in particular: how did West Africans react to education in Latin and the classics; how far did such education operate as a sign of oppression, of the 'colonisation of consciousness',[2] and how far as a means for personal and social advancement, or even as a tool for forging an anti-colonial politics? Why did Europeans bring the classics to West Africa, and how did they respond to the developing dynamic when West Africans laid independent claim to the classical heritage? In sum, how were the classics interwoven with the power struggles that characterized colonial systems and the resistance to them?

The answers that this study advances focus on the West African countries of Sierra Leone, the Gold Coast (which became Ghana on independence) and Nigeria. The period in question is approximately 1827 to 1957, a timeframe which extends roughly from the beginning of formal Western education in West Africa until the date of Ghanaian independence. For the purposes of this study I define 'classics' quite broadly. On the one hand, I am interested in the teaching of the ancient languages, Latin and Greek, in secondary schools and post-secondary institutions (neither Latin nor Greek was normally taught in primary schools). On the other, I also make use of a notion of 'the classics generally', the 'classical repertoire', in which I include the kinds of references to ancient history, literature and myth that might constitute 'cultural capital'. The very term 'cultural capital', drawn from the work of Pierre Bourdieu (1986), indicates how such a stock of reference might be useful for ambitious people who needed to work, and work against, systems, like that of colonial governance, which they did not help to build. While such a repertoire does not always presuppose acquaintance with the languages, it does usually accompany such knowledge, and in the West African colonial context, Africans who had been educated to the secondary level were likely to possess both the symbolic repertoire of classical reference and some acquaintance with Latin.

Although there is an obvious historical dimension to this inquiry, it is written not by a historian, but a classicist, and specifically a classicist with an abiding interest in classical reception. By 'classical reception', I mean the redeployment of classical texts and artefacts by subsequent societies and cultures. Within the discipline of classics, research into classical reception is a burgeoning sub-field, and within research into classical reception, the role of classics in colonial and postcolonial cultures has in recent years taken on a very high profile. This study hopes to promote further understanding in this area, and it therefore investigates not only the educational context but also the wider cultural, political and social contexts where classical materials are deployed by Africans and Europeans alike to support, resist or analyse the workings of colonialism. My inquiry is correspondingly targeted towards postgraduate students and scholars in several disciplines. The analyses and arguments are offered to scholars and students with interests in classical reception, in postcolonial cultural politics, in the history of education and in African history.

The materials for this study comprise evidence for the role of classics in educational establishments and in the wider cultures involved. I have drawn on British Parliamentary papers, school and university histories, autobiographies, essays, journalism and creative literature to construct a narrative in which classics emerges as a sign simultaneously of British cultural imperialism and of African cultural agency. While the situation of classics in formal education can often be read as a microcosm of the cultural conflicts attendant on colonialism, classics also has an important part in the articulation of African autonomy. As it did in Europe until very recently, knowledge of classical material in the British colonies of West Africa – the history and literature, but especially the languages – provided huge amounts of cultural capital, and in the colonial context, the acquisition of such capital by Africans became extremely controversial. Overall, I shall seek to show that in the very early period, Africans' classical qualifications contributed to the formation of an African 'middle class', and thus were welcomed by the imperial authorities as proof of the success of the 'civilizing' colonial mission, while occasionally deplored by other commentators both African and European. Yet the symbolic repertoire of classical literature and history was very soon pressed into service by supporters of African self-government like James Africanus Beale Horton, who promoted their arguments for African autonomy in part by showing that relations between ancient Greece and Africa predated the colonial construction of the 'classical tradition'. In the early twentieth century there were systematic attempts to withhold classical education from Africans, who by now were often equally, or more, determined to acquire it. Even the establishment of the new West African universities in the post-war period did not put an end to the conflicts over this prized cultural resource.

This narrative about classics is, as one might expect, related to the narrative about colonial education in general in the British African colonies, as discussed by, for example, Foster 1965 and Sivonen 1995. I suggest, however, that the classics held a special place, and warrant a dedicated inquiry, insofar as even from the earliest period, Latin was a prerequisite for university study, and thus either a gateway to the professions or a gatekeeper which prevented access to them. The ancient languages were also distinguished by the fact that, like mathematics, they offered a high degree of abstraction and so approached the status of an objective standard of achievement, something which became increasingly important in the educational context in the period under scrutiny.[3] On a different level of significance, the classical heritage of Europe which positioned British colonists to teach Latin and Greek to Africans, was also a major part of the claim to cultural superiority which fuelled much of the imperial project. Lord Frederick Lugard, whose works articulated some of the most compelling contemporary justifications for imperialism, suggested that (1926: 618):[4]

> As Roman imperialism . . . led the wild barbarians of these islands of Britain along the path of progress, so in Africa today we are repaying the debt, and bringing to the dark places of the earth . . . the torch of culture and progress.

If Britain can be aligned with the most prestigious cultures of antiquity, in terms of claiming a benign influence on other cultures, then its imperialism in Africa will be validated. The classical heritage thus plays a part in European cultural arrogance and in the corresponding intellectual subjection among colonized peoples, the 'mind-forged manacles' of cultural dependency, which anti-colonial writers have so often decried.[5] Yet even from the outset of such culturally colonizing activity, Africans drew on the classical tradition, including accounts of African contacts with ancient Greece, both to symbolize independence and to fight for it. The claim of Africa to its own classical tradition, and to relations with Rome and Greece that were independent of modern European imperialism, is a feature of several texts examined here.

To investigate the cultural politics of classics in the British colonies of West Africa is, then, to study a complex and often dialectical situation. This

Introduction will discuss the theoretical contexts in which I see my work unfolding, before moving to some facts and figures which help to situate the specific account constructed by this study. The Introduction will close with a preview of chapters.

Classical reception studies and postcolonial classics

The taxing dialectic between subjection and resistance – between British imperialism and African agency – is highly recognizable from other work on classics in colonial and postcolonial contexts, and also finds analogies in work on 'black classicism', the name currently given to classics within African-American culture.[6] It is arguable that a dialectical quality is characteristic of work in classical reception generally; classical reception interrogates the model of tradition which would involve classical cultures handing themselves down transcendentally to aftercomers, in favour of a dialogic model in which modern cultures appropriate elements of an antiquity that nonetheless potentially resists incorporation. In other words, classical reception studies hold that 'tradition' is never a one-way street in which the power or authority ultimately rests with the 'origin'; access to the classical repertoire is likely to be marked by conflict as well as homage.

In the colonial and postcolonial contexts, and in the case of African-American culture,[7] the new strategies of classical reception have led to a series of inquiries which broaden the scope of what is perceived as the 'classical tradition' and simultaneously develop an account of its politics. The notion of the 'classical tradition', as the sum of those texts and artefacts which draw on classical models or referents, in cultures subsequent to and different from ancient Greece and Rome, thus becomes inclusive rather than evaluative. Some inquiries in postcolonial classical reception have focused on literature by writers of African descent which explicitly draws on classical genres, including epic and tragedy.[8] Other work has adopted a wider-ranging field of inquiry and a different approach to what constitutes the materials of a tradition, going beyond the category of the 'literary' and directing attention to different kinds of texts and artefacts by people of African or Asian descent which had earlier been overlooked.[9] Taken together, this work has expanded our understanding of what counts as the 'classical tradition', and has correspondingly suggested its diverse political significances. Some commentators tend to emphasize the difficulty of remoulding the tradition so that it no longer confines or judges; others celebrate the ability of subsequent literatures and other discourses to escape the weight of the past. Still others seek to show that the classics themselves can be enabling and liberatory. All recognize the resourcefulness with which different populations seize on the traditional materials and make them work in new circumstances.

Recent studies have elaborated a series of different theoretical models with which to approach the phenomenon of colonial and postcolonial classical reception. In an earlier work, about African, African-American and Caribbean adaptations of the tragedies of Oedipus and Antigone, my co-author Michael Simpson and I offered the construct of the 'Black Aegean'. The 'Black Aegean' built on both Paul Gilroy's 'Black Atlantic' and Martin Bernal's 'Black Athena' to theorize a 'fluid and multi-directional'[10] zone of linked or networked sites which trade in representations of ancient Greece. This trade is 'undertaken by the colonizers as part of enforcing cultural superiority, and by the formerly colonized, both as "writing back" to the empire and as more or less direct, bilateral, creative negotiations with Greek works' (Goff and Simpson 2007: 39). Within the Black Aegean varying models of cultural transmission are available, so that violent, destructive versions of relations between the cultures of colonizer and colonized can be interrogated, and even overcome, by more generous, open-ended, or creative versions of exchange.

A similarly reciprocal model is discernible within Emily Greenwood's work on 'Afro-Greeks' in the Caribbean, which argues that 'reception of ancient Greece and Rome in anglophone Caribbean literature works both ways'. Her book thus examines 'how Caribbean authors have "received" Greece and Rome, as well as how they have returned original conceptions of Graeco-Roman texts' (2010: 2). The resulting 'dialogues' between the literature of Greece and Rome, and the anglophone literatures of the modern Caribbean, are characterized by 'frail connections' as well as by 'ruptures' (2010: 1, 3). The editors of *African Athena* make a similarly dialectical argument when they reassess the debates generated since Martin Bernal published *Black Athena* in 1987. In an endeavour to move beyond the polarities to which those debates have become subjected, the editors claim that 'we wish to emphasize the potent ambiguity of the phrase "African Athena": our self-consciously ambiguous title refers to both directions of cultural influence and diaspora, as they have occurred across centuries and millennia rather than at any arbitrary and specious "original moment'" (Orrells, Bhambra and Roynon 2011: 3). All these approaches valorize the circulation of the classical repertoire beyond its source and implicitly reject any hierarchy of origin and aftercomer. Together they provide one of the lenses through which the present study views classics in the British colonies of West Africa; the specific historical and political context in these colonies further modifies the account of cultural transmission which has been developed across the earlier studies.

The models built by classical reception studies for examining colonial and postcolonial cultures are thus highly significant, but within classical reception studies as a whole, another strand also has an important bearing on the present project. Much of classical reception studies seeks to describe and explain the role of what we are calling the 'classical tradition' in the formation of modernity.[11] At first, such a collocation appears paradoxical, insofar as antiquity is the antithesis of modernity, and European culture, at least, has often been divided between advocates of the 'ancients' and supporters of the 'moderns'. Yet a number of recent studies on historiography, philosophy, and psychoanalysis make clear how closely implicated are classical texts and metaphors in the defining discourses of modernity.[12] In the West African colonial context, classical education was an important dimension of the move into modernity which was also identified with Christianity and the use of English, and which was promised to Africans as the prime reward of colonial occupation. Appropriation of the classical tradition by nationalists subsequently ensured that classics would participate in the forging of postcolonial modernity in West Africa. The two strands of work in classical reception meet when we consider Paul Gilroy's argument, in *The Black Atlantic* (1993), that modernity is in fact generated by the encounter between Europe and black culture. To study classics in Africa is thus to study an encounter that potentially symbolizes modernity in particularly acute and demanding ways.

Empire

While classical reception studies are very important to the project of this book, I also acknowledge a debt to other types of inquiry. A huge body of work on the cultural politics of empire has suggested different models of how colonized peoples might approach the resources of the colonizing culture. Recent work has shifted focus away from accounts of colonial power as simply violent mastery, towards models which draw on notions of Gramscian hegemony, with its interest in consent, or conversely on James Scott's theorization of everyday resistance. Among theorists of colonial domination Homi Bhabha is important to this study for his discourse on 'mimicry', which is one of the major terms by which both Europeans and Africans have denigrated Africans' educational achievements. The line between the colonized subject who is not enough of a mimic, and the one who is too imitative, exercises the imagination of imperial pedagogy throughout this study.

Also particularly relevant to the issues raised here is the work of Simon Gikandi, on the investment in colonial culture on the part of the colonized. His work makes it clear that (1996: xviii):

> The colonized cannot continue to be conceived as victims of a triumphant Englishness that imposed its rule and civility on its radical other; on the contrary, the colonial space was to reconstitute itself in response to the imposition of Englishness.

His notion that the colonized helped to make colonial culture, and to redefine it (1996: xv), and that the culture of colonialism is one of 'mutual imbrication and contamination' (1996: xviii), is highly pertinent to analysis of the West African relationship to Western education generally and classical education in particular. For the purposes of this study an especially telling formulation is the following (1996: xix):

> One of the things that puzzled me about my people [East Africans] . . . is how strongly they detested colonial rule, which they fought tooth and nail, often ending up in prison, and how passionately they believed in the efficacy and authority of colonial culture. For many of them, this was not a contradiction: the reason they were fighting colonial rule was not because they wanted to return to a precolonial past . . . but because they wanted access to the privileges of colonial culture to be spread more equitably, without regard to race or creed. They wanted African children to be taught English so that they could have access to the institutions of colonialism, so that they could read Shakespeare in the original instead of having to rely on translations and adaptations.

Mutatis mutandis, this is a perceptive account of West African relations to Latin and the classics generally.

Gikandi's work implicitly builds on that of Valentin Mudimbe in *The Invention of Africa* (1988) and the later *Idea of Africa* (1994) which constructs and analyses the 'colonial library', the set of texts and representations which deliver Africa as locus of difference and alterity and thus enable it to be mastered by colonial discourse. The 'colonial library' is an almost entirely negative entity; in *The Idea of Africa* Mudimbe (1994: 29) cites the

> late eighteenth and early nineteenth conjunction of anthropology and colonial projects that hones the concepts and actualises, in the image of the colonized, all the negative metaphors worked out by five centuries of European explorations of the world.

In relation to a discourse of classics, a 'colonial library' would use classical texts and metaphors as weapons for the subjection of the colonized and to consolidate their cultural dependency. As does Gikandi, however, Gaurav Desai furthers and complicates this analysis by noting that the colonial library must also include the Africans who produce their own inventions of Africa (2001: 7). Desai's emphasis, throughout his analyses of pedagogic and anthropological discourse, is on the agency of the colonized subject and on subjectivities 'formed through resistance and accommodation' (2001: 174). Conversely, colonialism is described as fraught with contradictions and tensions, not singular or monolithic in its representations (2001: 10). When Desai writes that 'subalterns resisted, adjusted to, or even appropriated the changes that colonialism engendered among and around them' (2001: 165), we might align such 'subalterns' with Gikandi's collaborators in the making of culture.

Desai, and Gikandi, have some intriguing reflections on the differences, or rather lack of them, between the colonial and the postcolonial periods and discourses. Since this study spans these eras, such discussion is pertinent, particularly since we find classically educated proto-nationalists producing 'postcolonial' discourse in the late nineteenth century (Chapter 2), and texts from the mid-twentieth century, again produced by the classically educated, which explicitly seek to respond to the shift from dependency to postcolony (Chapter 4). Desai makes the point that texts produced by Africans under colonialism, rather than in the postcolonial period, are sometimes treated as suspect and even 'unreal', incapable of affording access to a lived history (2001: 162–3); his work sets out to recognize such texts instead as 'dangerous supplements' both to the colonial library and to 'our own postcolonial sensibilities' (2001: 170). It is insufficient, he argues, to declare the postcolonial identity as 'authentic' and 'liberatory', while consigning all former colonized persons to only one possible view of colonialism (2001: 175). For the purposes of the current study, a focus on classical references and metaphors brings to light a whole series of African-authored texts which do not simply articulate resistance to the imposition of European culture, but which coordinate different traditions, African and classical, with ingenious subtlety and sophistication, and make them serve a range of political stances.

Any study of classical education in British colonies must acknowledge the founding work of Gauri Viswanathan (1989) on Western education in India, and the more recent analysis of Sanjay Seth (2007).[13] How colonial India is relevant is because British authorities in Africa spent much of the period worrying that Africans would reproduce what they regarded as the undesirable trajectory of Indians, with respect to Western education, and they took the 'Mutiny' as an awful warning about the effects of a misguided education policy. Viswanathan clarifies the role of literary education 'as a major institutional support system of colonial administration' (1989: 4), which enabled 'the humanistic ideals of enlightenment to coexist with and even support education for social and political control' (1989: 3). Her formulations shed light on classics in the West African context. More incisively, however, following the lead of Edward Said, who posited a relationship of mutual implication between colony and metropolis, Viswanathan shows that English literature was codified as a subject in the colonial curriculum long before it was institutionalized in England (1989: 3). If the metropolis imposed its culture on the colony, via literary education, it is no less the case that the colony reciprocally remade the culture of the metropolis in a new image. This is also part of the argument of Gikandi 1996, in which the signs of Englishness are elaborated in colonial culture and return to interrogate, and remake, the metropolis.

Seth 2007 pursues the uneasy relation between colonialism and education. In his account, European colonizers assumed that Western education would naturally produce properly modern subjectivities in the Indian colonized, and concluded that Indians were inferior because they did not respond in predictable ways to Western education. Seth's analyses indicate instead that Western education did not in fact produce the subjectivities that colonizers had assumed were natural to it (2007: 43). Many of Seth's observations about colonial, Western education are relevant to the West African context; he reiterates the insight from postcolonial theory that colonial modernity did not simply 'stuff the heads' of existing people with new ideas, but made new people (2007: 4), and sums up usefully that 'colonial education is not simply a site where the skills of the modern could be acquired, because it was also a site where identities were produced and secured' (2007: 178). His work also points to one of the fundamental contradictions of colonialism, whereby it is a pedagogic project (2007: 2) that has grave reservations about the development of the educated (2007: 122):

> Colonial governmentality functioned to at once posit the possibility and desirability of governance through liberty, but always within a frame where that possibility was deferred, and where autonomous conduct was not possible – yet.

This contradiction was worked through in all its painful detail in the West African context of classical education, as is examined particularly in Chapter 3.

The studies of Viswanathan and Gikandi show how the cultures elaborated in the colonies return to inform the culture of the metropolis, remaking 'Englishness' as a colonial construct. While this study does not encompass classics in the metropolis, it shows how the discourse of the colonizers can mutate in response to African pressure. In particular, as Chapter 4 investigates, the European discourse of humanism, with its reliance on the classical tradition, is brought sharply into focus as a response to African articulations, both of the desire for self-determination and of the desire for classical education. African resistance and tactical appropriation of European symbols thus push at the frames of European discourse. In some of the official utterances which organize cultural transmission in the 1940s, the cross-fertilizing energies of the Black Aegean bring to light new ways to imagine and describe the relations between Africa and Greece. When early-twentieth-century commentators conclude, as they did, that no tradition is 'classical' unless it can resonate on the African continent, they implicitly redefine the classical as tested by Africa rather than simply guaranteed by Europe.

The triangulation of Africa, the classics and imperial Europe featured prominently in Martin Bernal's *Black Athena* (1987), and the current study, like much recent research on associated topics, comes in the wake of that seminal work. Bernal's analysis brought together what European tradition had often opposed to one another, the Greek and the African, and in a move indebted to deconstruction went on to show not only that they had always been mutually implicated, but also that the African came before the Greek, in the sense that African (and Asiatic) societies provided some of the materials for ancient Greek culture. Bernal's historical argument, by now largely familiar, is that the 'Ancient' model, espoused by ancient Greeks themselves, which describes Greek origins in interaction with African and Semitic cultures, was overthrown by nineteenth-century racist scholarship, but can be reinstated as the Revised Ancient Model. Mudimbe suggests that the work's significance lies in the fact that it is not just a revision but a reversal of perspectives (1994: 24): it 'witnesses to a reversal of what made possible and founded the slave trade since the fifteenth century; imperialism and colonialism' (1994: 104). Although Bernal's text is aware of certain accounts by writers of African descent which elaborate on the connections between Africa and Greece, it does not engage with the alternative histories provided by Mazrui's chapter 'Ancient Greece in African thought' (1978: 81–102), which were already interrogating the definition of Greece as European. Subsequent to *Black Athena*, Mudimbe 1994: 17–27, Selden 1998, and several chapters in Orrells et al. 2011, show that African and African-American writers repeatedly analysed the complex relationship between Africa and ancient Greece, contesting the 'white' ownership of classical antiquity from at least as early as the eighteenth century.[14] In the present investigation, we shall see West African proto-nationalist writers drawing on this tradition of contest from the mid-nineteenth century onwards.

Despite any apparent forerunners, however, Bernal's accomplishment marks the point where the classical establishment itself contributes to the project of 'universalis[ing] the Greek heritage and break[ing] the European monopoly on identification with ancient Greece' (Mazrui 1978: 94). I am aware, of course, that Bernal sited himself as an outsider vis à vis the classical establishment, and conversely that the outcry that greeted his work in some quarters might have suggested that classics as a discipline was still invested in Western cultural superiority. (I note also that classicists had many other, technical and scholarly objections to Bernal, separately from those which might appear ideologically motivated.)[15] But as I have indicated earlier, the last decade or so has seen an outpouring of studies of classics within non-European contexts, and this is one highly positive way in which the classical establishment has responded to Bernal. Although other pressures, political and cultural, have been brought to bear on the discipline of classics in recent years, the fact that Bernal invited classicists to be so self-conscious about the origins and commitments of their profession might even help to explain the phenomenon of classical reception studies overall.[16]

This study, then, acknowledges a variety of collaborators in its efforts to comprehend and describe the cultural politics of classics in the British colonies of West Africa. One other comparative context, which may shed further light, concerns how classics in African education may relate to classics in the education of other ideologically excluded groups, such as women or working-class people. There are very clear continuities. Bourdieu's notion of 'cultural capital' (1986) is perhaps tailor-made for understanding the prestige of classics within societies that are divided by class and status. Correspondingly, Christopher Stray 1998 and forthcoming, Françoise Waquet 2001, and Edith Hall 2007 and forthcoming have explored classical education as a means of class and subject formation and a method of patrolling, as well as permeating, class boundaries. These various studies show that classical education is regularly implicated in the maintenance of discriminatory structures, excluding women and workers from the educational ladders that lead to major social and financial rewards. Many aspects of the West African situation, especially as explored in Chapter 3, could be summed up with reference to the following account from Waquet (2001: 218) of Europe in the late eighteenth century; all we would need to do would be to replace 'peasant or artisan' with 'African' or 'native':

> Latin was not of the slightest use to the son of a peasant or artisan whose life would be spent behind a plough or bent over a counter or workbench, while for a merchant's son mathematics would serve better than Latin verse. In fact learning Latin was not just useless to the children of the lower classes, it might even be harmful, and not just to them but to the whole social fabric. For with Latin these children might also absorb ambitions above their station, which they would not be able to satisfy; so there was a serious risk that these men in adult life might become embittered enough to embrace extreme opinions or even rebel.

In the context of such strictures, the comment of the prominent liberal educator Victor Murray, who worked primarily in Africa, seems highly enlightening: the race problem is an aspect of the class problem (1929: xi).

Yet such studies as those by Stray, Waquet and Hall also show that the classical languages, with their highly formal patterning and explicit progression, enable mastery by talented individuals even outside of formal educational establishments, thereby providing routes to advancement in the teeth of rigid social expectations. Formal education generally is, of course, often responsible for the move from ascribed to achieved status which some commentators see as constitutive of modernity (Kendall 2008). While classical education can be seen to have operated in an analogous way in the British West African colonies, the overall context of colonial struggle means that classics can be called upon to play other significant roles as well, for instance providing models of cultural change which implicitly undermine imperial ideology (Chapter 2). Yet classics continued to exclude certain social groups in West Africa, as it did elsewhere; girls did not regularly learn Latin in West African secondary schools until very late in the period, and the schools which offered Latin and the classics, even when they began as philanthropic institutions, gradually consolidated identities as elite foundations which were financially unavailable to most students and families. While classical education might render porous certain boundaries between colonizer and colonized, it remained implicated in the construction of class and gender.

Numbers

Although this Introduction has suggested that the classical education of Africans could cause lively controversy, such education was only ever available to a tiny percentage of the African population. Sanjay Seth makes the point (2007: 2, 129) that agitated discourse about literary education in British India was in inverse proportion to the number of colonized people with such an education, and the situation in British West Africa was exactly comparable: classical education was of disproportionate interest, and provoked disproportionate anxiety, in comparison to the miniscule numbers of people involved. Such disproportion alerts us, of course, to the weighty ideological significance of the education at stake. Although the 'educated elite', as they were often known, were few, they exerted considerable influence across West Africa because they provided the professionals – the teachers, preachers, clerks, journalists and lawyers – who both served the colonial establishment and very quickly became some of its fiercest critics. Almost all exposed to Latin and to classical culture, they were the subjects of controversy throughout the period.

That said, the numbers of people who had access to classical education increased considerably during the period under examination. Although we cannot assume that all secondary schools taught classics, the growth of secondary education in the region is significant. As I shall discuss in greater detail later on, the nineteenth and early twentieth centuries saw just a handful of secondary schools in the region, but the number of establishments increased particularly after the twenties. What the basic numbers do not show is the various geographical imbalances, so that in 1914, for instance, there were 11 secondary schools in Southern Nigeria, of which 8 were in Lagos, but there was none in Northern Nigeria (Fafunwa 1974: 110); in 1938 Southern Nigeria had 33 secondary schools and Northern Nigeria 1 (Crowder 1968: 377). In the same year, 1938, Sierra Leone had 9 secondary schools, but overall, the coastal region of Sierra Leone educated perhaps half of its school-age children and the rural areas, fewer than 1 in every 33 (Crowder 1968: 376). For the Gold Coast, which is usually considered the most advanced British West African colony in terms of education, Foster calculates 400-plus secondary school students in 1930 and 1,200 in 1930, compared to 4,000 in 1940 and over 11,000 in 1950 (Foster 1965: 115). To put that in perspective, Mayhew calculates that the population of Nigeria in the 1930s was 20 million, that of the Gold Coast 3 million (Mayhew 1938: 194). In 1952 the region as a whole shows 68,000 students in secondary schools (Nuffield Foundation 1953: 4–5).

Other figures, including those for primary education, which grows apace during the period, can give further context. In 1920–1 the Phelps-Stokes Report shows one-tenth of the school-age population of the Gold Coast in school (Jones 1922: 57), and one thirty-fifth of the school-age population of Nigeria (Jones 1922: 156). Mayhew (1938: 200) suggests that in 1881 there were 500 Gold Coast children in school, in 1900 12,000 and in 1937 63,000. Crowder suggests that the 1938 figure was 76,000 (1968: 376). The compilers of *African Education* show 336 primary schools in Nigeria in 1920–1, but in 1952, 9,000 primaries educating over a million children; in the Gold Coast, *African Education* shows 35,000 children in school in 1920–1 but 300,000 in 1952 (Nuffield Foundation 1953: 4).

So far in this Introduction I have used the term 'West Africa' or 'British colonies of West Africa' without discrimination, but we should note some salient differences as well as similarities among Sierra Leone, Nigeria and the Gold Coast (which became Ghana on independence). Owing to their possession of coastal regions which had a history of trade with Europe, including the trade in slaves, each colony developed a coastal area that was relatively Europeanized, and usually housed some secondary schools, and a more rural hinterland where, in the cases of the Gold Coast and Nigeria, much indigenous resistance to the British was located, and where correspondingly few or no secondary schools were located until after the First World War. In each colony, the first establishments of European education, including the classical languages, were the work of missionary activity; the missions had usually arrived in the wake of the slave trade. Protestant missions, prominently including the Church of England and the Wesleyan Methodists, made the first running. Sierra Leone is distinguished by the particular history of the Church of England's initiatives; the Gold Coast is distinguished later on by the economic success brought about by the farming of cocoa (Agbeti 1980: 71), and the British government's corresponding openness to more educational initiatives. Nigeria is distinguished, for the purposes of this study, by the less happy legacy of Indirect Rule, and perhaps not coincidentally, the British establishment in Nigeria seems to show more resistance to Africans' classical education. All three colonies discussed here share, at least in their coastal areas, the culture of the 'educated elite', riven by the contradictions that classical education addressed and promoted.

One important element of the West African context that I have not felt qualified to discuss is the prevalence of Islam in the north of the region. The presence of Islamic communities and loyalties exercised considerable influence on British government policy, and constituted part of the overall culture of the area. The prominent politician and educator Edward Blyden, who was fluent in several ancient and modern European languages, was also equipped with Arabic, and was very interested both in the influence of Muslim culture on African communities and in the ways that Muslims in Africa might profit from European (colonial) education. Although the drama of classical education in the British colonies of West Africa played out in the Anglophone, Christianized context, for classical reception generally it seems likely that one of the next moves will be to examine more closely the relations between the classical tradition and the Islamic.[17]

The plan of this book follows a chronological order in which related issues emerge in different guises at different periods. For the first chapter, which considers nineteenth-century developments, the documents include the various Parliamentary reports which discuss the first advanced educational establishments in Sierra Leone and elsewhere, missionary reports, and some of the earliest histories authored by Africans. The chapter examines the role of classical education in the production of a new 'middle class' among freed slaves in Freetown, Sierra Leone. Contradictory reactions to Africans' acquisition of the classics are read in various different documents, and especially in representations of Samuel Crowther, the first African bishop in the Church of England. Chapter 2 reads the classical references in the texts of African 'cultural nationalists', from the nineteenth and early twentieth centuries. The essays and novels of James Africanus Beale Horton, Edward Blyden, Kobina Sekyi and Joseph Casely Hayford are mined for their classical tropes, which the texts put to work to construct different models of political change and of personal development, in order to combat denigration of African culture by European colonialism.

In Chapter 3, the focus is on the first decades of the twentieth century, when marked political and cultural transformations were brought about by the First World War. These decades saw perhaps the most energetic struggle over classical education, with British authorities now wishing to withhold it from Africans, against their vigorous opposition. The evidence includes prominently the Phelps-Stokes Report of 1922 and De Graft Johnson's *Towards Nationhood* of 1928, as well as autobiographies of African students and the history of Achimota, a school which endeavoured to combine the classical with the African tradition. Some of the prominent figures discussed include Lord Lugard, Henry Carr (the first African inspector of schools), and the educator James Emman Kwegyir Aggrey, all of whom were caught up in different ways in the controversy surrounding the figure of the 'educated African'. The final chapter examines the period leading up to independence, where the significance of classical education shifts, to some extent, and more of the relevant sources are generated by Africans. This chapter draws on articles in the termly magazine of Mfantsipim school to detail the tensions surrounding classics in the mid-twentieth century, and also examines the autobiographies of the prominent mid-century nationalists Robert Cole and Joseph Appiah, to investigate how classics might be deployed to produce a gendered, class-conscious, and nationally focused subjectivity. In this chapter I examine too how the colonizers' discourse of humanism responded to African pressure. The chapter closes with an account of the still-conflicted roles of Latin and classics in the new universities of West Africa, and a coda analyses Abioseh Nicol's short story 'The Devil at Yolahun Bridge'. This remarkable story in many ways captures the contradictions that marked the whole history of classics in the British colonies of West Africa.

I have worked on this study with the support of many different audiences and colleagues. I would like to acknowledge debts of common gratitude and various magnitude to: David Carter, Michael Gagarin, John Holton, Lorna Hardwick, Katherine Harloe, Bart Moore-Gilbert, Stephen Harrison, Matthew Nicholls, Kunbi Olasope, Daniel Orrells, Tessa Roynon, Michael Simpson, Christopher Stray, Susanne Turner and Phiroze Vasunia. I would also like to thank engaged and thoughtful audiences at the Society for the Promotion of Hellenic Studies, the University of Liverpool, the University of Reading, the Classical Association, the Archive of Performances of Greek and Roman Drama, the American Philological Association, and the Ancient Greek Breakfast Club at Godolphin and Latymer School. I would also like to recognize the work of the staff at the British Library and at the Library of SOAS, a remarkable institution without which this project could not have been undertaken, let alone completed. Deborah Blake, and her colleagues first at Duckworth and then at Bloomsbury Academic and Continuum, have supported the project with admirable energy and dispatch.

At another level of magnitude I would like to honour the mighty scholars of West African history, upon whose shoulders I certainly would not presume to stand. At another order of magnitude entirely, I thank the boys, all three of them.

Notes

1 I discuss this quotation at greater length in Chapter 4.

2 The phrase 'colonisation of consciousness' comes from Comaroff and Comaroff 1991.

3 But see e.g. Bishop 2006 for an interrogation of colonial mathematics.

4 See also Vasunia 2005 on the invocation of classical empires by Great Britain.

5 Among these, Ngugi Wa Thiong'o 1986 is one of the best-known and most incisive polemics.

6 'Black classicism' was a term used by Rankine 2006 to differentiate African-American authors' creative engagements with classics from the archival work undertaken by Michele Ronnick and named by her 'Classica Africana'. 'Black classicism' is now applied across the spectrum of studies of the intersections between classics and African-descended traditions; see e.g. Greenwood 2009, who implicitly applies 'black classicism' to African work as well as to African-American.

7 Space does not permit me to enter here into the debate over the extent to which the United States is a postcolonial society with regards to its African-American population; see Goff and Simpson 2007: 70–3 for a discussion.

8 Such work includes Wetmore 2002 and 2003, Hardwick 2007, 2006, 2005, 2004, Budelmann 2005, Goff 2005, Goff and Simpson 2007, Rankine 2006, Walters 2007, Cook and Tatum 2010 and Roynon 2013.

9 Here we might think of Ronnick 2005, Ronnick 2006, Hardwick and Gillespie 2007, Hilton and Gosling 2007, Greenwood 2010, Lambert 2011, Hall and Vasunia 2010, Stephens and Vasunia 2010, and Vasunia 2013. On these developments in scholarship see in particular Greenwood 2009.

10 See Greenwood 2009: 89.

11 I define 'modernity' as the assemblage of cultural forms promulgated by the West over the last two centuries, conditioned above all by industrial capitalism, rationalist science and social democracy. Other forms attend these, such as urbanization and the development of professionalized disciplines.

12 See e.g. Leonard 2005 and 2010, Miller 2007, Bowlby 2007, Morley 2008, Willis 2011 and Harloe 2013.

13 Much work is also currently being undertaken on classics in the education and culture of colonial South America. See e.g. Laird 2006, Fradinger 2011.

14 See in particular, within *African Athena: new agendas* (2011), the chapters by Keita, Malamud, Goings and O'Connor, and Roynon.

15 See Orrells et al. 2011 for the latest (positive) take on Black Athena from the classicists' side.

16 By 'other pressures' I refer to the persistent undervaluing of classics as irrelevant, still to be found in the utterances of Anglo-American politicians; an alternative threat, in the eyes of many classicists, is co-optation by the political right in the name of values, virtues or Western civilization. Pressure of yet another, more welcome kind is perhaps offered by the creative flowering which has seen so many new adaptations of Greek tragedy, and now of Homeric epic. See e.g. Hall et al. 2005, Unsworth 2002, Malouf 2009, Oswald 2011, Miller 2011.

17 This work is underway, but does not as yet occupy centre stage; see e.g. Pormann 2006–7, 2009.

1

Colonial Contradictions

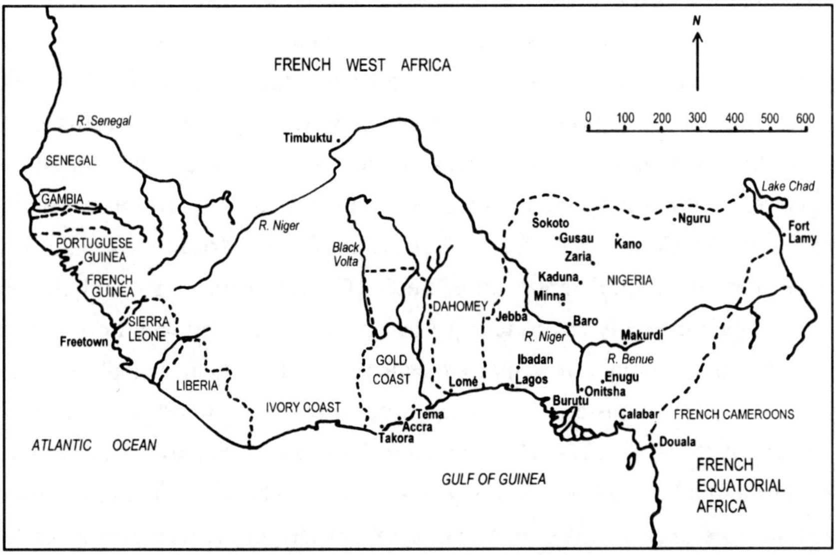

Map 1 Map showing the British Colonies of West Africa, ca. 1918.
Source: Adapted with permission from J. F. A. Ajayi and Michael Crowder ed. *History of West Africa*, vol. 2 (London: Longman, 1974): 426–7.

Although the west coast of Africa first attracted Europeans by means of trade in exotic commodities like gold and spices, the most important trade for many years was that in humans. From an early date the slave traders were shadowed, and usually opposed, by Christian missionary enterprises. By the middle of the nineteenth century, missions had entered into what are now Sierra Leone, Nigeria and Ghana (then the Gold Coast); because of the slave trade, the coastal areas had been open to European influence for a long time, so the missions established themselves first in these areas, and rarely made much headway into either the interior, or predominantly Muslim areas such as northern Nigeria, whose cultural influences came more from the east. From this missionary activity resulted the introduction of formal classical education among indigenous West Africans. From the first such educational initiative to the achievement of political independence, we can study over 100 years during which the relationship of West Africans to classical education underwent several shifts, provoking conflicts that were symptomatic of, even as they contributed to, the profile of culture under colonialism.

In this chapter I shall first examine the early accounts of classical education among West Africans, and the ways in which it contributed to the formation of an emergent class of often Christianized, Europeanized professionals. Although the formation of this class depended on a particular notion of the imperial project, which was in turn closely allied to the work of the British government and the Church Missionary Society in Sierra Leone, the class itself spread across the region, and classically educated men became prominent in all three colonies. When the ideas of empire modified and became more aggressive, in the movement which led eventually to the partition of Africa at the Berlin Conference of 1884 (the 'scramble for Africa'), this class was likely to produce vocal opponents of empire. Classical education could thus be lauded, by Europeans, as producing Africans who identified with Europe and the 'civilizing mission', or suspected, as fostering discontent. I shall examine these two perceptions of classical education with special reference to Samuel Ajayi Crowther (ca. 1807–91), the first non-European bishop to be consecrated in the Church of England.[1] In the final part of this chapter I shall move from mainly European sources to examine the variety of African responses to classical education in the early period.

Why classical education took root in West Africa is a question with complex answers. The region had long had various kinds of intercourse with Europe, although for centuries that intercourse had included the highly toxic element of the slave trade, and the establishment of the empire on the west coast was certainly not a simple matter of British military force against primitive tribesmen. Britain had, in fact, a series of treaties with some of the peoples of the region,[2] and was invoked as an ally in various conflicts among different peoples, especially in the Gold Coast. Relationships between Britain and the inhabitants of West Africa were thus only gradually codified into the starkly unequal terms of imperial domination.[3] A recent commentator notes that 'the weight of imperial authority' could be lighter in this region than in other parts of Africa (Caine 2010: 159). To say this is not to assent to J. R. Seeley's notion that Britain acquired her empire in a fit of absence of mind,[4] but it is to note the complexity of colonial relations in the area, which made possible some of the ways in which European culture became embedded in the region, with the consent and cooperation of some of the indigenous peoples. F. Ugboaja Ohaegbulam claims that there is 'abundant evidence to document the ease with which various African societies adopted specific European values and practices which they believed to be beneficial' (2002: 5).

West Africans then had long-standing relations with Europeans, which had not always been characterized by the binary of force and resistance. West Africa was, moreover, characterized by persistent social mobility which made it often receptive to new cultural imports – such as, in this case, classical education. Stephanie Newell characterizes West Africa via a 'migratory subjectivity', with a 'cultural and economic vitality that pulses through the region', further noting that (2006: 13):

> The popular image of a remote African village tucked away in a forest, bound by tradition and untouched by external influences, is a myth invented by colonialists and cultural nationalists to serve their own ideological purposes . . . human beings are constantly on the move in west Africa ...

Terence Ranger, in his seminal work on the invention of tradition within colonial Africa, underlines how 'competition, movement, fluidity' were features of societies which colonial authorities sometimes wished to see as static and unchanging (1983: 248), and several authorities have also pointed to the figure of the 'mediator', or cultural 'middleman' (Koehl 1971, Peel 2003: 8), translating one group to another, as a prominent part of West African society and one which facilitated the assimilation of European culture in the region. Ajayi (1965: 20–1) notes also the movement of peoples consequent on the slave trade and the Yoruba wars, which facilitated missionary penetration into the area. West Africa was, then, relatively prepared both in historical and in cultural terms to encounter European and specifically classical education.

This is not to say, of course, that the European colonial incursions met with no resistance. Although some West African communities identified certain opportunities in the contacts with Europeans, others worked energetically to preserve their own values and traditions, and made the Europeans pay in blood and treasure for the huge territorial gains that they eventually achieved.

Varieties of resistance and cooperation will be part of the account here of the cultural politics of classics. While some critics conclude that the West Africans who embraced European education were simply deluded as to the ultimate goals of the Europeans, others suggest that they were trying to respond creatively to the forces unleashed on their continent.[5]

The first West African to learn Latin and ancient Greek within the British colonial context may have been Philip Quaque (1741 to 1816), who was born in the Gold Coast, and sent for education in Britain by the Methodist missionary Thomas Thompson, who had been successfully working in the Gold Coast since 1751.[6] Quaque studied at the Islington establishment of the Society for the Propagation of the Gospel, and was ordained in 1765 – the first non-European to be ordained in the Church of England (Bartels 1965: 4). On his return to the Gold Coast he remained as missionary and schoolmaster at Cape Coast Castle, where a school had been founded for the children (by African women) of the European traders and soldiers who were stationed there (Bartels 1965: 23–4). Although the Revd. Quaque calls himself 'unletter'd in the many Branches of the Greek and Persian Sciences' (Carretta and Reese 2010: 47), he would have had to learn Latin for ordination, but no commentator concludes that he taught Latin or Greek to the students in his school.[7] We should note that these few students were children of mixed parentage, the offspring of European men and West African women, so they were already perhaps positioned between cultures before they were exposed to Western education. The connections between such education and anomalous cultural positioning will be a keynote of the present investigation. As sons of white men, Quaque's students may have been regarded as elite, and indeed Philip Quaque was himself the son of an indigenous chief (Bartels 1965: 23–4). The 'elite' nature of classical education in the British colonies of West Africa is another theme that will recur in the present study.

The story of the Revd. Philip Quaque brings out a few other important issues, which remain critical throughout the period under discussion. Of the two other boys who were sent to London to study with him, one died of tuberculosis and one went mad and died in an asylum (Carretta and Reese 2010: 9). To survive the acculturation to Western education was no easy task. Conversely, missions in the British West African colonies suffered well into the nineteenth century from very high mortality among Europeans, and this was to have a noticeable effect on the acquisition of classical education by Africans.[8]

A further important point is the close connection, in the early period, between the establishment of Christianity in the region and the acquisition of classical languages by Africans. Not only was Quaque both missionary and schoolmaster, but all the other early educational initiatives in the area were undertaken by missions. Since the first in the region were the Protestant missions, they taught classical languages in order that Africans might be able to read the Bible in the original languages.[9] To this end they quite often taught Hebrew as well as Latin and Greek, and New Testament Greek as well as the Attic of standard texts like Plato. As missions gained in confidence and experience, the close relations between education and Christianity meant that education could often be a part of mission attempts to break down indigenous cultures and draw children away from their family context into new ways of living and thinking.[10] Where Christianity was embraced, then, it was likely that education would also find favour; conversely, both the new religion and the new cultural equipment might be rejected in order to preserve a society which rapidly, and correctly, perceived itself as under threat. Over time, these projects of the missions could conflict with government ideology about education and acculturation generally, and the changing relations between the missions and the colonial administration will be a further strand in the present account. The school of Quaque at Cape Coast was anomalous in being supported by the British government as well as by the missionary Society for the Propagation of the Gospel.[11]

Although the classical languages first took hold because of the access they afforded to Christian texts, they also bore with them the huge weight of the cultural authority which they had accrued over centuries in Europe, so that they were not ever simply handmaidens to scriptural reading. We shall see some of their other pivotal roles in the course of this study, but should note that although the first Christian institutions taught Hebrew, as well as Latin and Greek, to their young men, once secondary schools were founded which purveyed a more general education, Hebrew became less central. Although the classical languages were usually taught in the context of Christian establishments, they gradually became a sign less of preparation for ministry and more of professional, elite aspiration.

One final point to note overall is that classical languages were taught in an environment where the cultural politics of English were also at stake, and Latin in particular was often ostensibly prized because of its support for the learning of English. From one perspective, the issue of classics is a cadet branch of the issue of English, which was debated more extensively and intensively throughout the period because of its status as the language of the empire. Numerous policy documents and anecdotal accounts discuss the merits of keeping primary education in a vernacular or insisting on English at that relatively early stage; almost all agree that in the secondary context, English is necessary. Those Africans who learned Latin or Greek, then, learned it while speaking another foreign language, albeit one which they had probably been practising since the primary years. Within the debates about English versus vernacular languages, some of the positions we shall encounter are the same as are rehearsed regarding Latin and Greek; on the one hand, there is perhaps less cultural imperialism about the gesture of teaching in the vernacular, but on the other, Africans could readily see that English would serve them better in their attempts to negotiate with the colonial structures that were rapidly consolidating. To withhold English, then, becomes as aggressively imperialist as to impose it – and the dynamics of the colonial situation are very similar when it comes to Latin and Greek.[12] Within such a dynamic, the classical languages carved out for themselves further specific roles – upholding imperial ideology, fostering cultural dependency, yet also articulating autonomy and resistance.

The Freetown experiment

Although the slave trade in the British colonies was abolished in 1807, the British took if anything more of a proprietary interest in West Africa after that date. Slaving itself persisted, and British naval vessels were subsequently stationed along the west coast of Africa, principally in Sierra Leone, to intercept any ships which were receiving slaves captured in the interior. These slaves would be bound for transportation to the Americas, but if 'recaptured' by the British, they would be set free. At the same time, the British government and missions too were engaged in developing 'legitimate' trade in West Africa, and above all, in bringing the contemporary trinity of 'Christianity, commerce and civilisation' to those who could be seen, at that historical juncture, as the benighted heathen.[13] What is most interesting for our present purposes is that the freed slaves, those recaptured by the British anti-slavery ships, were largely settled by the British government in the coastal areas of Sierra Leone, where they eventually formed a recognizably new kind of society. In 1787 Sierra Leone had been the scene of an early philanthropic experiment when freed slaves living in London were settled there under the leadership of the abolitionist Granville Sharp. They nearly all died, but in 1794 a second wave of freed slaves, emigrating from Canada, was more successful in surviving the difficult conditions. Such freed slaves and 'recaptives' or 'Liberated Africans' were, of course, of African descent, but although in West Africa, they were often far from their ancestral territories. Since they also included numerous African ethnicities and native languages,[14] they faced multiple obstacles in developing a working society and culture in their new land.

On arrival in Sierra Leone, the recaptives were granted some land and other resources by the British government, and from an early date they were also offered education and church membership by the missionary arm of the Church of England, the Church Missionary Society (CMS), which in 1816 entered into an agreement with the British government to educate the children of the colony (Wyse 1989: 3, cf. Sumner 1963: 20–32). Over time the people thus settled in Sierra Leone came to be called Krios, or Creoles,[15] and to form a particular society with recognizable characteristics. Distinguished by conversion to Christianity and the use of both English and a new English dialect, also called Krio, they shared as well a high level of exposure to classical education. Because of the initial philanthropy of the British government, moreover, the Krios were likely to consider themselves loyal to Britain, and even to identify wholeheartedly with English culture and mores. The notion of the 'Black Victorian', which later came to identify people in other regions as well, had particular relevance for the Krios (Dixon-Fyle and Cole 2006: 3), indicating not only commerce and Christianity, but also 'Victorian' qualities such as industry, sobriety and moral rectitude.[16] Although the settlements began as agricultural, the land proved less than cooperative, with the result that the recaptives or Liberated Africans were likely to turn to trade, and in a couple of generations were producing middle-class professionals, lawyers and doctors, as well as teachers and religious personnel (Wyse 1989: 5–7). Within these new social formations the classical languages played an important role as a form of cultural capital.

It was quickly recognized that this settlement in Sierra Leone was an experiment, testing how Africans would fare under a benign European paternalism rather than as victims of institutionalized European violence.

As such, it was host to educational initiatives of extraordinary ambition, and as early as 1821 the Christian Institution, founded by the CMS, had eleven boys beginning 'the Latin grammar, which they found a very difficult study' (Walker 1847: 121).[17] In 1827, the British government received the Report of the Commissioners of Enquiry into the State of the Colony of Sierra Leone, which opined that: 'The great increase in Freetown, and the circumstances of its inhabitants, seem to require the establishment of a seminary where a limited number of youths might receive a more liberal education than is at present afforded' (Rowan and Wellington 1827: 70). In the same year the Christian Institution moved to Freetown and became the Fourah Bay College, with the explicit aim of offering an advanced education to selected African boys.[18] Designed ultimately to fit such boys for ordination, it was in effect a seminary education, and included the classical languages from the outset. By 1842, it could also be described by an official missionary source as preparing teachers, not only for Sierra Leone but also for other parts of Africa (Sandon 1842: 461).[19] The plan of instruction, as communicated by the secretaries of the CMS in 1842, included (Crowther 1970: 391):

> (1) English Composition, Geography, and History; (2) Arithmetic, Euclid, Algebra, Trigonometry, and the branches of Natural Philosophy; (3) The Elements of Latin and Greek; (4) the most considerable of the Native Languages of West Africa; (5) Vocal Music; (6) Drawing and Perspective; (7) Scriptural Instruction, including the Holy Scriptures, as the basis of all Religious teaching; (8) Ecclesiastical History, with the Government, Formularies, and Articles of the Church of England; (9) Exposition of Scripture, composition of sermons, and the method of communicating knowledge to others.

While this programme of education is clearly shaped towards the ministry, it also represents an ambitiously academic training, and is remarkable in valuing the native languages along with English, Latin and Greek. In 1845 a Grammar School was founded, also by CMS, in order to feed better equipped students into the College, and it provided instruction in Latin among other subjects.[20] In 1875 the Methodists founded a rival Boys High School in Freetown which offered 'Latin, Greek, French, Ancient Histories, English and its usual branches, Arithmetic, Algebra, Geometry, Trigonometry, Mensuration, Book-keeping, Phonography, Physical Science' (Wyse 1989: 8).

Thus by mid-century the classical languages were well established as an integral part of what British colonialism had to offer to the ambitious and able among its African dependents. Their role as preparation for ministry meant that they were seen as conducive to positions of leadership within the newly developing colonial society, and within a few years, boys from other parts of West Africa were also attending the Freetown schools. Aaron Belisarius Cosimo Sibthorpe, the African who published the first *History of Sierra Leone* in 1868,[21] indicates that he went to school with boys from the Gold Coast, Nigeria and the Gambia (1970: 167).[22] Conversely, recaptives from Sierra Leone migrated into Nigeria in the 1840s, and established a mission and a seminary at Abeokuta, near Lagos.[23] The culture of European education, with its role for the classical languages, thus spread throughout the region, and was instrumental in providing the contours of an educated, professional identity. That such an identity should develop in the colonial context of West Africa attracted comment both favourable and hostile.

Contemporary government and missionary sources are loud in their praise of Freetown's College and Grammar School. Walker's history of the Church of England Mission in Sierra Leone suggests that the ten boys in the College in 1845 appear 'to be engaged in a curriculum of studies such as it is probable few public schools in our own favoured land impose among their youthful alumni' (1847: 556). The Revd. Edward Jones,[24] an African-American clergyman and head of the College, wrote in his official report (Walker 1847: 556) that:

> The students have gone over, verse by verse, the first eighteen Chapters of St. Matthew's Gospel; have read through Parts I and II of Horne's Compendium, on the genuineness, authenticity, and inspiration, literary history, and interpretation of the Scriptures; and have committed to memory the whole of the Articles of the Church of England, referring other works bearing on the subject. The Greek class have read Valpy's Grammar, through a portion of the Syntax, with the first twenty pages of his Delectus.[25] With two exceptions their progress is very encouraging. In Geography, the portions relating to Africa and British North America have occupied the class. The text-book, is Ewing's, and they possess a creditable knowledge of it. Euclid and Algebra have been taken up by them with some earnestness. They have gone over the first thirty Propositions of the First Book of Euclid, and through Involution in Algebra. In general History, with Keightley's Outlines as a text-book, the history of Rome has been proceeded with, from its origins

> to the commencement of the reign of Diocletian. English Grammar and composition may be truly called our 'questiones vexatae'. There is, however, a slow but manifest improvement. On the whole, I must say that their progress and diligence have been praiseworthy.

We may note that the classics here appear under the sign of history as well as of language. There is here no Hebrew, although it will appear shortly, so we may see the classics serving the same 'liberal' purposes that they did in comparable European institutions. In the same volume, the Revd. Thomas Peyton reports on the newly founded Grammar School, which had taken the younger pupils from the College (Walker 1847: 557). Here, there are more students, and they are divided into different classes, which are distinguished partly by the presence or absence of Greek:

> The number of pupils is now thirty.... The whole are divided into two classes. The course of instruction pursued by the first division embraces English Grammar and composition, Greek, Mathematics, Geography, Astronomy, with the use of the Globes and Mapping, Bible history, the thirty-nine Articles, English history, writing, and recitation from the English reader, and music. The second class follows the same courses, with the exception of Mathematics and Greek.

A few years later, another Report to the British Parliament, on the State of Her Majesty's Colonial Possessions, explained the educational provision in Sierra Leone in even greater detail (Macdonald 1851: 191).[26] Again it is interested in both Fourah Bay College and the related Grammar School.

> The first [of the leading educational institutions in Freetown] is the Fourah Bay institution, under the personal superintendence of the Revd. Edward Jones, of the Church Missionary Society, in which the students receive instruction in the following branches of education: namely–
>
> For the First Year. – in Arithmetic, English Grammar and Composition, Geography, Greek, Hebrew, Algebra and Scripture History.
> For the Second Year. – in Algebra, Euclid, English Grammar and Composition, Greek, Hebrew and Scripture History.
> For the Third Year. – Trigonometry, Greek, Hebrew, Arabic, Introduction to the Bible, Articles of the Church, General History. And –
> For the Fourth Year. – Greek, Hebrew, Native Languages, General History, Church History, Introduction to the Bible and the writing of Sermons.
>
> . . .

> The second educational establishment, belonging to the Church Missionary Society, is the Freetown Grammar School, under the superintendence of the Rev. T. Peyton.
>
> The students of this school are divided into classes.
>
> The first class, as appears by the plan of instruction pursued at the grammar school, are educated in Lineal Drawing, Nicholl's Help to the Bible, Arithmetic, Algebra, Greek and Grecian History, Mensuration, English Grammar, Geography and the use of the Globes, Latin, Euclid, Music, Writing and Drawing, Singing and in writing Themes.

From these reports we may conclude that the College is distinguished by its teaching of Greek and Hebrew, while the Grammar School lays a foundation in Latin. The teaching of history quite often includes either Roman or Greek.

A. B. C. Sibthorpe, the Sierra Leonean historian cited above, describes the situation in slightly different terms and explains that the 'schoolmaster's' class at the Grammar School enjoyed only the 'English studies', which included 'Grecian, Roman, and Bible histories', but the 'foundation pupils' added, 'as they were intended for the Fourah Bay College, classics and mathematics rightly so called' (1970: 167). The classes below the first or 'foundation' thus did not enjoy the benefits of Greek or Latin, or Algebra and Euclid. Sibthorpe goes on to demonstrate the symbolic heft of classics and mathematics when he proclaims: 'The writer belonged to the former ["schoolmaster's", "English studies"]. No sooner, however, had Mr Quaker taken up the school than he ordered publicly in the school: "Sibthorpe must take up mathematics and classics; English studies are too easy for him"' (1970: 167–8).[27] Sibthorpe devotes a good proportion of his history to schools (1970: 147–89), showing us that there were a handful of other schools as well as the CMS Grammar School in late nineteenth-century Freetown, including one for girls, the Annie Walsh Memorial School (founded 1849). While the girls' school did not offer classical languages, others such as the Wesleyan Methodist Boys' High School (opened 1874) and the Leopold Educational Institute (opened 1884) did so.

The outlines of this education, with its emphasis on literary rather than practical activity, and its high regard for religious instruction and ancient languages and history, are typical of English secondary education at the time and indeed, as Françoise Waquet 2001 has shown, of education across Europe. The classics and mathematics, from which the less advanced classes are excused, will for the rest of the period under examination afford the touchstone of an aspirational post-primary education. They are also, of course, what European missionaries would expect to teach, because they are what they learned themselves when at school, and what they conceive of as appropriate preparation for those called to lead the church. Thus one of the missionaries sent out to teach at the Christian Institution, later Fourah Bay College, who died in 1823, wrote (Walker 1847: 191):

> I commenced a regular course of study. In the morning I translated a chapter of the epistle to the Ephesians from the Greek; and have begun with the assistance of the best German critics, to write a brief explanation of the epistle. In the afternoon I either write sermons or translate Psalms out of the Hebrew. These employments afford me many pleasures; – and I often think – How delightful will it be, to be able to instruct one of those African youths, who will be entrusted to my care, in the sacred languages, and in the elements of christian [*sic*] theology.

Since the missionary's own work is to grapple with the ancient languages, it is this work that he will impart to and share with his students. In the words quoted by an important history of Nigerian education, 'The missionaries had come with the Latin service-book in one hand and the Latin grammar in the other' (Fafunwa 1974: 81).

This literary, classical education quickly came to be identified as a sign of the progress that the colony in Sierra Leone could make. Sibthorpe closes his history with an exhortation that assumes the close connection between the colony and its classical languages: 'My dear good people of Sierra Leone, read Greek, read Latin, read Hebrew, add Arabic to your readings . . .' (1970: 217). He goes on to encourage Sierra Leoneans to pursue English literature as well, but it remains relevant that the first descriptors of Sierra Leone in this context are Greek and Latin. We have seen that the Commissioners of Enquiry of 1827 understood 'liberal education' as the sign that the colony was progressing and that families were becoming wealthier. In 1845 Governor Fergusson, the first person of African descent (from the Caribbean) to hold the governorship, wrote on the topic again, in a despatch home to the British government, and made even more explicit the link between education and material progress. The importance of this letter caused it to be reproduced in several histories of the period (Walker 1847: 557–8; Sibthorpe 1970: 175–6):

> [The schools] will, at no remote date, be the means of establishing a new, most important, and influential grade in the society of Sierra Leone; among

> which the husbands, the wives, and the domestic intercourse, of the middle classes of England, will, for the first time, find representatives in western Africa. It may be taken as neither an unfair nor an unfavourable criterion of the position in the social scale at which the people have arrived, that these establishments are at length acknowledged to have become necessary.

This view is also quoted by Governor Pine as endorsement for his own celebration of the CMS Grammar School in Freetown, when he notes the classical component of the education there purveyed (1848: 199).

At least two points may be noted here. The first is that the West African population is understood to develop along exactly the same lines as the British, impelled by the same needs and desires. That the goal is to reproduce the British 'middle classes' is assumed as natural and uncontroversial. This confident cultural imperialism is unsurprising in its historical context, and it is connected to the prevalence of classical languages in West Africa. At this early period, in these sources, no difference is assumed between the aspirations and eventual destinies of Britons and Africans, and Africans' exposure to classical languages is a symptom and sign of this assumption. Moreover, the British are well aware that education along European lines is conducive to identification with the West, as in this recommendation from the 1842 Report from the Select Committee on the West Coast of Africa (Sandon 1842: vii):

> We would recommend that further provision should be made for these objects . . . by encouragement to schools of a higher class than any which are found there at present; to which, among others, the neighbouring Chiefs should be invited to send their sons to receive an education which might fit them to be of benefit to their own people directly, if they returned to their families, or indirectly, if they remained by entering into connexion with British interests.

Western education here leads effortlessly to Africans making common cause with 'British interests'.

The second point to note overall is the huge stake that the quoted sources have in the enterprise of Western, missionary education. Even though comparatively few Africans were ever educated in the classical languages and histories, their education attracted substantial rhetorical resources.[28] Since very few indigenous African voices make their way into the sources at this stage, we hear from the British government, which needs the settlement to succeed so that British philanthropy is vindicated and British expense not wasted; and we hear from the missionary bodies, who need proof of their good offices and of the inevitable spread of Christianity among the 'heathen'. For these diverse purposes the African acquisition of Greek and Latin takes on substantial symbolic value.

The multiple significances of Samuel Ajayi Crowther

Only a few years after its foundation, Fourah Bay College achieved an immense success in the education of Samuel Ajayi Crowther, a Yoruba who was to become the first African to be ordained as a bishop in the Church of England. He was captured as a child when his town was sacked; he was then passed from owner to owner before eventually reaching the coast, from where he would have been transported to Brazil by Portuguese traders. Once the Portuguese slave ship on which he was embarked was captured by the British, he was settled in Sierra Leone as a 'recaptive', and entered the Christian Institution (Fourah Bay College). In 1841 he helped to lead an expedition up the Niger river, to explore the possibilities of establishing missionary bases in the interior, away from the coastal settlements, and later in life, as Bishop Crowther, he became the head of the Niger Mission, the first all-African mission within West Africa.[29] Such was his academic progress at Fourah Bay that he is regularly mentioned in official documents of the period. In 1842, when he left Africa for further training in England, he was cited in the Report of the British Parliament's Select Committee on the West Coast of Africa (Sandon 1842: v), as being one of those who proved that Africans are

> fitted for every branch and grade of service . . . The gentleman lately Acting Governor of Sierra Leone, and the Queen's Advocate there, are both gentlemen of colour; and it appears that an Akoo [Yoruba], lately a liberated African, is now on his way to England, to be ordained a clergyman of the Church of England, having been instructed in Greek under the care of the Church Missionary Society established in the same colony.

This quotation comes from the Select Committee's own conclusions, indicating that they have been convinced by the testimony which they have heard about Crowther. One such piece of testimony comes from Dandeson

Coates, Secretary to the Church Missionary Society, and one of the signatories to the 1842 Fourah Bay curriculum quoted above. Eager to establish the good record of the CMS, Coates claims that 'Education is considerably advanced in the colony' and cites the case of the African who 'has made so much progress in theological and general knowledge (he is able in fact to read the Greek Testament) that he has been called to this country by the Committee with a view to his being presented as a candidate for holy orders to the Bishop of London' (Sandon 1842: 97). In subsequent sources Crowther will regularly appear as both exceptional and as proof of what Africans can naturally achieve.

The Committee also interviewed the Revd. J. F. Schön, a missionary with the CMS, and enquired about the nature of the education purveyed in Sierra Leone.[30] 'What is the system of instruction pursued in the higher schools supported by the Church Missionary Society . . . Do they read anything of general literature or history . . . Do they learn anything of the classical languages . . . Do you teach anything of the exact sciences?' (Sandon 1842: 461). A question about the boys' exposure to classical languages is regularly posed in connection with any ambitious school. Enquiring of the career destinations of the boys so educated, the Chair comes round to the famous African with Greek: 'Have any of them [the boys] become clerks in shops or in merchants' houses? . . . Is there not a black person who has received his education in Sierra Leone, who is coming over to be ordained?' Schön agrees that 'There is one, Samuel Crowther, who by a course of missionary and private instruction, has received this education' and the proceedings go on to establish, in response to the Committee's question, 'He has learned Greek as well as Latin, has he not?' that 'He reads the Greek Testament; he knows nothing of Latin' (Sandon 1842: 461).[31] The emphasis on Greek to the exclusion of Latin indicates that this classical learning was indeed undertaken for the purposes of scriptural reading, rather than for exposure to the classical heritage as it is understood nowadays. Since the course of instruction outlined earlier, however, at the Grammar School and Fourah Bay College, included both Greek and Latin, it would have qualified as 'liberal' in the sense of the Commission of Enquiry's remarks quoted above.

During the mid-nineteenth century, Samuel Crowther and his acquisition of Greek are regularly mentioned when an argument needs to be made about the progress of Sierra Leoneans and West Africans generally, and especially if the nature or quality of mission education is at stake. Crowther's achievement is a sign that the experiment at Freetown is working properly, all the more so since the narrative arc is genuinely impressive, taking him from slavery to a bishopric, and from the coastal settlement to missionary work on behalf of the CMS in the interior of what is now Nigeria. Unlike Philip Quaque, but like many other West Africans who entered the system of Western education, he was uprooted from his ancestral lands and participated in a new formation, the polyglot and multicultural society of 'recaptives' in Freetown, where cultural exchange was facilitated by shared exposure to English and Christianity. As we have seen, the new inhabitants of Freetown had been separated from their original homes, and often had also experienced different backgrounds including England, the Caribbean, Brazil and the United States. Strenuous acculturation via English and Christianity worked to bind the new society together, and the advanced educational facilities helped to produce a new 'middle class' among the 'Liberated Africans'. Those Africans who could take advantage of the educational opportunities – supported by family, friends or missionary societies – came to constitute a recognized group, an 'intelligentsia' and even an elite, distinguished by conversion, education, and, often, Western dress. In many of these respects Crowther was emblematic of the 'new elite' discussed by historians such as Ajayi (1965) and Ayandele (1966, 1974).

As a person on the cusp of a changing society, Crowther was exposed to the various pressures of Freetown culture, and has been described as a 'mediator' in the sense investigated by Koehl 1971. He can be understood as part of a tradition of individuals whose task it was, in a commercially and culturally mobile region, to interpret communities to one another.[32] He was also an 'interpreter' in another sense, in that he was a gifted linguist who translated much of the Bible into Yoruba, working from the original New Testament Greek. Another African minister, J. K. Solomon, wrote from the Gold Coast to the secretaries of the Wesleyan Mission in London, in 1869, to point out that 'to have a Gospel in Fanti required a man who is well acquainted with Greek to translate it properly' (Graham 1971: 127). Solomon continued 'and such a man we have not', which might indicate the value of such as Crowther. Crowther amassed a personal library which he left to Fourah Bay College, and is on record as a supporter of academic education for West Africans. Simultaneously, however, he found less educated men to be better at missionary work among ordinary Africans (Ajayi 1965: 221–2).

Despite this alleged preference, Crowther is one of the first people to be explicitly recognized as a successful 'Native Agent', an indigenous missionary who preached to and converted other Africans.[33] The role of the Native Agent was produced by the particular circumstances of early missionary enterprise in West Africa, where as we noted, mortality was very high among Europeans whose systems, unable to cope with the climate, ended up as prey to malaria, dysentery and numerous unspecified 'fevers'. From the very beginnings of colonial activity, the West African colonies were not 'settler colonies', like Kenya or Uganda in British East Africa, or like South Africa, but rather 'colonies of exploitation' where Europeans administered and extracted value, but did not settle in serious numbers. Indeed, Sierra Leone was known as the 'White Man's Grave'. This situation entailed that if the gospel was to be spread effectively among West Africans, it would have to be done by native converts, and this meant in turn that natives must be trained up to serve the church. This is perhaps the most compelling reason why West Africans were initially introduced to the ancient languages and why, conversely, there is a much slighter history of classical education in the British East African colonies.[34] Although various missionary sources had been insisting for years that their enterprise needed Africans for full success, Ajayi 1970 suggests that the necessity was formally recognized only after 1841, when Crowther accompanied the European missionary Schön on an ill-fated expedition up the Niger into the interior of West Africa. Fully one-third of the 150 European missionaries on the expedition died, leaving the ordained and classically trained Crowther as living proof not only that Africans must be missionaries to other Africans, because the enterprise killed Europeans, but also that Africans were completely equipped for the task. Henry Venn (1796–1873), then secretary of the CMS, was particularly influential in conceiving and designing the 'native pastorate'.[35]

In other government sources, such as the Report from the Select Committee on the Final Extinction of the Slave Trade, questions about Africans' expertise in classical languages come second only to questions about their character and general ability (Oxford 1850: 96–7). This Committee called the Revd. Charles Frederick Childe, who taught at the Church Missionary College in Islington, London, to answer for the two Africans from Sierra Leone, Nichol and Maxwell, currently in Britain for ordination by the Bishop of London. While they have made some progress in Latin, the Committee hears, they are much further forward in Greek, and can read the Testament very well; these young men evince great natural aptitude, may very well excel Europeans in their work, and even demonstrate 'literary ambition', which the Revd. has 'sometimes thought it necessary to check, lest it interfere with higher objects'. They thus follow in the footsteps of Crowther and Thomas Macaulay, who are also discussed in this interview. Unsurprisingly, the men who are mentioned by name in such reports, distinguished for their religious and intellectual aptitudes, went on to occupy positions of leadership in their home communities.

The curriculum of the Freetown Grammar School and the Fourah Bay College, and the intellectual achievements of such as Crowther, Macaulay, Nichol and Maxwell, can be cited by contemporaries as signs that colonialism works and that Africans can take full benefit of European civilization. Not all Europeans shared this investment in African achievements, however, and in the later decades of the nineteenth century some of the public rhetoric about Sierra Leone, and West Africa generally, adopted a different tone. Many modern commentators agree that as the century moves towards the Berlin conference of 1884, when Africa was partitioned in the 'scramble', a much more racist discourse emerged in the statements of prominent Europeans on the nature and potential of Africans, conditioned partly by far-ranging European doubts about the value of the colonial enterprise, partly by sheer territorial ambition – and by African resistance to the latter. Within this racist or sceptic discourse, Africans' relation to classical education is a matter for negative comment.

Some of this negative discourse can be read in the proceedings of a Select Committee of the British Parliament, which reported in 1865. The Committee was tasked with considering the state of the British establishments on the western coast of Africa, and among its first determinations was that (Adderley 1865: iii):

> all further extension of territory or assumption of Government, or new treaties offering any protection to native tribes, would be inexpedient; and that the object of our policy should be to encourage in the native the exercise of those qualities which may render it possible for us more and more to transfer to them the administration of all the Governments, with a view to our ultimate withdrawal from all, except, probably, Sierra Leone.

The Report thus envisaged self-government, and to that extent was welcomed by the West African intelligentsia.[36] Yet withdrawal from West Africa was also suggested by other motives, among them the unhealthy effects of the location on Europeans, which seemed to make long-term engagement an impossibility, and the fact that not all missionary activity had succeeded in 'civilizing' the Africans.[37] Not only this, but where Africans were 'civilized', or at least educated, Europeans began to suspect that they thereby became proud and intransigent, and possibly immoral. Education is thus of great concern to this Committee, and the provision in Sierra Leone is discussed several times, with Latin and Greek coming under scrutiny because they signify either the great aptitude of Africans for 'civilization', or the utter fatuity of the missionary endeavour. Questioning a range of witnesses, including missionaries, traders and military men, the Committee is faced with the whole gamut of attitudes towards Africans and British colonization. Sceptical witnesses decry missionary work as being so unsuccessful as not to warrant its continuation, but where it has achieved success, in the field of education, the Africans products are decried as so educated as to make them unmanageable. Burton (1821–90), the famous explorer, claims that (Adderley 1865: 105):

> the general voice of the coast is against the Sierra Leone men; they are looked upon as men who have sufficient education to deceive others and not sufficient to keep themselves straight . . . The civilized Christian convert of Sierra Leone is dreaded on the rest of the coast; he has been trained up in police courts; he can examine a witness as well as any lawyer in England; he has great missionary interest, which enables him to raise a cry at once.

The overwhelming articulacy of the 'civilized Christian convert', especially if prepared for the law, would regularly include acquaintance with the ancient languages. From other witnesses the Committee hears that the products of the mission schools are dishonest, unwilling to work,[38] convinced that they are 'above' other natives, but in fact unsuited to a useful life because 'when they come out of the school they have nothing to do; no trade has been taught them; they know nothing but reading and writing; and very little of that' (Adderley 1865: 201).[39]

On the other hand, missionary and other witnesses cite classical education, in a move that is by now familiar, as a sign not only of actual historical progress but also of Africans' ability to improve still further. They explain hostility to mission education not as objective criticism but as reaction to the fact that the missionaries expose the shortcomings of the traders in guns and liquor, as they had earlier worked against the slave trade.[40] The Revd. C. A. Göllmer, asked about progress since 1844, replies enthusiastically, and does not omit to mention the Revd. Samuel Crowther, the first native pastor (Adderley 1865: 236):

> the progress of the Colony of Sierra Leone might be seen, first, in a religious point of view, by the great increase of native Christians and scholars, and by the superior educational establishments, both for young men and young women, even the classics and the mathematics being taught to young men, and then by their liberal contributions to the work, they supporting their own churches and schools, and especially by the transfer of the missionary churches and missionary work to native pastorates; in 1841 we had but one native pastor, and now we have 12.

He goes on to show how the Grammar School at Lagos (founded in 1859), and the seminary at Abeokuta (both in modern Nigeria), which teach English, mathematics and Greek (Adderley 1865: 237), help to confirm that the 'native' is thoroughly 'educable' and can equal or surpass the European in virtue (Adderley 1865: 240). Such reassurance will also, of course, go to support the case for eventual self-government, a connection which is made explicitly by some witnesses (e.g. Adderley 1865: 133, 220, 283). Other witnesses, while admitting the quality of classical education, are concerned that it is too narrow. Sir Samuel Blackall, Governor of Sierra Leone, articulates a reservation which will reverberate into the twentieth century (Adderley 1865: 312): 'It is a good educational establishment, so far as the classics go; they are very well taught, I think; but I think what we want more is to enlarge their mind . . . '.

The Committee's questions to Colonel Ord, of the West Indies, at first express some reservations about classical education, but later work towards establishing a parity or comparability between West African and British education that is highly significant (Adderley 1865: 39):

> Generally speaking, are the means of education considerable in the colony? – The means of such education as I conceive to be required, are very readily attainable.
>
> The course at the grammar school is not a bad education, is it? – No.
>
> Whether that be right or wrong, there is Latin, and so on, taught there, is there not? – Yes; I am of opinion that such education as is requisite is readily attainable. (Adderley 1865: 63):
>
> You have mentioned the [Lagos] Grammar School; have you any information with regard to the quality of the education furnished in that school? – I

have not; I understood it was a school founded on the principle of the Sierra Leone Grammar School, which I inspected on more than one occasion at Sierra Leone, and which I thought very highly of.

Does it correspond with our idea of a Grammar School in this country, Greek and Latin being taught for instance? – I imagine that Greek and Latin would be taught there as they are at Sierra Leone.

Then, in fact, the grammar school does correspond with our idea of a grammar school in this country? – Yes, the grammar school began on 6th June 1859, with six pupils; that number was increased to 22, which has been sometimes more and sometimes less; there are now 25 on the list, and there have been registered 41, who have left the school to be variously employed; some as merchants' clerks, and some in higher pursuits.

Colonel Ord's testimony allows the conclusion that the African and the Briton are equally capable of classical education, and logically then of everything else. The testimony of the Revd. Elias Schrenk goes perhaps further in proclaiming the necessity of a classical education, for Africans and British alike, simply in order to function in the modern world. The Revd. Schrenk is a member of the Basel Mission in the Gold Coast, who are German Protestants,[41] but the education on offer differs only in degree from that offered by other Protestant missions in West Africa. The Revd. Schrenk's testimony is emphatic (Adderley 1865: 141):

Akropong [northeast of Accra] is one of our principal stations, because there is a college for the native missionaries, and another school, where young men receive a good education. There we teach also the old languages.

Do you teach the native boys Latin, Greek and Hebrew? Yes; Latin has not commenced, but Greek and Hebrew they have learnt already.

Is that of any use? They must read the Bible in the original languages; we only teach it to those who will be missionaries and teachers.

You only teach the classics to the boys or young men who will be missionaries? – Yes, but there will be others who will learn at least Latin when we introduce it.

. . .

You teach English, do you not? – We teach English.

Would you not find the English language and literature a sufficient means of developing the minds of those Africans, without teaching them Latin and

> Greek? – I think we must have a larger view than that; it is our resolution to make the negroes independent, and therefore we think that the native minister must be able to read the Bible in the original language if he would be independent; we should respect no minister here at home if he could not read the Bible in the original language, therefore it is our decided aim to make them independent …
>
> Does that apply to the ordinary pupils in the schools? – No, I do not know of what use Greek and Hebrew would be for them, but the more intelligent of them will learn Latin, because we cannot read a newspaper without having learnt Latin.

The 'independence' of the Africans here is a new note in the discussion, and it is not clear that the Revd. Schrenk envisages political independence rather than the intellectual independence prized in the Protestant tradition, but in any case it is a significant contrast to the views expressed elsewhere to the Committee, and perhaps also to the Committee's own assumptions. The Revd. Schrenk goes on to address the comparability between Europeans and Africans on a slightly different topic, but again is helped by the classical languages. The Committee asks (Adderley 1865: 144):

> When you spoke of the education you gave the [African] missionaries, you mentioned the difficulty of developing the thinking faculties of the native children; how does that operate; do you find that, after a certain time, they seem to lose their power of advancing further, and remain stationary, or fall back? – No; that is a point which has been touched upon here and there to me, since I came back; but for a man who knows our life at home it is no mystery. Here, at home, when they are 17, youths lose, sometimes, their energy, and you know the reason of it; but that is much more the case among such people as the Africans, for where there is no moral power there is no resistance. If they come under the influence of Christianity there is moral power in their heart, and we do not find, that when they are 14 or 15 years of age, they do not make more progress. We have in our college young men of 24 or 25, who study just as we do here at home. We opened the college in 1863; I was there at the opening of the college, and three months afterwards I was again there, and I saw that those young men had made very nice progress in Greek; so much so that they can be compared with Europeans who have learnt Greek for three months.

The Revd. Schrenk thus seems to accept the racist commonplace that eagerness for study, and ability to apply oneself, fall off in the African after a certain age, which is usually understood as the age of puberty. To this extent, intellect and developing sexuality are assumed to conflict with one another in the African; but in the Revd Schrenk's discourse, the African who is fortified with Christianity has the moral power to resist, and so can continue to excel in Greek and Latin.[42] The ancient languages here are represented as helping to overcome the natural disposition of the African, and offer a crucial sign of commensurability with the European. The African's nature, in this discourse, is not such that he can withstand sexuality by himself, but fortified by Christianity and mission teaching, he can make the same progress in Greek and against temptation as does the European. There is nothing inherent in his African identity that precludes access to classical languages.[43]

From the European testimony given to the Select Committee it is clear that education, and prominently classical education, is a touchstone for all sides of the argument, and also that even those who favour the eventual independence of the West Africans, discourse of them in ways that we may today find gratingly patronizing. Much more disturbing, however, are the terms in which the argument is mounted in the contemporary discussions at the Anthropological Society of London consequent on a lecture given by Winwood Reade (1865). Reade, a British explorer and an atheist (1838–75), had recently returned from travels in West Africa, and delivered a paper in which he claimed that missionary endeavour there was bound to be fruitless because Africans were incapable of improvement; their conversion to Christianity was mere lip-service and the alleged converts were likely to be the most immoral people of all.[44] The Journal of the Anthropological Society records the response of a missionary, H. Burnard Owen (1865), and the subsequent discussion. Unsurprisingly, Samuel Crowther makes an appearance in Owen's case, and this time the native Bishop is accompanied by further proofs (Owen 1865: clxxxix):

> The case of Bishop Crowther is an effectual refutation of the assertion that the native African is incapable of being raised to a very high standard of intellectual advancement. Does the request of another native minister (the Rev. G. Nichol) betray incapacity for education? He desired a friend to send him from England some books, foremost on the list of which was Alford's *Greek Testament*, next an Arabic Lexicon, Maunder's *Treasury of Universal Knowledge*, Maunder's *Biographical Treasure*, Melville's *Sermons*, Spurgeon's *Sermons*, etc.

> To the Church Missionary Society he applies for two first-rate university men to superintend the studies of the African theological students, adding, 'It will not do to send men of ordinary capacity now-a-days; our students are too well taught in their Greek Testament not to catch their professor tripping if he displays insufficient knowledge'. That this assertion is not unfounded the Freetown Grammar School examinations in 1859 conclusively show. The governor, expressing his astonishment at the intelligence of the pupils 'I had no idea that you had such youths,' he said; 'they can learn anything.' The intelligence and quickness of the negro child is very great.

Staking his claim to the ancient languages, the Revd. George Nichol, a product like Crowther of Fourah Bay College, strikes a new note when he incidentally makes sure that his British correspondents are aware of the Africans' attainments. Owen represents him as implying not only the commensurability of African and British language training, but also the possibility of African superiority, and it is perhaps this slant to his correspondence that draws out the vitriolic responses of the sceptical, or should we simply say racist, parties to the debate.

Burton takes up the challenge of the African scholars by suggesting, basically, that they do not exist. Of Crowther he claims (Owen 1865: ccvii):

> Bishop Crowther I know; he is, perhaps, the best African, or rather the only good one I have met on the West Coast, but I am unable to tell you whether he is a negroid or a negro. There were even at his birth Moslems in his native village, and there have been usually Haussa blood in their veins.

Crowther thus proves nothing about African abilities because he is at some level not 'African' at all, or at least not a 'negro' of West Africa. Burton continues: 'Of the Rev. G. Nichol, I cannot say anything, except that if what we have heard is true, he must be a *rara avis* [rare bird], and most dissimilar to "Niger" generally'. Burton would abandon missionary efforts because he cannot bear the British government to spend money on the 'hopeless barbarous blacks of west Africa' rather than on relieving domestic poverty (Owen 1865: ccix). Mr Carter Blake (ca. 1840–ca. 1887), a palaeontologist, comparative anatomist and founder member of the Society, is similarly scornful and dismissive: 'As to the remarks made by Mr. Owen, I am not allowed to reply to them. Mr. Nichol and his *Greek Testaments*, the paradise of Wilberforce and Regent;[45] let any person who knew those places ten years since go there now, and say if he finds those places progressed or otherwise' (Owen 1865: ccxxxix). But John Harris, the Gold Coast trader, goes furthest in contesting both the African identity of Crowther and the achievements of Nichol. Crowther's parentage becomes a matter of 'delicate' avoidance, suggesting perhaps that he is the illegitimate product of miscegenation, and his consecration is placed in inverted commas. Nichol is demoted from Reverend to student, 'begging' for books rather than sending to his friends, and becomes not so much a *rara avis* as a figment of Owen's imagination (Owen 1865: ccxliv):

> 'Bishop' Crowther is frequently cited as an example of the civilised negro, improved by the missionaries out of the hold of the slaver. Now, unless Mr McArthur has had some positive physical evidence of 'Bishop' Crowther's truly negro parentage (I mean such physiological evidence as would satisfy a jury in the Divorce Court), I must throw all the weight of proving his improbable thesis on himself. The predominance of Haoussa blood in the neighbourhood where 'Bishop' Crowther states that he was born is significantly omitted from the discussion, and those who have ever seen this highly educated African will, while admitting the darkness of his complexion and the woolliness of his hair, prefer, as in many other cases where the parentage of the negro is discussed, to avoid this delicate question. The story which is cited by Mr. Burnard Owen of the negro student who begged for copies of Alford's *Greek Testament*, Maunder's *Treasury of Universal Knowledge*, Spurgeon's *Sermons*, and other depositories of critical, elementary, or superfluous information, he must pardon me for saying that I take 'cum libro salis'. If any of our West African travellers will tell us what the negroes do with these books, even supposing them to be ever sent, I am sure that anthropologists would be highly gratified.

The naked antagonism of these responses needs little comment, but we might want to pause briefly at the Latin phrases. As we shall see, the notion that Africans learn only phrases of the ancient languages, parrot-fashion, without true understanding, exerts a stranglehold on debate in later years, and there may be some buried reference to it in the Europeans' strictures here. More pertinent, perhaps, is the fact that they insult the Africans in the classical idiom that is at stake in the debate. In particular, Harris rings the changes on the phrase 'grain of salt' by claiming that he takes Nichol's achievement with a 'pound of salt'; his reinvention of the Latin phrase here demonstrates precisely that ability with the language which he doubts in the case of Nichol's Greek.

African responses to missionary classical education

That Africans' aptitude, and indeed appetite, for classical education remained controversial was ensured partly by the numerous contradictions within colonialism itself. Those I have called the 'racist' commentators, like Hunt, Reade, Burton, Harris and Blake, complain that Africans are 'savages' and 'barbarous', but colonialism requires that they be so, or there is no excuse for occupying their lands or extracting their mineral wealth. Simultaneously, however, they must be amenable to civilization and specifically to Western, European culture, or there is no reason to assume and celebrate the superiority of the latter. Bhabha's analysis of 'colonial mimicry' demonstrates how colonialism desires 'a reformed, recognizable Other, as a subject of difference that is almost the same, but not quite' (1994: 122) and Newell agrees, writing that 'colonial discourse paradoxically requires the "native" to be both . . . incapable of being civilized and fully available for domestication' (2006: 51). For some voices in the mid-to-late-nineteenth-century debate, then, Africans' alleged progress in classical education must be denied, so that the native remains savage, while for others, the progress must be patronized, so that the domestication remains incomplete and does not seriously threaten European superiority. The progress is, in any case, vulnerable to the charge of special pleading on the part of missionaries with much at stake in the educational enterprise.

Despite, or perhaps because of, the suspicions of some Europeans, West Africans in the later decades of the nineteenth century took steps to acquire even more classical education. As we have noted, boys came from other regions to be educated in Freetown, and conversely several secondary schools were founded in Lagos and the Gold Coast during these decades. In Lagos, secondary schools were founded by CMS in 1859, Wesleyan Methodists in 1878 and Baptists in 1885.[46] Most of these schools offered some elements of a classical education; the Wesleyan school offered Latin, Greek, Hebrew, ancient history and mythology as optional extra subjects (Ajayi 1965: 154), but by contrast, the Hope Waddell Training Institute, founded at Calabar in 1895 by the Church of Scotland (Presbyterian) Mission, eschewed academic education in favour of practical and vocational. Other schools which pursued the academic track were St Andrews at Oyo, founded in 1896, and in the Gold Coast, the Wesleyan Boys' High, founded in 1876, and the Cape Coast Grammar, founded by the nationalist educator Egyir Asaam in 1896.[47]

Some prominent West Africans went further and agitated for a West African University, in which they expected classical languages to play a leading role even if other disciplines such as science and the law were also emphasized. From the early 1860s, James Africanus Beale Horton (1835–83), one of the first Africans to qualify as a physician, wrote on this topic, and in 1868, in his *West African Countries and Peoples*, recommended that Fourah Bay College become the University of Western Africa, with lectures in (1969: 184):

> the theory and practice of education, classics, mathematics, natural philosophy, mensuration, and book-keeping; English language and literature; French, German, Hebrew, history in general, mineralogy, physiology, zoology, botany, chemistry, moral and political philosophy, civil and commercial law, drawing and music, besides the various subjects which might be included under the term of theology.[48]

The role of the classical languages in the university may be understood from another of Horton's texts, on medical education. In 1861 Horton had also recommended the establishment of a medical training institution in Sierra Leone, which would take 'certain young men . . . who have made some proficiency in Latin, Greek, and Mathematics' (Horton 1969: 44n).[49] Horton thus assumes, along with other Africans and also Europeans of his educational background, that the demanding secondary-school subjects qualify the student for advanced work in other areas.

Horton was not the most famous African to agitate for higher education; in 1872, Edward Blyden (1832–1912), then working in Sierra Leone, wrote repeatedly to Governor Pope-Hennessy on the subject of a secular West African university (Blyden 1978: 95–9).[50] As we can see from his work in Liberia College, to be discussed in Chapter 2, this institution would have foregrounded classical languages and literature.[51] Although the idea of a West African University was looked upon with favour by Pope-Hennessy, it excited no interest at the Colonial Office in London. Yet partly as a result of this and related pressure, in 1876 Fourah Bay College gained affiliation to the University of Durham, and thus enabled its students to read for degrees without having to travel abroad.[52] In the twentieth century, other institutions enabled students to read for the BA Intermediate Arts degree of the University of London too, usually by private study, sitting the exams while in West Africa. Since the only degrees initially offered at Fourah Bay were in Classics and Theology, the ancient languages retained their hold over the education system, and garnered enough support that local enthusiasm for the academic education purveyed there helped to ensure the College's survival at several subsequent moments, e.g. 1909 and 1929, when shortage of funds made the authorities consider abandoning the higher-level education and concentrating solely on ordination (Bradshaw 1977: 22). As modern commentators note, Horton, Blyden and other educators such as James Johnson were far ahead of their time in their pioneering visions for modernity in West Africa; university education there did not come into full flower until the middle of the twentieth century.[53]

In the early years of the twentieth century, several more secondary schools were established throughout West Africa, either by missions or by independent African initiative, and occasionally by government.[54] In Nigeria, the CMS founded Abeokuta Grammar School in 1908, Ibadan Grammar School in 1913, Ijebu-Ode Grammar School in 1913 and Ondo High School in 1919 (with a great deal of African input; cf. Ogunkoya 1979: 48); other churches founded Oron Boys High School and Wesley College Ibadan in 1905. The government founded King's College Lagos in 1909, and Eko Boys High School was founded by private initiative in 1913, so that by 1914 there were eleven secondary schools in southern Nigeria (Fafunwa 1974: 110).[55] In the Gold Coast, the Accra Grammar School was founded in 1903 by the nationalist educator Attoh Atuma, and Adisadel was founded by the Anglicans in 1910. Ajayi and others have shown how even very early missionary contacts were often initiated by Africans in order to serve their own political, commercial or educational ends,[56] and the foundation of new secondary schools in this period indicates that missions and other bodies were responding to pressure from African communities who were eager to take advantage of secondary schooling. Although all secondary schools served a tiny percentage of the West African population – 2 per cent in the years before the First World War[57] – and were moreover geographically distributed in very unequal ways, they testified to West Africans' increasing desire for advanced education, which almost invariably included the classical languages. Some scholars see independent African foundation of schools as part of a response to the growing racism among Europeans, and it may also suggest a response to unsatisfactory provision by missions. For instance, schools of different denominations might compete for the few students available, each providing a small school for an area rather than cooperating to provide a larger and more efficient one, and often underfunding their foundations (Berman 1974: 533, Bassey 1999). Primary schools were often started by Africans, who sometimes remained the sole teachers, but since secondary schools were routinely judged on whether or not they provided European staff, the independent African initiatives were significant.[58]

Investment in a classical education was thus part of West African response to rapidly changing economic, political and cultural circumstances, in which Africans took the tools of colonialism and used them to their own advantage. As several critics have shown, colonialism was not exclusively a case of brutal imposition on helpless people, and the issue of classical education in the British West African colonies suggests, alongside rampant cultural imperialism, a dynamic in which indigenous people determined their own educational trajectories and articulated their own, albeit highly conditioned, preferences. Gikandi has written perspicaciously, for instance, on the appeal of the 'middle-class' ideal to colonized peoples, which in view of Fergusson's explicit formulation quoted above is very relevant to the issue of Africans' classical education (Gikandi 1996: 32): 'The most attractive and persistent ideal of colonial culture, as far as the colonized were concerned, was the idea of bourgeois civility and identity . . . we cannot ignore the affinity between colonization and the making of – or desire for – middle-class sensibilities'. Provision of secondary and classical education was increasingly geared to this desire rather than exclusively to the need for 'native agents'. For instance, when the new secondary schools taught ancient languages, they usually dispensed with Hebrew but retained Latin and, often, Greek. Since Hebrew was not regularly offered in schools, it would appear that the provision of Latin and Greek was designed to equip boys not so much to read scripture independently as to acquire a 'liberal' education recognizable in European terms. Such an education proclaims itself valuable in a general intellectual sense rather than directed to particular vocational ends, and thus offers to furnish boys with the means to a modern professional identity.

There were also immediate practical and instrumental reasons for prizing the classical languages; an education that included Latin and Greek helped the boys of West Africa to develop into the 'Black Victorians' that the colonial communities required and rewarded. Latin was useful as an aid to learning

English, which was the language of the colonial administration and thus of importance to any even moderately ambitious West African. Once Fourah Bay College offered degrees, there emerged another important motivation towards classical education. This was simply that the requisite number of 'credits' in Latin (or Greek) at Cambridge School Certificate level (roughly equivalent to GCSE) was necessary to 'matriculate', to qualify for University entrance.[59] Any West African student who envisaged a university education, in Sierra Leone or abroad, had to do well in a classical language at secondary school. Permitting thus access to a valuable higher education for some, while keeping out the huge majority, just as they did in Europe, the classical languages also represented for any post-primary school with aspirations an objective standard which was assessed by public examination.[60] This dimension of classical education would prove increasingly significant in the early twentieth century.

Although many of the new secondary school foundations constituted responses by missions to African pressure, some were, as we have seen, founded by Africans, sometimes in the face of missionary opposition.[61] Ayandele goes further and claims that educated Africans began, in the 1880s if not earlier, to be perceived as competitors by the missionaries (1974: 23). Although the CMS had founded Fourah Bay and the Freetown Grammar School, their European head of mission at Abeokuta, in Nigeria, the Revd. Henry Townsend (1815–86), wished to avoid academic training for Africans and the 'pride' that allegedly came with it (Ajayi 1965: 150). He maintained a lengthy quarrel about the content of the boys' education with the Revd. G. F. Bühler, head of the Training Institute at Abeokuta, founded in 1853 by CMS. In 1861, Bühler was teaching history, including that of ancient Rome, geography and arithmetic, as well as scripture history and English; a year later he had introduced Greek and Latin to the more advanced boys (Ajayi 1965: 151). Townsend had earlier removed the native minister Thomas Macaulay from the mission at Abeokuta, claiming that he was more suited to work at the Freetown Grammar School, but Macaulay, with Samuel Crowther on his side, asked the CMS to allow him to found a grammar school in Lagos instead. The list of books which Macaulay ordered for the Lagos school includes Euclid, Eaton's *Latin Grammar* and Valpy's *Greek Grammar*, as well as books on English, history and geography (Ajayi 1965: 153). Such a list indicates the academic aspirations of the school and its resistance to Townsend's strictures. Even at Abeokuta in 1874, the books of the

Revd. Thomas J. Marshall included eight volumes of *Rollins' Ancient History*, the *Student's Gibbon*, and a Greek/English dictionary, as well as numerous works on Bible history and interpretation, devotional works and inspirational biography (Ajayi 1965: 148).

In Sierra Leone, the Wesleyan mission opened the Wesleyan Methodist Boys' High School in 1874, 30 years after the CMS Grammar School was opened in Freetown. Ten years later, the Leopold Education Institute was opened by an African, without missionary input. In the Gold Coast the Methodists opened the Wesleyan Boys' High School, in 1876, which showed 2 out of 28 studying Latin and Greek, and 12 offering Latin 2 years later (Boahen 1996: 30–1). The 1876 prospectus showed Latin and Greek as extras, at 7s 6d per quarter (Graham 1971: 146), but Latin and Greek were shortly made part of regular offerings. The Principal reported that: 'We have added Latin to the course and find that it has not interfered with the English studies, but has rather been an inducement to greater diligence, much interest being paid when attention is turned to the part which it plays in the structure of the English language' (Boahen 1996: 31). Later in its history the school suffered from various kinds of controversy and opposition, including briefly from its own Principal, and after some temporary closures it was refounded in 1905 by a consortium of West African leaders (Boahen 1996: 61). Among them were John Mensah Sarbah and J. Casely Hayford, who had been themselves students at the school, and who as prominent journalists, lawyers, educators and authors, were serious thorns in the side of the British authorities. The consortium, titled Fanti Public Schools, renamed the school 'Mfantsipim', a word which may be translated as 'a thousand Fantes' or 'soul of the people', or simply 'Fanti Public School' (Boahen 1996: 117–18). However translated, the name constituted a clear challenge to the missionary usage characteristic of most other secondary schools. Very deliberately, the school was given a motto, devised by Sarbah, which was in Fanti rather than being English or a Latin 'tag' (Boahen 1996: 115); Dwen Hwe Kan translates as 'Think and look ahead'.

A slightly later account can suggest something of what was at stake in the prominence of classics within post-primary education in this period, in terms of aspirations, standards and community identity. In 1913 Bishop A. B. Akinyele founded the Grammar School at Ibadan, Nigeria, which was the first secondary school in that town. Bishop Akinyele had taught himself

Latin in order to matriculate and be admitted to Fourah Bay College, where he had obtained the Durham University degree in BA Arts, the first native of Ibadan to gain a degree (Adebiyi 1969: 39). This is his biographer's account of the role played by the classical languages in the early years of the school (Adebiyi 1969: 54):

> The first thing he did was to inculcate in the students the spirit of belonging to a grammar school no matter where it might be . . . by including in the school's curriculum such impressive subjects as Greek, Latin, Shorthand and Physiology. The boys responded eagerly and after a few months, they could conjugate some Latin verbs fluently and write and pronounce some simple Greek words. They felt big indeed, those boys, and expressed this feeling loudly on the streets and at their homes by throwing Latin and Greek words and phrases at one another for all ears to hear even though they could not be jarred when these words were wrongly used. Phrases like 'Today, aurum et argentum non habeo' (Gold and silver have I none) to express 'I have no money today' and 'I shall see you in church on Sunday, Deo volente' (God willing) or 'This book was given to me by Amicus Davidus, anno Domini 1913' were not uncommon in the company of these gentlemen.

Adebiyi goes on to claim that this method of publicity proved efficacious, and that the school rolls soon increased. The pleasure that the boys took in their own accomplishments met the insistence of the bishop, as represented here, that secondary education was a matter of particular high-status subjects, to form a virtuous circle.[62] Latin and Greek are described, moreover, as the sign of belonging to a special group, one which aspires to high standards, as well as satisfying a recognizable juvenile desire to speak in code. In these ways they function for the African youth as they had done for centuries for European youth,[63] with the caveat that Africans under colonialism were structurally liable to the suspicion of not being able to attain high standards.

External standards are perhaps particularly relevant to the classical languages because at least in the early stages of acquisition, they lend themselves to a form of digitization. Academic progress can be readily marked off in terms of declensions and conjugations, although this point has less force in a system, like that of the late nineteenth century, where almost all education was conceived of on the model of rote learning. Certainly the available reports on boys' progress, such as those from the CMS concerning the Freetown

Grammar School and Fourah Bay College, were scrupulous in describing the specifics of texts read. In 1854, for instance

> The first class, of four students, have completed their course of study in the Institution [of Fourah Bay]. The entire New Testament in Greek has been read by them, and the two most important Epistles, Romans and Hebrews, have been pursued three several times. . . . The second class contains three students. Two have read, during the half-year, from Romans to 2d Timothy in the Greek. The other is only reading the Delectus and Arnold's Greek Accidence. All three read Hebrew with Mr. Reichardt. . . . [At the CMS Grammar School] Sixteen pupils are studying Latin. Ten of these are reading the Delectus and grammar, and six, Cornelius Nepos. Nine study Greek, six of whom are reading the grammar, and three the grammar and the Analecta Minora. (*The Foreign Missionary* 12: 246)

A year later, the Report shows three students in the first class at Fourah Bay, who have studied 'the first three centuries of Mossheim's Church History, Plato's Apology of Socrates in the original, half the first book of the Aeneid, and Cornelius Nepos, from the life of Thrasybulus to the end of the work.' They have also worked on Hebrew and Arabic, and on mathematics. The Report goes on to state that (*The Missionary Register* 1855: 140):

> The second class, consisting of four students, have read in the Greek testament from the twelfth chapter of St John and the whole of St Matthew's Gospel. . . . The third Greek class contains two students, who have finished the Delectus, and have read the first five chapters of Xenophon's Anabasis. . . . The remaining students, six in number, have been pursuing English studies . . .

At the CMS Grammar School, Freetown, the first class contains two pupils, who have read (*The Missionary Register* 1855: 141):

> the Analecta Minora as far as to the end of the eighth chapter of Lucian's Dialogues. These two pupils have also read in Latin Cornelius Nepos to the end of Dion. The second Greek class consists of five, who are still in the grammar, but will shortly take up the Delectus. These, together with two others, have read the first twenty-five pages of the Latin Delectus.

The students also perform satisfactorily in their English, geography, history and other customary subjects. The Wesleyan Mission reports that 'In addition to the usual branches of an English Education, the senior class have read parts of St John's Gospel and the Epistle to the Hebrews in Greek, and in Latin, Vergil's Fourth Eclogue' (*The Missionary Register* 1855: 12). This last entry is doubly interesting in that only the classical languages are digitized; all else that the students may have done is simply summed up in 'the usual branches'.

The digital quality of these accounts shows how they may be used to describe progress with a measure of objectivity, proceeding from the grammar to the Delectus and thence to the standard authors, and it also holds out the possibility of comparing African boys' academic development directly with that of British or European boys. While the Reports of the various Select Committees occasionally implied such comparison, some of the reports from the new secondary schools were explicit. Thus in 1878 the inspector of the Wesleyan Boys' High School (later Mfantsipim) in the Gold Coast wrote (Boahen 1996: 32): 'The boys in the first class are progressing favourably and would compete very fairly with English boys of the same age. Besides the ordinary subjects they take Physiology, Greek and Latin . . . ', and in 1882, the Principal records that 'They would fill many English boys with blush over their Latin grammar' (Boahen 1996: 39). In 1887 the Report of the Wesleyan Methodist Missions, Sierra Leone, congratulates the community on the performances in the High School, Freetown, where there are 39 boys in the higher 'classical' division reading large portions of Vergil's *Aeneid*, acquiring 'considerable ease' in translation, and turning in exam papers which 'would compare favourably with papers executed in an English school' (Boahen 1996: 12). These reports, then, directly compare the African boys with English pupils, on the grounds of facility with Greek and Latin. Later communications from principals of Mfantsipim indicate that the boys' achievements could put pressure on the teachers; in 1903 the Revd. Bartrop wrote back to the London Methodist headquarters that 'I would rather have a Westminster man with the adequate classical knowledge, than wait a year for a minister' (Boahen 1996: 98), and in 1912, the Revd. Sneath asked for leave because 'It has become clear to me that I cannot continue to perform my duties here officially without a better knowledge of Greek, Hebrew and Theology' (Boahen 1996: 213).[64]

Classical education as sign of aspiration and effort, and a passport to further opportunities, was thus often embraced by those West Africans in a position to afford secondary schooling. In mid-century, such education helped to enable some Africans towards positions of community leadership and 'middle-class', professional standing. It formed part of the package of 'civilization', which we might nowadays call Europeanization, or modernization, and which some Africans initially welcomed as a corollary to the Christian conversion and the developing economic opportunities that colonialism brought in its wake. After the Select Committee of 1865 expressed a commitment to eventual self-government, there was further incentive to exploit the resources of the alien incursion that had now apparently renounced its long-term ambitions. Such Europeanization saw some members of the Christian, educated elite take not only English names but even classical ones. Thus A. B. C. Sibthorpe, himself boasting a 'Belisarius' element to his name, went to school with one Lysias Turner (Sibthorpe 1970: 169), and a member of the Yoruba elite, a Christian and a musician, emerges into the sources with the name of Joseph Pythagoras Haastrup (Ayandele 1966: 257, 1974: 19).[65] But by the end of the nineteenth century the British government had abandoned its goal of self-government, had annexed Lagos (1861), and had made the Gold Coast into a colony rather than a protectorate (1874). The last military action in West Africa took place in 1902. Not only had the racist discourse flourished to the extent that Samuel Crowther had been forced out of his bishopric in 1890 (Ajayi 1965: 238–55), but the Berlin Conference of 1884 had implicitly accepted its terms in order to partition Africa. Higher grades in the colonial administration were closed to Africans no matter what their qualifications, and there was reluctance to promote Africans to positions where they would have Europeans serving under them (Taiwo 1975: 7, 57). Ajayi concludes that 'the transmutation of Europeans from guides to rulers was becoming complete in the administration of the country, and that the earlier policy of encouraging the growth of an African middle class was completely overturned' (1965: 269). In this context, the cultural politics of both Europeans and Africans underwent some changes, and objections to Africans' classical education were formulated by both sides.

From an early date some African families had resisted sending their children to European mission schools because they would thereby lose valuable labour; some simply took their children out of school when extra hands were needed (Taiwo 1975: 46, 49), and others demanded that missionaries pay them for their children's schooling rather than, as the missionaries sometimes expected, the other way round (Ajayi 1965: 135, Fafunwa 1974: 88). Families had also registered that mission education could alienate children from their parents, leading to 'pride', 'disrespect' and 'idleness' (Ajayi 1965: 135). While the missionaries did aim at detaching the children from their traditional worldviews, they balked at rearing a generation of 'proud' or 'superior' Africans (Ajayi 1965: 143), and were quick to criticize their own students if such outcomes threatened. We shall see further developments in this kind of criticism in the twentieth century. Both Africans and Europeans could, then, express concern about the moral effects of missionary education; where they might disagree would be over other dimensions of its suitability for Africans.

We have seen that Africans' classical education could be dismissed in overtly racist terms, by Europeans. It could also be dismissed in different terms, as being of little use to Africans, even if they were objectively very good at it. Thus Governor Blackall expressed the reservation, to the Select Committee of 1865, that a classical education was too narrow for the needs of the colony (Adderley 1865: 312). In 1852 Governor Macdonald of Sierra Leone had used harsher words (Macdonald 1852: 183):

> I regret sincerely that I cannot report any departure from, or change for the better in, the existing very defective system of education pursued at the Church Missionary schools in this colony. I allude here more especially to their two principal establishments, the one at Fourah Bay, under the superintendence of the Reverend Edward Jones, the other the Grammar School at Freetown, under the charge of the Reverend Mr. Peyton. The subject of educating the African youth has, I am happy to say, been under the consideration of Her Majesty's Government for some time past, with the view of inducing the adoption by the Church Missionary Society of a more sound and useful course of education, one better adapted to the mental capacities of the youths intrusted [*sic*] to their care and training, and more suited to the real wants and requirements of this colony than a smattering and parrot-like education in Hebrew, Greek, Latin, and the higher branches of a mathematical education can possibly be for ages to come.[66]

His objection has two parts; the classical education on offer at Fourah Bay and the Grammar School does not answer the needs of the colony, and does not suit the 'mental capacities' of the Africans. Europeans echo both parts of this criticism throughout the period under study, while Africans do formulate the first but rarely articulate the second objection. Towards the end of the nineteenth century even those who had profited from a classical education, in the terms of the 'middle-class' aspirations and achievement outlined above, were aware that such education implicitly, and often explicitly, downgraded African culture and thus cut children off from their own traditions. In the face of increasing racism they began to demand secondary schools which had syllabi fitted to African requirements (Ayandele 1974: 16, 47).

The dynamic can be seen in action in the Gold Coast, where some of the most prominent African nationalists of the period went into action first to rescue the Wesleyan Boys' High School from decline, and eventually in 1905 to amalgamate it with their own new institution. While the new school, named Mfantsipim, often claimed a seamless descent from the Wesleyan Boys, the history, as reconstructed by Adu Boahen, shows a series of disputes among the European leaders of the Wesleyan Synod, the local press and the nationalists. When the Revd. Dennis Kemp was Principal of the High School, in the 1880s, he worked against its tradition of classical education. Repeatedly recommending industrial and agricultural institutes instead of literary education for African students, who 'are not built so as to be on an equality – intellectually – with white races' (Boahen 1996: 58), he describes the school as 'very feeble' (Kemp 1898: 34), the boys as 'abominably conceited' and 'unmanageable' (Boahen 1996: 78), and ridicules the notion that they should wear European dress at school. He also decries the school on the grounds that it separates out an elite group and discriminates against families who cannot afford its uniform (Boahen 1996: 82–3). His objections to advanced education thus conform to the parameters outlined above: the African students cannot manage the education, and in any case it is not suitable for the community, here because it is socially divisive and undermines an African identity. Although these two objections are often voiced in tandem by European commentators, they address very different aspects of the colonial situation, and as noted above, Africans cannot commit themselves to the 'inferiority' objection.

Nonetheless, complaints were also made by Africans about the classical aspirations of the Wesleyan Boys' High School, in terms of their use to society. In the 1880s the *Gold Coast Echo*, a newspaper founded by John Mensah Sarbah and edited by Joseph Casely Hayford, objected that 'doubtless some parents thought they were throwing away their money; and some boys considered their time was being wasted when the latter were made from day to day to run through Latin and Greek declensions, and to solve intricate [mathematical] problems' (Boahen 1996: 55). Even Old Boys wrote to the papers to complain about 'Latin and whatnot' and to point out that 'our elderly ministers and merchant princes know nothing of "x plus y minus z" nor the vocative of coecus, and yet how high, how rich in intellect, in morals and society' (Boahen 1996: 54, 55).[67] Over the next few years the school responded with reorganization of the curriculum, to make it more responsive to the needs of Gold Coast society. Yet even though Latin and Greek became less prominent, they were retained under the first African principal, the nationalist Egyir Asaam, who took over in 1891 (Boahen 1996: 67–72). Without Latin or Greek, of course, no boy could have proceeded to higher education, and the school could not have obtained that important external validation. In 1892, inspectors acclaimed the students' excellent performances especially in the iconic secondary subjects, Mathematics and Latin (Boahen 1996: 75), but insisted that 'higher studies', in their words, should be less important than sound instruction in more practical English (Boahen 1996: 84). In 1902 the *Gold Coast Leader* complained that the school was still too liberal and academic, without enough respect for African culture. 'Setting aside the cramming of one's head with Latin and Greek, and all the eulogies, for which there must be a very limited demand, can we say enough has been done to teach them how to earn an honest livelihood by giving them a plain and simple education?' (Boahen 1996: 109). Despite these criticisms, and despite the nationalism of the refounders, Mfantsipim School consolidated its reputation as an elite school purveying an advanced education, with the classics at its heart. In fact, the classical education purveyed by this and other secondary schools helped to produce the leading exponents of anti-colonial and nationalist politics.[68] In the next chapter we shall examine how the classical repertoire facilitated the cultural expression of proto-nationalist views.

Notes

1 There were African bishops in the early Christian church, such as Augustine and Tertullian, but they were not, of course, part of the Church of England.

2 On treaties and protectorates as means of imperial expansion, see e.g. Porter 1999: 13–15, Newbury 1999: 635–40.

3 One of the defining moments of British hegemony in West Africa was when Lagos was annexed as a colony in 1861, after a dispute between rival rulers, one of whom

managed to identify with British interests. The coastal areas of the Gold Coast became a colony in 1874, the Ashanti area in 1900. Some regions would become 'protectorates' before being reorganized as 'colonies'. In Sierra Leone, however, 'colony' referred to the coastal settlements and 'protectorate' to the interior. On protectorates generally see e.g. Burroughs 1999: 190–6.

4 In *The Expansion of England*, 1883.

5 See Ohaegbulam 2002: 5 for the variety of responses to European incursions by kings and traditional rulers, including diplomacy, violent confrontation, affirmation of traditions, revolts, non-cooperation, religious separatism and migration. Lulat's discussion of colonial education overall makes a strong case for understanding the 'educated elite' as the compromised 'comprador' class, 'tainted' by their investment in colonialism (2005: 3, 7, 11). He concedes that the situation is also complicated because colonialism is not a 'unitary totality' (2005: 10) and education always retained its 'subversive' potential (2005: 3, 12). Zachernuk stresses the complexity of the colonial situation and questions Ayandele's characterization of the 'educated elite' as 'deluded hybrids' (2000: 3–5).

6 The ex-slave Jacobus Capitein, who was educated in Holland, also learned classical languages in the eighteenth century, but not within the British context. Quaque is now often known as Kweku or Kwaku.

7 Some contemporaries claim he went to Oxford, but this testimony is not particularly reliable. For instance, John Beecham, who claimed in 1841 that Quaque went to Oxford (Carretta and Reese 2010: 203), was an opponent of black preachers, and makes his claim in order to denigrate Quaque.

8 On the representation of European deaths from imperialism, in the Indian context, see Arnold 2004.

9 The CMS was prominent in Sierra Leone, as we shall see, and in Nigeria. In the Gold Coast, the Methodist church made the early running, and the Basel Mission was also active. With reference to our focus, the classical training of West Africans, the missions had differing viewpoints. Of the three so far mentioned, the Basel Mission tended to concentrate on vocational training. It was driven out of British territories in 1917 and its activities taken over by the Scottish Missionary Society. The Roman Catholic missionaries entered Nigeria in 1862 but were not established in the Gold Coast until the 1880s; in Nigeria they did not build secondary schools or ordain an African until the twentieth century (Ajayi 1965: 150). The Roman Catholic church thus arguably contributed far less than the Protestant to the formation of the West African elite.

10 Smith 1966 offers a critique of mission activity along these lines.

11 See Bartels 1965: 64.

12 For some of the politics of the English language in Africa see e.g. Thiong'o 1981 and Achebe 1989.

13 The 'trinity' is attributed to David Livingstone, the explorer and missionary, and formed a large part of the 'remedy' for the slave trade proposed by Thomas Fowell Buxton in his 1840 book of that name.
14 A contemporary ethnolinguist, Koelle, identified more than 100 native African languages spoken in the colony in 1854. See Wyse 1989: 2.
15 Once Krios left Sierra Leone, as they often did, to trade and establish themselves in professions elsewhere in West Africa, they were often called Saros. For a general introduction to Krio culture see Fyfe 1962. For an excoriating analysis of the Saros as 'deluded hybrids', see Ayandele 1974: 9–52.
16 Compare Ranger 1983: 237 on the various appropriations by Africans of European symbolic capital. Of particular relevance to this enquiry are his identifications of aspirant Africans adopting middle-class attitudes and practices, and of uprooted Africans drawing on European culture to help make a new society.
17 It is intriguing that this very early reference to Latin stresses its difficulty, whereas, as we shall see, later references conclude that Latin is in some ways quite easy for African boys. West African languages did not offer much of a purchase on the classical ones; for instance, Yoruba is pitched, so in that respect it is akin to Greek, but it is not inflected (Ogunbowale 1970: 13, 37). Several commentators make the point that West African languages are routinely described in grammatical terms drawn from English, and ultimately from Latin, which are inappropriate and unhelpful (Echeruo 1998: xi–xii, xvi).
18 Until after the Second World War, 'boys' might attend school at different ages, and were often much older than their modern counterparts.
19 By 1891, 27 Africans had obtained degrees from Fourah Bay. Paracka 2003 is a comprehensive history of the institution.
20 This school started with 30 students, some of whom were adults, and ambitious (Agbeti 1986: 27). By 1853 this school had 78 students; by 1933, 250, and by 1935, 3,740 (Ayandele 1979b: 82).
21 Further editions were produced in 1881 and 1906. The 1906 edition is the one that is now most readily available.
22 On the 'cosmopolitanism' of the CMS Grammar School see Ayandele 1979b: 83.
23 On the early movements of the missions see Agbeti 1980.
24 Paracka 2003: 34–9 has further discussion of Jones' exacting academic standards. Jones rejected the notion that certain subjects made African students 'vain and proud' – 'arguments of which I could never see the force' (Paracka 2003: 35).
25 The *Delectus* of Richard Valpy, first published in 1815, accompanies his *Grammar and Syntax* by providing Greek sentences that practise the various points learned. The first sentences are very short, one or two words, and later ones increase in complexity. While some are made up, and others are derived from the New Testament, many are drawn from the range of classical authors. Some give access

to classical myths, e.g. 'Orestes killed his mother' to practise the second aorist; others paraphrase famous classical sayings. For instance, on p. 25 of the 1866 edition students could read, 'Agis the king said, the Spartans did not ask how many the enemy were, but where'. In 20 pages (of the 1866 edition) students would have practised all the tenses, moods and voices, and some of the cases too.

26 Another contemporary source mentions Hebrew, Greek, Mathematics, Mechanics, Mensuration, Navigation and Geography. See *The Baptist Missionary Magazine*, vol, 3 (1851): 185.

27 Compare Stray forthcoming, where he notes that in mid-century 'middle-class schooling and English schooling were seen as equivalent terms, denoting a world which had to be acknowledged and catered for, but which was inferior to the world of the classically-educated gentleman'. I am grateful to Professor Stray for permitting me to read his essay prior to publication.

28 Seth 2007: 3, 129 makes the same point about the perceived significance of the Western education of tiny numbers of Indians.

29 See Ajayi 2001.

30 The CMS frequently employed missionaries of German descent; see Agbeti 1980: 21.

31 Crowther's period of study in the United Kingdom brought forth praise from the Regius Professor of Greek, and from Bishop Bloomfield, who allegedly remarked: 'That man is no mean scholar; his examination papers were capital, and his Latin remarkably good' (Ajayi 2001: 132). Crowther wrote the first grammar of Yoruba, in which the terms were apparently transferred from Latin and even, possibly, from Thomas Arnold's Prose Composition as revised by Bradley (Oke 1968: 10–11).

32 See e.g. Yankah 1995, especially Chapter 3, on mediation in West Africa. The Gold Coast (Ghana) had the particular institution of the chief's linguist or interpreter, who spoke for the chief and for the community.

33 See e.g. Ajayi 1970.

34 On the different trajectory of classics in the settler colony of South Africa, see Lambert 2011.

35 See Schenk 1983.

36 This Report, for instance, helped to spur the production of James Horton's *West African Countries and Peoples*, to which we shall return.

37 The late nineteenth-century development of quinine helped to eliminate one cause of anxiety.

38 Africans' alleged natural idleness is regretted by both detractors and supporters with tedious regularity, e.g. at 13, 28, 36, 95, 200, 226 and 281 in this document, and throughout other documents from the period.

39 This quotation comes from the trader Andrew Swanzy; see also the trader John Harris in Adderley 1865: 206–7.

40 Thus Livingstone, the famous missionary and explorer, on 228, and a less famous missionary, the Revd. Elias Schrenk, on 140. On the liquor trade see Ayandele 1966 chapter ten. An earlier report (Rowan and Wellington 1827) is explicitly attributed, by Sumner 1963: 32–5, to the conflict between missionaries/abolitionists and slave traders.

41 The German missions were closed down after the First World War and their work was taken over by the Free Church of Scotland. The Basel Mission, which was established in 1813 and entered West Africa in 1828, was later known for its commitment to practical education in the vernacular. See e.g. Agbeti 1980: 62–72. The Basel Mission is also interesting because its first two attempts to establish a base in the Gold Coast, in 1828 and 1831, were thwarted by the deaths of all the missionaries; in 1836 the move to a healthier location in Akropong then allowed the educational institutions to take root.

42 Crowder 1968: 397 shows this canard about intellect and sexuality, buttressed by racist anatomical studies as well as by sheer fantasy, documented throughout the period up until 1949. See also Desai 2001: 28–9.

43 Compare the kind of prohibition implied in the encounter between Mary Church Terrell, an African-American student of Greek, and Matthew Arnold. This scene is quoted in Haley 1993: 25:

> One day Matthew Arnold, the English writer, visited our class and Professor Frost asked me both to read the Greek and then to translate. After leaving the class Mr Arnold referred to the young lady who read the passage of Greek so well. Thinking it would interest the Englishman, Professor Frost told him I was of African descent. Thereupon Mr Arnold expressed the greatest surprise imaginable, because, he said, he thought the tongue of the African was so thick he could not be taught to pronounce the Greek correctly.

44 See Driver 2001: Chapter 4 on the controversy. Reade's paper came in the wake of the even more notorious 'On the Negro's Place in Nature', delivered to the Society by James Hunt in 1864, which draws on comparative anatomy to prove the negro closer to ape than to other humans.

45 These are Sierra Leonean towns near to Freetown.

46 Ajayi 1965: xiv discusses the relative dates of mission entry into Nigeria, and explains the prominence of the CMS with reference to its close relations to the British government.

47 Girls' schools were also founded in all three colonies, but none of them taught Latin until the 1920s. The Wesleyan Methodist mission to the Gold Coast was led by an Englishman of African descent on his father's side, T. B. Freeman, who worked successfully in the Gold Coast and Nigeria from 1838.

48 In Horton's plans, four regional grammar schools would feed this University, teaching 'Geography, Rudiments of Latin and Greek, Euclid, Geometry, Botany, Mineralogy and Music' (Horton 1970: 145). We may note incidentally that

Horton sees the classics as separate from 'theology', and as part of a much broader curriculum aimed at preparing young men for a range of modern roles.

49 See Patton 1996: 78–87 on Horton's achievements and some of the racially prejudiced responses which he encountered.

50 The correspondence is also printed in Ashby 1966: 452–69.

51 James Johnson, another member of the West African intelligentsia and first advocate of an independent African church, joined this agitation, but did not focus on the classical languages. See Ayandele 1966: 252, 1970: 59.

52 In 1875 Codrington College in Barbados similarly affiliated to Durham University and offered its degrees in Classics and Theology.

53 See e.g. Ayandele 1971, Nwauwa 1999. For James Johnson see note 51 above.

54 Yet as late as 1933 one African founder says that he was laughed at, because only Europeans founded secondary schools (Barber 2006a: 387).

55 There were none in the predominantly Muslim northern region of Nigeria, which was under a separate educational administration until 1929.

56 Ajayi 1965; see also e.g. Berman 1974.

57 See Ohaegbulam 2002: 223.

58 On primary schools, often 'bush' schools, the classic text is Murray 1929.

59 Ashby 1966: 473 lists the courses of study prescribed for the Ordinary Durham degree in 1877, the degree for which the Fourah Bay students read. The first and second readings comprise Herodotus 1–3, Virgil 1–6, Gospels of St Mark and St John in Greek, Greek Grammar, Latin Grammar, Ancient History from Herodotus, English History, Scripture History, Arithmetic, Euclid 1 and 2 or Logic, Latin Composition. The final exam added Paley *Evidences of Christianity* and *Natural Theology*, French or German.

60 The mechanism of public examination facilitates the move from 'ascribed' to 'acquired' status, which by some is seen as characteristic of modernity. See e.g. Kendall 2008: 117.

61 Berman 1974: 529–30 has a good account of this activity. Well into the twentieth century, some missions might resist African desire for post-primary education. As late as 1938, African Presbyterians in the Gold Coast 'pursued the vision of a Presbyterian Secondary School against strong opposition from the Basel and Scottish missionaries, who did not believe that it was their responsibility to provide higher education beyond their mission of training teachers and catechists' (Djangmah 2008: 2). See also Taylor 1996: 205, who claims that the Presbyterian missionaries 'prevaricated'.

62 The bishop took all the classes in Latin, Greek, Bible Knowledge, Geometry, Algebra and English. He was given to asking the boys to decline the words 'Dives' and 'Lazarus' instead of studying the 'parable of the rich man' (Adebiyi 1969: 55–6).

63 See Waquet 2001 and Stray 1998 on the roles of Latin for educated European youth.

64 Other colonial syllabi show similar progression through Latin and Greek as do the mission schools of West Africa. For instance, in Caribbean schools the Delectus, Ovid, Vergil, Cornelius Nepos and Caesar are the texts of choice, but these schools were designed first for white pupils. At Colombo, in what was then Ceylon, in 1852, boys at the Colombo Academy similarly moved from Grammar and Delectus in both Greek and Latin to Cicero and Xenophon (Anderson 1853: 311). They also learned Scripture by heart and studied the History of England, Rome and Greece. In 1905 boys in Lagos progressed from Grammar and Delectus to Caesar *de bello Gallico*, Vergil *Aeneid* I, Xenophon *Anabasis* I and Homer's *Iliad* I (Carr 1905: 67). Translation to and from Latin and Greek was a constant.
We may note that the Senior Cambridge School Certificate for 1869 required in Latin and Greek Cicero *Pro Milone*, Horace, Thucydides 6.1–51, and Aeschylus' *Prometheus Bound*. See Bacchus 1994: 257. This exam was taken by the boys of Queen's Collegiate School in Trinidad, which was the first institution to set this exam outside the United Kingdom (Campbell 1996: 26). Campbell thinks it unlikely that black students attended such schools until the 1870s (1996: 16).

65 Haastrup changed his name to Ademuyiwa (Peel 2000: 293). The later years of the nineteenth century saw many 'cultural nationalists' reject European names and take traditional African ones (see e.g. Boahen 1996: 71). Yet even in the 1920s Robert Wellesley Cole attended Fourah Bay College with Aristarchus Peter Davies (1988: 24).

66 Governor Macdonald had, only five years earlier, given five sovereigns as prizes for the students of the Grammar School, that 'valuable institution', including for performance in Classics, Scripture, Arithmetic, for general progress and for morality. See Oxford 1850: 184. We should note that this complaint comes only a few years after the praise of advanced educational institutions by Governor Fergusson, who was from the Caribbean.

67 Echeruo 1977: 59 notes a similar letter to the *Lagos Record*, 6 January 1894: 'Had I not wasted my time and energies on the mastering of Latin and Greek, and learning the histories of those same people, but had been initiated thoroughly in shorthand, typewriting, book-keeping or any foreign language, I would now be able to earn a living . . . How many men are there nowadays who have reached most enviable social and financial positions without this absurd cramming of Latin and Greek or mathematics in their teens?'

68 On this connection between the nationalists and the secondary schools see Moumouni 1996. Chanaiwa 1996 argues contra, at least for South Africa.

2

Classics and Cultural Nationalism

Classical education formed an integral part of the cultural imperialism that accompanied the economic and territorial imperialism in West Africa. Once the Christian establishment, both missionaries and government officials, had accepted the need for 'native agents', education in Greek and Latin for selected West Africans followed as a matter of course, and the drive for conversion ensured that other forms of education were more or less excluded. From the beginning of missionary activity in the region, Africans' ability with the classical languages was a matter for remark, whether positive or critical, and the languages became a significant part of a new identity within an educated, Christianized, polyglot society. Although the early sources at first retail European views of Africans, rather than independent African testimony, commentators agree that Africans prized the languages as a means of advancement to modern, demanding but rewarding trajectories, part of a newly valued aspirant middle-class culture.

Such a dynamic can be read not only in the African foundation of secondary schools, but in other cultural developments too. We have already noted the phenomenon of classicizing names. By the last decades of the century there is also the phenomenon of African-owned newspapers in the region, often full of classical quotations. As an egregious example we might cite the *Lagos Observer* of 20 July 1882, which suggests that a young African might study his mother tongue only when he

> has already successfully developed his intellectual capacity by mastering the principles underlying a sound European civilised education . . . not only of English but of classical Latin and Greek, when he has delved into the hidden mysteries of universal grammar and philology and has been able to hold sweet communion with the sages of all times from Aristotle to Darwin, and from Homer to Longfellow and Tennyson.

Such rhapsodizing might make it clear why other newspapers took schools to task for excessive concentration on classical languages and the concomitant denigration of African culture. Yet African investment in the classical languages and classical education generally did not always conform to the somewhat slavish hierarchy that this quotation can be seen to subtend. Classicizing newspapers also delivered anti-colonial critique of British policy, and in the late nineteenth and early twentieth centuries, classical tropes were pressed into service for a newly confident agenda of political and cultural emancipation. Even in the same newspaper, in the same year, another article uses classical references precisely for the purpose of extolling indigenous poetry (*Lagos Observer,* 1 June 1882):

> The legends of Troy, it must be admitted for interest stand pre-eminent; but what can equal for beauty and poetry embellishment the legends of Ile-Ife – that cradle of mankind – as tradition relates. Their oratorical powers have immortalised the names of Demosthenes and Cicero, but their orations in many points can hardly be said to excel those that have been delivered in the house of Ogboni at Abeokuta or those in the palace of the Alafin of Oyo, or those that have moved the soldiery to deeds of bravery in the camp of Field-Marshal Ogedengbe of Ilesha . . . [1]

Such cultural self-confidence was hard-won. It developed partly as a response to the increasingly racist discourse emanating from European sources, itself fuelled by the naked territorial ambitions thrown into relief at the Berlin conference of 1884.[2] Despite the commitment of the West African educated elite to the promotion of modernity within their society, European powers largely abandoned the project of 'civilizing' Africans and creating 'Black Victorians'. Resistance to the British empire began to take two forms, which were held in a productive tension: the educated elite worked both with their own tools, in the rediscovery of the excellences of African culture, and with the tools that they had been given, the discourses of the west, often including Christianity but also prominently classical tropes. A powerful conjunction was on occasion offered by the claim that ancient Greece had been partly formed by contact with Africa.

The movement to re-value African culture and customs, in the period roughly from the 1880s to the First World War, has often been termed 'cultural nationalism', as in the pioneering analyses of Ajayi (e.g. 1961). Although there is some difficulty with the term, in that no 'nation' as such was at stake, it has gained considerable currency among scholars, and thus continues useful. While the political and cultural leaders whose texts I examine here are likely to subscribe to a pan-African politics rather than a national, most of them were also active in the politics of specific West African communities, and some were part of what may be termed the earliest anti-colonial or 'nationalist' movements in West Africa, namely the Aborigines' Rights Protection Society of the Gold Coast and the National Congress of British West Africa.[3]

As well as rejecting European names, such as Pythagoras, and adopting African names again, some members of the educated elite ceased to wear European dress – up until that point, a sine qua non of Christianity and civilization – and favoured native clothing instead (Ayandele 1966: 254–9). Yet some of the most prominent advocates of cultural emancipation made a point of likening native dress to the ancient Roman toga. John Mensah Sarbah (1864–1910), a graduate of the Wesleyan Boys' High School (later Mfantsipim) in the Gold Coast and the first West African to qualify as a barrister, was described thus in the newspaper *Gold Coast People* of 30 November 1893: 'Mr J. Mensah Sarbah, who in his native cloth looked like a Roman in toga garb at the forum . . .'. Sarbah emphasized the point himself, at greater length, in the Introduction to his *Fanti National Constitution*, first published in 1906 (1968: xvii–viii):

> [I am] fully convinced that it is better to be called by one's own name than to be known by a foreign one, that it is possible to acquire Western learning and be expert in scientific attainments without neglecting one's mothertongue, that the African's dress has a closer resemblance to the garb of the Grecian and the Roman (the acquisition of whose languages and philosophies is still promoted in modern European universities, and the knowledge of them the standard of liberal culture) and should not be thrown aside, even if one wears European dress during business hours.

The resemblance between native dress and toga here might stand as a metonymy for Sarbah's desired amalgam among mother tongue, Western learning and scientific attainments, which he implicitly promoted at Mfantsipim.

The use of classical tropes to promote African identity and political development can be found within the writings of several other late-nineteenth-

and early-twentieth-century West Africans who were recognized by their contemporaries as cultural and political leaders. In this chapter we shall read the classical references within the texts of James Africanus Beale Horton, Edward Wilmot Blyden, Kobina Sekyi and Joseph Ephraim Casely Hayford. Within many of these texts, classical literature and history provide a symbolic repertoire of considerable authority. Often, the repertoire is more resonant in general application rather than in specific quotation; Rome and Greece are invoked in their overall contours rather than detail, as they frequently were by Europeans too, and certainly without the armature of scholarly footnotes which we might now expect. These West African texts demonstrate the use of classical material as cultural capital, wielded in a particular struggle, and implicitly going beyond the pragmatic, if controversial, learning of the languages which was the focus of the first chapter. The classical material is often used to make claims about Africa's own antiquity; while the cultural nationalists do not routinely claim that classical civilization descended from Africa, as do some later commentators, they do point to early exchanges between Africa and Greece in order to claim for Africa both history and autonomy.

James Africanus Beale Horton

James Africanus Beale Horton (1835–83) was a Yoruba by parentage, but born in Sierra Leone and a member of the 'educated elite' by upbringing and education. Having studied at Fourah Bay College and then at King's College London, he qualified in medicine at Edinburgh, and served as a physician in the British army in West Africa. His adoption of the name 'Africanus' might suggest the Europeanizing disposition of the West African elite in the middle of the nineteenth century, but Ayandele calls it a 'significant, emotive, self-advertising word' (1970: 14). It may also have been a practical way of distinguishing himself in Britain, and indeed Adell Patton (1996: 78) suggests that it was standard professional practice among 'scholars of rank' to Latinize one's name. Approaching his African identity by way of the Latin language in these multiple ways, the name perhaps models a subjectivity produced by two cultures and the relations between them.

Horton's writings are political, historical, medical and scientific, rather than avowedly literary, but they deploy the kind of knowledge of the classical literatures that identified them as authoritative. A number of his publications concern medicine, public health and the physical and human geography of West Africa, but he also published the very important *West African Countries and Peoples* (1868), in which he analysed the possibilities of self-government for each of the contemporary colonies, and *Letters on the Political Condition of the Gold Coast* (1870) which examined recent history. While his targeted audience presumably included the educated among European colonizers as well as among West Africans, his assertive politics may be discerned from the title of an earlier (1865) pamphlet, 'The African's View of the Negro's Place in Nature'. In this he 'signified' on the infamous article by James Hunt, 'The Negro's Place in Nature', which claimed to prove that the Negro is closer to the ape than to the European, or more circumspectly that 'the analogies are far more numerous between the Negro and apes than between the European and apes' (1864: xvi). Within Horton's work, Greece and Rome give depth and authority to his analyses of contemporary African states.

In the introductory paragraphs of *Letters on the Political Condition of the Gold Coast* Horton makes the point that (1970: vii):

> The history of a country forms a part of the history of the world, and its publication is necessary for its preservation. Thus Caesar preserved his brilliant conquests over the Gauls in his Commentaries, and Cicero the glorious history of the Roman Republic in his voluminous writings. With the view of preserving in a continuous form the history of the Gold Coast for the last ten years, I have . . . given a full account of the political atmosphere of the Gold Coast a few years prior to and since the transfer to territory between the English and Dutch Governments . . .

The appeal to classical sources counters the European assumption, often identified with Hegel but legible in many other texts, that Africa has no history, and here the appeal is extremely self-confident in implicitly equating the history of West Africa with that of the most prestigious ancient cultures.[4] A similar boldness in asserting equality can be read in gestures like the use of a Homeric quotation to describe the Elminas (1970: 46) or in the outburst, on the occasion of an atrocity during the Ashanti wars, 'I would cry credo quia impossibile est, were I not in possession of sufficient testimony on oath to corroborate every tittle of the statement' (1970: 123). This last quotation employs the classical language but quotes from the early Christian source

Tertullian (*On the Body of Christ* 5.4). As a native of North Africa, Tertullian has a significant role overall in Horton's writings.

In other references, Greece and Rome are mobilized as signs of pervasive historical change which shifts the relative status of the ancient civilizations, the modern European powers and the nations of Africa. The opening paragraph of *West African Countries and Peoples*, decorated with five footnotes to classical texts,[5] offers a broad sweep of history which takes 'mankind . . . from a primitive state of barbarism' to the 'benefits of civilized life'. How we may know this history is explicitly said to be by 'ingenious demonstrative analogies of the manners, customs, and tenets of the inhabitants at present occupying this globe, as compared with those of a few centuries ago' (1969: 3). Geography is bound to history, in that certain present inhabitants indicate the state of some previous ones, and these analogies also indicate how we should choose among different models of historical change. Thus, the comparisons between past and present validate 'the speculative traditions of the ancient Romans', which describe an 'advance from a rude and helpless state to the formation of political society' rather than the Greek 'mythological legend' which offers a primary 'state of innocence and bliss' (Horton 1969: 3). Once the classical authorities are laid under contribution, the narrative can proceed to build the future prosperity of West Africa on the basis of its previous 'barbarism', and two chapters are particularly significant in Horton's attempt, 'Erroneous Views Respecting the African', and 'The Progressive Advancement of the Negro Race'.

In 'Erroneous Views Respecting the African' (1969: 19–30), the argument is to 'claim the existence of the attribute of a common humanity in the African or Negro race' (1969: 27), and in this essay, the common humanity is guaranteed by reference to classical authorities such as Aristotle (1969: 27) as well as to Christian teachings. Furthermore, Africa under the British is compared to Britain under the Romans, to the disparagement of the latter (1969: 26):

> It would be as absurd to attempt to compare the civilization of Britain fifty years after the landing of Julius Caesar with the civilization of Rome, then in the zenith of her prosperity, as to attempt to compare the result of civilization of a savage, barbarous race of Africa, during fifty years' feeble attempts at civilization, with the civilization of the nineteenth century in England. And, in fact, if the comparison be made between the degree of improvement exhibited by the two countries, history informs us that the

> present degree of improvement exhibited by the liberated Africans under missionary influence far exceeds that of Britain under Roman influences during a similar period of time.

According to the Romans, such as Cicero and Caesar who are quoted extensively, the ancient Britons were 'very barbarous', and were not even prized as slaves, on account of their inability to learn music or letters (1969: 28). If Britain was not 'condemned . . . to an eternity of Boeotian darkness' by the Romans' strictures, the inference is that 'untutored negroes' should not be so condemned by the writings 'of members of the Anthropological Society' (1969: 29).

In a subsequent chapter, 'The Progressive Advancement of the Negro Race' (1969: 52–61), another side of this version of historical change is given. Classical authorities are now called upon to show how Africa was itself the teacher of Europe, specifically of Greece and Rome. Although no precise classical references are cited, unlike in the opening pages, Solon, Plato and Pythagoras are listed as eminent men who made pilgrimages to Africa in search of knowledge, 'and several came to listen to the instructions of the African Euclid who was at the head of the most celebrated mathematical school in the world . . . The conqueror of the great African Hannibal made his associate and confidant the African poet Terence' (1969: 59). After also invoking the numerous African fathers of the early church – Origen, Tertullian, Augustine, Clement and Cyril – Horton enters into the debate about whether the 'Ethiopians' of antiquity were 'negroes', and calls on Herodotos to show that they were (1969: 60):

> The accounts given by Herodotus, who travelled in Egypt, and other writers, settle the question that such they were. Herodotus describes them as 'woolly-haired blacks, with projecting lips', and further notes that the people of Colchis 'were Egyptian colonists, who were "black in complexion and woolly-haired."'

In the face of prejudices like that articulated by Hegel, Horton establishes Africa's claim to its own history by showing that it predates that of classical antiquity. What modern Europe is now to Africa, Horton's model shows, Africa was to Greece and Rome, affording modern Europe no exclusive ownership either of the classical heritage or of civilization itself, and proving from a different direction that Africans are more than capable of emerging from 'savagery'. The narrative arc holds out to the 'nations of Western Africa' 'the hope that in process of time their turn will come, when they will occupy a prominent position in the world's history, and when they will command a voice in the council of nations' (1969: 61).

Since Africa taught Europe, but now must learn from Europe again, Horton's historical narrative has another significance, in that 'civilisation must come from outside' (Horton 1969: 175); no country can civilize itself. 'As it was with Europe and America, so it must be with Africa' (1969: 175); the civilizing power moves across the globe as the concomitant of what might otherwise appear as invasion. But since Rome and Greece can demonstrate that Europe used to be 'savage', and thereby guarantee that Africa will soon be 'civilized', Horton can also claim that Africa will civilize much more swiftly than Europe, because she has modern invention on her side as well as the weight of historical precedent. Thus his *Letters on the Political Condition of the Gold Coast* opens with the confident flourish (Horton 1970: i–ii):

> 'Rome was not built in a day'; the proudest kingdom in Europe was once in a state of barbarism perhaps worse than now exists amongst the tribes chiefly inhabiting the West Coast of Africa; and it is an incontrovertible axiom that what has been done can again be done. . . . The civilisation of France and England, and even of Germany, dates from the time when Rome, agitated by social contentions, made Julius Caesar proconsul of Transalpine Gaul; the brilliant conquest which he made over the then savage tribes who lived in caves and miserable huts, and the wise but rigid government which he enforced, led in eleven hundred years to the gigantic discoveries and improvements which now startle the denizens of less favoured climes.
>
> But I argue that modern inventions . . . leave not a shadow of doubt in my mind that, although it took eleven hundred years to bring France and England to the high standard of civilisation which they now occupy, it will take far less time to bring a portion at least of Western Africa to vie with Europe in progressive development.

The classical examples here offer an implied rebuke to Europeans who claim 'civilization' as their own, reminding them that they acquired it only as victims of Rome, and threaten them with the possibility of being overtaken in the race for 'progress' by Africa. At that point in the cycle where Africa achieves 'civilization', however, the narrative stops; although Horton subscribes to a cyclic model of history (Shepperson 1969: xx), the cycle does not need to move into Africa's decline and the rise of another culture, because it was Africa that initiated the cycle much earlier, when Solon and Plato made their pilgrimages.

When Africa is 'civilized' again, then, the cycle will be complete. Certain European theorists, including Matthew Arnold and Lord Lugard, had already argued that civilization had shifted from the ancient world to modern Europe via the Roman conquests (Mazrui 1978: 82). In their models, civilization had then stopped, as it does in Horton's, but in Europe rather than in Africa. Horton's model is thus a development and an interrogation of theirs.

Although Horton seems to have accepted without question the judgement that contemporary Africa was largely 'savage' and uncivilized, his own career offers evidence to the contrary,[6] and his prose often delights, correspondingly, in a highly telling classical quotation. Shepperson draws attention to his 'assurance in handling classical quotations' (1969: iv), and I have suggested above that several of them can be read to make quite bold assertions about the equivalent historical value of the Gold Coast and the classical cultures. Others have a more purely rhetorical force. When the claim to 'the existence of the attribute of a common humanity in the African or Negro race' is substantiated by the quotation from Spinoza 'Natura una et communis omnium est' ('Nature is one and common to all', Horton 1969: 27), the very possibility of offering the quotation, in the original language, enacts what Horton claims.[7] In a similar vein Horton ends 'Advice to the Rising Generation', which closes *West African Countries and Peoples*: 'Then there will be the real exercise of those qualities which will gradually lead to the attainment of the power of self-government and the contemplated improvement of the House of Commons Committee will go on *tuto, cito*, and *jucunde*' ('safely, swiftly, and sweetly', Horton 1969: 249).[8] In both these quotations, the African ability to command Latin bears out Horton's contention. His commitment to the classical languages is also shown in a quotation from the *Christian Messenger and Examiner* (Horton 1969: 103), which first extols the African's 'wonderful gift of learning a foreign language, such as is seldom met with in any other part of the globe', and goes on to stress the importance of the 'study of old and modern languages among the educated and gifted Africans, to make the riches of classic and foreign literature accessible to them, to translate them into the native languages, and by that means make them by-and-by the property of all'. This acquisition of language and literature is not, however, to produce young men who 'forget and despise the mother-tongue', so that the deployment of the classics takes place within a context of cultural independence that is appropriately African.

Although classical references form only a small part of Horton's oeuvre, it is no coincidence that both his major publications open with invocation of Greece and Rome, and that it is classical history, and Africa's relations to the classical world, which ground his model of historical change in general. His work thus shows an early and highly politicized awareness of the need to combat European cultural arrogance by 'breaking the European monopoly on ancient Greece' (Mazrui 1978: 94). While some modern commentators have acclaimed his vision as 'far ahead of his time' (Nwauwa 1999) in its assumption of independence and mass and higher education, others have critiqued Horton's apparent inability to understand either the underlying power structures of colonialism, especially in the run-up to the 'scramble', or the ways in which the educated elite could be seen as compromised by their admiration of Western culture (Ayandele 1971). Commentators have not shown interest in Horton's classical references, but these sum up the paradox of his publications very well, in that he draws on the past to forge a future. The role of the classics in his argument is to prove not only Africa's centrality to history, but also its right to modernity, or as Horton calls it, 'civilization'.

We may note a couple of further points about Horton's use of the classical repertoire, which will also be significant for other authors canvassed here. There is some difference between the invocations of Greece and of Rome, since the latter appears more often in contexts where politics and history are under discussion, and the former where culture in a more general sense is at stake. While Rome enables very useful temporal arguments, particularly when Roman Britain is concerned, ancient Greece provides the text with a version of Africa productively different from that offered by contemporary European ideology. For modern readers, the version of the relation between Africa and Greece purveyed in Horton is recognizable from the work of Martin Bernal.[9] Bernal's *Black Athena* (1987) suggested that ancient Greeks' views of their cultural dependence on Egypt and Phoenicia were historically valid, but had been largely obliterated by the racist desire of nineteenth-century scholarship to derive Europe solely from itself. Although Bernal does not discuss the work of Horton or other cultural nationalists, their work is important in showing that Africans were well aware of a tradition which offered an alternative to the pure descent of Europe from Greece, and that they made creative use of it from a relatively early stage in their dealings with imperialism.[10] Horton's texts also suggest that the rigorously digitized classical education which we encountered in Chapter 1 could, almost paradoxically, give access to a breadth and depth of cultural reference which grounded the authority of a radical discourse.

Edward Wilmot Blyden

If Horton's classical cultures were deployed as part of an historical argument, as well as of his pointed rhetoric, those in the writings of Edward Wilmot Blyden (1832–1912) first constructed a version of history and then subverted and transcended it. Of African descent, Blyden was born in the Caribbean but, repulsed by the racism of the United States, which would not permit him to study at theological college, emigrated as a young man to Liberia, in 1850. In this West African country a new settlement was developing under the patronage of the American Colonization Society, which aimed to find a home for Africans displaced by slavery to the United States. Although he occupied many posts in Liberia, Blyden also spent some time based in Lagos and considerable periods in Sierra Leone, as well as travelling to Europe and the United States; as he repeatedly traverses the Black Atlantic, he is perhaps a prime example of the 'migratory subjectivity' that Newell identifies in West African culture (2006: 13). At different times Principal of Alexander High School, Professor of Classics, President of Liberia College and Ambassador to Britain, Blyden also founded and edited several newspapers and wrote numerous essays in which he developed a 'pan-Negro' ideology, rooted in the idea of Africa as a homeland for all those of African descent.[11] Disseminated throughout the region, and even into Europe and the United States, his writings on 'Negro' identity, abilities and destiny were inspirational to the cultural nationalists of the late nineteenth century, and Blyden was widely recognized as a leader, even a 'colossus', among the West African intelligentsia.[12] Among his contributions, his early version of pan-Africanism, and his resolute resistance to racist ideologies, stand out; his identity as a classicist is less often celebrated.[13]

Extraordinarily adept at many European languages, Hebrew and Arabic, Blyden wields his classical learning in his voluminous writings as part of a strategically assertive personal and political identity. Throughout his various publications, the rhetorical register is very high, forceful and intellectually demanding, with a wide access to various cultures, including but not limited to ancient Greece and Rome, that implicitly commands respect. Like Horton, he addressed an audience of the West African educated elite, but unlike him, Blyden also found receptive readers in the United States. While Horton was chiefly preoccupied by the destiny of West Africa, Blyden elaborated a pan-African vision and, especially, a new account of African identity. To do this, he draws on multiple traditions. The biblical tradition is crucial, and probably provides his texts with more figures of speech than any other discourse, as one might expect of a writer in the mid-nineteenth century. Although much of his rhetoric draws on Christian tropes, and he is also very much at home in Islamic discourse, all of the European tradition is laid under contribution, so that not only Homer and Horace, but also Goethe and Pope, find a place in, for instance, an address given in 1865 to the Mayor and Common Council of the City of Monrovia on the anniversary of Liberia's independence (Blyden 1865). But the symbolic repertoire of the classics plays a crucial role in his texts, important for the various different perspectives that they can offer, and also because, given their familiarity to an educated audience, classical references can be twisted and turned to make less familiar points. The classical references in his work range from a simple Latin 'tag', of the kind often deployed in order to indicate the education of the writer and his targeted audience, to sustained metaphoric flights which turn received versions of Africa and Europe on their heads.

Some of his classical quotations are fairly standard, for instance variations on the theme of 'non omnis moriar' ('I shall not entirely die', 1994: 348–9),[14] but many others make new connections and arguments. As a student and teacher, Blyden uses classical expertise as a practical way of judging others' fitness for the ministry,[15] and he regularly writes to colleagues asking for more books with which to equip his classes.[16] Famously, he initiated a long-lasting correspondence with Gladstone, in which he discusses Gladstone's work on the classics, invites support for his own educational ventures, and deploys substantial quotations both as a *captatio benevolentiae* and as a proof of the common ground between them. Thus in the letter of 20 April 1860, Gladstone is feted with the words 'you may adopt the languages of Horace "exegi monumentum aere perennis" . . .' (I have built a monument more lasting than bronze) whereas Blyden adopts for himself, the struggling classics teacher in the newly developing society of

Liberia, a quite different persona: 'I do not know that I could give you a better idea of my efforts than referring you to the labours of Sisyphus when Ulysses saw him'. He then quotes *Odyssey* XI. 593, 'And indeed I saw Sisyphus, suffering terrible pains'.[17] Although he acknowledges his poverty and membership of a race 'down-trodden and despised' (Blyden 1978: 98), the fact that he couches the complaint in a quotation from Juvenal means that he more than holds his own in the encounter with the British statesman. The quotation is 'Haud facile emergent quorum virtutibus obstat/Res angusta domi', which may be translated 'With difficulty shall they emerge whose virtues are obstructed/by poverty at home' (1978: 29).[18]

Blyden himself later became, like Gladstone, a statesman as well as a classicist, although his bid for the Presidency of Liberia failed and at certain points he was forced to live in exile from his adopted country, often in Lagos or Sierra Leone. While still a teacher, on 13 April 1867, he wrote to Gladstone in more conventional vein, on the connections between classics and the public role. While the paragraph corresponds to much that has been written about the educational value of classics at different times and places, it also shows us that students in Liberia did not always accept those arguments, and it perhaps has an added poignancy in that the challenges facing the Liberians were considerably greater than those that the 'white Victorians' like Gladstone would encounter (1978: 77):

> I have just come across a most exquisite passage from your pen – a translation of Homer's *Iliad* (Book IV – 422–432). It is the most beautiful and the most exact translation of the passage I have ever seen. It strikes me that the most fastidious admirer of the Maeonian bard – Mr. Matthew Arnold himself – must be satisfied with the idiomatic English as well as the Homeric idea brought out in the felicitous rendering of
>
> So mute they marched, thou couldst not ken
> They were a mass of living men.
>
> Sometimes my pupils get restless, and not being able to see the connection between their present intellectual drudgery, as they call it, and their future usefulness in subserving the diversified needs of their race on this continent, or in promoting their personal advancement, they are anxious to leave school and plunge into trade, which is a great temptation on this coast. They want to know what will be the use to them of classical lore. Sometimes they put

> the very question of Strepsiades. [Aristophanes *Clouds*, 648, which could be roughly translated, 'How will poetry get me fed?]
>
> I then point them to yourself and other statesmen in England, and show them how you were trained to be the men you are; and when I can exhibit to them such translations made by the great men of the earth – not extorted by the necessities of a daily recitation, but voluntarily produced as a pleasant relaxation in the midst of most onerous duties – they are encouraged and betake themselves with fresh avidity to the foot of Mount Parnassus.

In the poetry of Blyden's prose we are perhaps invited to see the Liberian students as themselves 'mute marchers' in the uphill struggle.

Blyden mobilized the classical repertoire to represent himself occasionally, and again in conventional ways, as in his letter to Gladstone quoted above. On 12 July 1877 he longs for the 'eyes of Argus and the arms of Briareus that I might do the work of 50 men' in the service of Liberia, and conversely on 24 January 1910 he foresees only 'dark prospects' for himself, likening himself to Cicero, Demosthenes and Socrates who 'must go if the unprincipled demagogue so wills'.[19] A few of his classical quotations seem to be used chiefly for rhetorical effect with little further resonance, but many more labour to construct a revised version of history and of African identity. In the service of an independent African identity, which Blyden saw as crucial for overcoming the harmful effects of colonialism, his texts elaborate on an 'Ethiopia' which is offered both by the biblical quotation, 'Ethiopia shall soon stretch out her hands to the Lord' (Psalms 68.31) and by the verses from Homer's *Iliad* in which Zeus is described as absent from the scene of the Trojan War because he is visiting the 'blameless Ethiopians' (1.423). Although there was and is some controversy about where ancient and biblical Ethiopia was located, Blyden, like Horton, argues for Ethiopians to be understood as 'black' and their country to be equated with the continent of Africa.[20] Once this is in place, a history of Africa can be written which counters the racist assumption that the 'dark continent' had no history or identity before European colonialism. The Ethiopians are thus the subject of long excurses in Blyden's major work, *Christianity, Islam and the Negro Race* (1994: 132–3, 174–8).[21]

Blyden's texts convene Herodotus and the *Periplous of Hanno*[22] as well as the early Church Fathers, like Augustine and Tertullian, to write the narrative of an Africa which combines the Homeric and biblical virtues and thus offers a pride in 'the race' that will overcome Africans' more recent colonial inheritance of self-doubt and self-condemnation. Having asked Gladstone, on 16 April 1862, for 'the sources of information on the subject of the Ancient Ethiopians', he sent him on 11 May 1869 a copy of the pamphlet 'The Negro in Ancient History', 'the first article in an American review from the pen of a Negro' (1978: 78),[23] and this topic informs a good many of Blyden's classical quotations. While other authors also draw on the Ethiopian quotations from Psalms and Homer, Blyden ups the ante by retelling in addition the story from Herodotus of the king of the Ethiopians who saw through the ruse of Cambyses, when the latter plotted to extend his territory. The king warned Cambyses off his territorial ambitions, reminding him to thank the gods that the Ethiopians were not inspired by the desire to add another's land to their own (Kedourie 1970: 269, cf. Herodotus 3.21).[24] Blyden's texts can thus have Ethiopians who are not only virtuous, refraining from imperial adventures, but also implicitly threatening to potential colonizers, well able themselves to carry out such adventures if they wish.

The most crucial of Blyden's writings are collected in *Christianity, Islam and the Negro Race*, first published in 1887. As with many of the early anti-colonial texts, much of the rhetoric draws on biblical tropes and quotations, but classical antiquity is also an important resource throughout, and offers a range of rhetorical and political effects. Within the history of 'Ethiopia', Blyden notes the Greeks who learned from Africa, as did Horton, but he is not deploying antiquity in order to prove Africa's claim to modernity. Instead, antiquity offers a model of African independence and cultural autonomy; so, Blyden lists the foreign cultures who have tried to gain a foothold on the African continent and have been driven back. Since these include the Egyptians (counter-intuitively, as he admits), the Carthaginians, Romans, early Christians and Portuguese (1994: 179–83, 274–5), Blyden's conclusion is that Africa must be for the Africans. The African republic of Liberia, and the concomitant departure of the contemporary European colonizers, form the logical conclusion of this argument.

Within this construction of a usable African past, the classical repertoire can be pressed into service in order to resist harmful European histories and representations. For instance, classical quotations are deployed to defend the reputation of Africans, Blyden's prose simultaneously advertising his own extensive acquaintance with the classics and his adversaries' obliviousness. Deprecating European misrepresentations of Islam in West Africa, Blyden describes the futility of current efforts at Christian proselytizing by quoting the account, at Vergil, *Aeneid* 2.543–5, of the spear thrown feebly by the aged king of Troy, Priam, which, failing to penetrate, hangs uselessly from the shield of Achilles' murderous son Pyrrhus (1994: 72). Comparing the treatment of African soldiers among the Portuguese, French and British, to the detriment of the last-named, Blyden concludes (1994: 47)

> If it is asked why Protestant Negro soldiers are not equally efficient – why the West India troops did not distinguish themselves in the recent Ashantee war – we have no other reply than the query of the poet:
>
> Quis enim virtutem amplectitur ipsam
> Praemia si tollas?

(Who embraces the virtue itself/if you take away the rewards? [Juvenal Satire 10, 141]). Africans will not fight if their prowess is not recognized; Blyden's rhetoric of reciprocity undermines other imperial assumptions of hierarchy.

A more sustained attack concerns Sir Garnet Wolseley, who in his battles against the Ashanti had famously addressed his troops to this effect: 'it must never be forgotten by our soldiers that Providence has implanted in the heart of every native of Africa a superstitious fear and dread of the white man that prevents the Negro from daring to meet us face to face in combat' (1994: 21).[25] To counter this extraordinary assertion Blyden points out that 'Sir Garnet also deemed it important to bring to bear against these awe-struck Negroes armed with cheap flint muskets, all the appliances of modern warfare, and, no doubt, bore in mind the Roman poet's advice – *Ne crede colori*' (1994: 21). The 'awe-struck Negro' writer thus adeptly reinterprets the Vergilian quotation, which is usually translated 'Do not trust in your good looks', to mean more bluntly 'Do not believe in the colour', and implicitly admonishes Sir Garnet for not taking full account of this useful maxim when he so sweepingly underestimated the Ashanti troops. Blyden continues by noting that (1994: 21–2)

> the statement served its purpose, and is one among the many evidences of Sir Garnet's skill and readiness in not only availing himself of advantageous elements in the situation but of creating them, if they do not exist. In this case, he adroitly played upon the 'superstition' of white men: 'an dolus an virtus, quis in hoste requirat?'

Blyden adroitly plays upon the absurdity of Garnet's claim by terming it a 'superstition', turning Garnet's own word against him. He adds the pertinent Vergilian quotation, which comes from *Aeneid* 2.390, when the Trojans left alive at the fall of Troy arm themselves from fallen Greeks in order to escape. Fitzgerald translates this in context: 'Trickery, bravery; who cares, in war?' and his translation captures the ambivalence of the phrase, which could be voiced either by Garnet, happy to use trickery rather than courage against his enemy, or by Blyden, predicating trickery rather than courage of his enemy. In context the quotation is a very neat way to put European and African on the same footing, each having his valour questioned by the other side. Garnet accuses the Africans of cowardice but Blyden's quotation suggests that Garnet is as capable of *dolus* as of *virtus*. The Vergilian quotation itself seems almost to be assimilated to superstition, in its pithy folk wisdom, as well as representing a critical commentary on Garnet's rhetoric.

Other quotations underline Blyden's arguments when he describes how Africans must resist being made over in Western form, invoking Xenophanes's account of how humans make gods in their own images. 'The saying is attributed to an ancient philosopher that if horses, oxen, and lions could paint they would certainly make gods in their own image . . . This is no doubt true, and the Negro who grew up normally would certainly not be inferior to lions, horses, and oxen' (1994: 18). Discussing how Africans react to exile in the Americas (1994: 44), he uses the Horatian image of the hybrid monster:

> Every intelligent Negro, in the lands of his exile, must feel that he walks upon the face of God's earth a physical and moral incongruity, and as legitimate a subject of laughter as Horace's famous heterogeneous picture, the creation of 'a sick man's dream':
>
> > Humani capiti cervicem pictor equinam
> > Jungere si velit . . .

(As if the painter should wish to join/ a human head to a horse's neck, Horace *Epistle to the Pisones* [*Art of Poetry*] 1.) In the same essay he quotes the newspaper *The West African Reporter*, of Sierra Leone, which called African children 'the Polyphemus of civilisation, huge but sightless, – cui lumen ademptum' (1994: 86) – whose light is taken away – as a result of being exposed only to European and not African cultures and history.[26] The classical repertoire is here not opposed to the African; the antiquity of Europe is a resource in the struggle against its modern aggression.

Conversely, the classical world is also brought in to demonstrate how early Britons were uncivilized (1994: 225), or that Romans themselves performed human sacrifice and engaged in the 'brutal' pursuit of the gladiatorial show (1969: 56, 59). Unlike Horton's model of history, these examples are not assembled in order to suggest a cyclical movement whereby Africa is 'savage' but will become civilized; they go rather to show that 'civilization' is a relative term and that Africa can be proud of her own institutions. Similarly, although Blyden elsewhere subscribes to the Christian viewpoint, he also draws parallels between the paganism of Africa and of classical culture (1994: 259–60, 279–81, 1969: 30), with a view to showing that underlying religiosity transcends cultural differences.

Blyden was committed to the return of Africans from the Americas to their native land, to settle in Liberia and there fulfil the promise of an independent African identity and history. In discussing this project his use of classical referents can become quite startling. Africans who remain in the United States are like the broken statues of the classical heritage (1994: 402): 'many, alas, who may never gain the fructifying atmosphere – who must always resemble those figures one sees in museums in Europe, which would be magnificent if they were complete; as they now stand, they are only splendid torsos – melancholy suggestions of unattainable possibilities'. Conversely, the African who returns to Africa will be like the 'giant of the ancients, who always gained strength, for his conflict with Hercules, whenever he touched his Mother Earth' (1994: 106). Here the myth is refocused away from the 'hero' Herakles and to the side of what is normally the 'monster', Antaeus. In this rescripting of the mythical antagonists we can perhaps read the wholesale re-evaluation of the 'Negro' that Blyden wishes his readers to undertake.

Blyden also re-uses the *Aeneid*, and specifically Aeneas' sojourn in Carthage, in novel ways. Pointing out that 'Emergencies drove homeless wanderers to the shores of Libya' (1994: 110), he argues for Africa's ability to save Europe from itself, as it saved the Trojans, by providing first the slave labour which helped to open up the continent of America, and then by providing new productive land and markets for European commerce. But later the focus of the citation of Aeneas changes, to celebrate a homecoming to the shores of Africa and implicitly to downgrade the other destiny that consisted in the founding of Rome. The African who returns to Africa will be like Aeneas, exclaiming 'O fortunati, quorum iam moenia surgunt' (Oh fortunate they, whose walls already rise, Vergil, *Aeneid* 1.437), but will not need to journey onwards (as Aeneas did to Rome), because he will be planning to settle in Liberia: 'unlike the mythical author of that exclamation, he feels that he has a part in the rising fortunes of the settlements; that what he beholds is not only what he himself may accomplish, but is the promise and pledge of the future greatness of his adopted country' (1994: 120).

Perhaps the most intriguing such rewriting of classical myth comes in an extended comparison in the essay 'Africa's Service to the World', dating to 1880 (1994: 146–7). Here, Blyden rejects one classical trope for Africa and elaborates on another, which he ensures leads back to his central point about African spiritual and intellectual independence. First rejecting the image of Africa as Niobe, because Africa is so much more resilient in the face of loss, he goes on to suggest that Africa is instead a Sphinx, waiting at the crossroads of the world, and dealing death to those who attempt to manage her. But the image does not end on a note of negativity, because the task of explaining the 'riddle' of Africa must consequently be left to the Africans themselves,[27] who alone are equipped with the relevant identity and history.

> Africa is often called the Niobe of the nations, in allusion to the fact that her children in such vast numbers have been torn from her bosom; but the analogy is not strictly accurate . . . The children who were torn from her bosom she could well spare. She has not been petrified with grief; she has not become a stone. She is as prolific to-day as in the days of yore. Her greenness and fertility are perennial. It was said of her in the past, and it may be said of her today, that she is ever bringing forth something new . . . No; if we are to gather an analogy to Africa from ancient fable, the Sphinx supplies us with a truer symbol. The Sphinx was said to sit in the road side, and put riddles to every passenger. If the man could not answer, she swallowed him alive. If he could solve the riddle, the Sphinx was slain. Has not Africa been, through the ages, sitting on the highway of the world? There she is, south of Europe, with but a lake between, joined onto Asia, with the most frequented oceans on the East and West of her – accessible to all the races, and yet her secret is unknown. She has swallowed up her thousands. The Sphinx must solve her own riddle at last. The opening up of Africa is to be the work of the Africans.

Both classical tropes are reworked so that Africa overcomes their possible negative charge, and Africa becomes as central to geography as the nationalist version of Ethiopia shows her to be to history.[28]

As well as rewriting classical myth, Blyden experiments with counterfactual history in order to vindicate the present state of Africa. While classical models are sometimes used to indicate a regularity in human affairs which helps to organize the future of Africans, Blyden's text is also keenly aware of the massive disruption to African history caused by the slave trade, which has produced so much of its present circumstances. He therefore points to the analogous institution of slavery in early Europe, among Angles and Saxons as well as among Greeks and Romans, and goes on to extrapolate a different history for Africa. 'Who was it that sold those Angles whom Gregory saw in the slave-market at Rome? Is it not well known that Saxon husbands and parents sold their wives and daughters? Did not slavery prevail in every country in Europe?' (1994: 309). Blyden then imagines the battle of Marathon with a different result, enabling Asia to invade a Europe thus weakened by slavery. Europe would then be like Africa, riven by the trade in slaves, and would be vulnerable to Asian colonialism in the same way as Africa was to that of Europe (1994: 309):

> Suppose that during the days of European ignorance and darkness, when the people sold their own children, the large alien populations of Asia had agreed to make constant incursions into Europe and stimulate the traffic in slaves. Suppose the result of the battle of Marathon had been different and Europe had become the vassal of Asia, and Asiatic hordes had entered its territory for the purposes for which both Europeans and Asiatics have entered Africa, and had continued their depredations to this period, what would be the condition of Europe today?

Later on in the same article, 'Africa and the Africans', the argument is pursued with additional comparisons (1994: 319):

> It is a fact that a description of the condition of things in portions of central Africa truthfully given would read like an account of the earlier ages of Greece and Rome . . . if the proceedings of chiefs in council which we have witnessed were written down in plain, unadorned style, the account would read like descriptions in Caesar's Commentaries on the doings of the Celts in the days of their unsophisticated habitudes. Now, if Greeks, Romans or Celts had been smothered in the cradle of their civilisation by extraneous violence perpetuated to this time, is it unreasonable to suppose that they would be found at this day in much the same condition that Stanley found some of the African tribes?

Although the text admits the underdevelopment of parts of Africa, the responsibility is imputed to modern Europe, and Greece and Rome work to help imagine a different history for Africa.

Blyden's mobilizing of the classical repertoire thus has varied functions, ranging from the conventional allotment of praise or blame to a wholesale rediscovery of African history, and rethinking of European history. In one of his more sustained discussions of the classics, 'The Aims and Methods of Liberal Education for Africans', his inaugural address as President of Liberia College, delivered on 5 January 1881, classical literature and culture is also of service because it helps to avoid the intersections between European and African history where repeated articulations of prejudice will do most harm to Africans. The address recommends study primarily of the classics at the university, not simply for access to authoritative cultural documents, as classical texts were then held to be, nor for the mental discipline and endurance required for their mastery, which Blyden like many others before and since claimed to provide a good training in itself and a solid foundation for many other enterprises (1994: 100–1). Instead, the address privileges classical civilization because it alone could be studied without encountering the racism that otherwise menaced the literate African (1994: 94–5, 97–8):

> We shall devote attention principally, both for mental discipline and information, to the earlier epochs of the world's history . . . Modern Europe boasts of its period of intellectual activity, but none can equal, for life and freshness, the Greek and Roman prime. No modern writers will ever influence the destiny of the race to the same extent that the Greeks and Romans have done. . . . These [later works, e.g. Shakespeare and Milton, Gibbon and Macaulay] are not the works on which the mind of the youthful African should be trained. It was during the [later] period that the transatlantic slave-trade arose, and those theories – theological, social, and political – were invented for the degradation and proscription of the Negro.

Blyden's analysis continues later:

> The instruments of culture which we shall employ in the College will be chiefly the Classics and Mathematics. By Classics I mean the Greek and Latin languages and their literature. In those languages there are not, as far as I know, a sentence, a word, or a syllable disparaging to the Negro. He may get nourishment from them without taking in any race-poison . . . Passing over, then, for a certain time, the current literature of western Europe, which

> after all is derived and secondary, we will resort to the fountain head; and in the study of the great masters, in the languages in which they wrote, we shall get the required mental discipline without unfavourably affecting our sense of race individuality or our own self-respect. . . . there is nothing that we need to know for the work of building up this country [Liberia], in its moral, political and religious character, which we may not learn from the ancients. There is nothing in the domain of literature, philosophy, or religion for which we need be dependent upon the moderns. Law and philosophy we may get from the Romans and the Greeks, religion from the Hebrews.
>
> Even Europeans, advanced as they are, are every day devoting more and more attention to the Classics.

The classics here provide all the intellectual grounding that Africans need, without subjecting them to the pernicious influence of more contemporary European culture. The timeless value of the classics, for Blyden's text, is not a product of a generalized humanism of European descent, but of an ahistoricity which avoids becoming entangled in a toxically specific history. In this respect too Blyden's use of the classics can be distinguished from that of Horton. Although Blyden draws on the model, shared with Horton, of Africa's originary teaching to Solon and Plato, he does not describe a movement of civilization across the globe, and so is not vulnerable to the colonial history whereby Africans only know Latin and Greek because of their exposure to European culture. Instead, Rome and Greece are in his model a fountainhead equally accessible to Europeans and Africans, and by this means the classics can play a role in the all-important independent African history and identity which Blyden's works construct. This history and identity are what will propel Africa into a viable modernity, rather than the productive contact with Europe described by Horton.

If there is a paradox here, threatening to undo the construction, the text indicates its awareness of the fact in a striking figure that Blyden uses when discussing the necessity for the African somehow to forget Western colonialism, in order to take possession of his own identity (1994: 92): 'Matthew Arnold (in his Preface to Johnson's *Lives of the Poets*) reminds us that when someone talked to Themistocles of an art of memory, he answered "Teach me rather to forget"'. The reference manages to transmit an entire tradition of Western literature, summoning Greece, the Enlightenment and the Victorian age, while demanding that it be transmitted no more.

Kobina Sekyi, the Anglo-Fanti

The redeployment of classical tropes in Blyden's works is probably the most inventive among the West African intelligentsia of the turn of the century. But in some later works by West African nationalists, the classical repertoire is re-used in fictional contexts which suggest further dimensions to West Africans' relationship to the classics. Kobina Sekyi (1892–1956), also known as William Esuman-Gwira Sekyi, was a lawyer and writer very prominent in nationalist organizations. Having been raised an 'Anglo-Fanti' (his own coinage), and taught the superiority of everything English to everything traditionally African, he reassessed his upbringing after experiencing England first-hand, and became a passionate advocate of cultural and political independence.[29] An early adopter of native dress, he also rejected his European name, was a member of the Aborigines Rights Protection Society and the National Congress of British West Africa, and published numerous critiques of the British administration. In 1915 he published the satirical drama *The Blinkards*, and it was performed by the Cosmopolitan Club of Cape Coast – the very club which is ridiculed in Act 3 Scene 2.[30] Formally, the play is not unlike a European 'well-made play',[31] but its satirical force means that its characters are larger than life in their ridiculous obsessions and egregious mistakes. While the plot structure and many of the episodes turn on the issue of traditional polygamy versus European monogamy, the butt of most of the jokes is the Anglomania of some of the West African elite, their wholesale rejection of indigenous tradition and consequent inability to construct authentic identities for themselves.

A major innovation in the play is its polyglot amalgam of English and Fanti, often representing the linguistic chaos that ensues when the Fanti-speakers cannot quite manage the beloved English that they aspire to. In Act 3 Scene 3, set at a wedding reception, the English is permeated with almost Aristophanic neologisms modelled on Latin. Mr Kyirewfu makes a speech in which he applauds, without due regard for syntax, 'the manifestations of incredible merrimentations has displayed in this capacious hall due to wedding matrimonial jollifications' (Sekyi 1974: 97). On sitting down, he asks his neighbour 'What did I say? Did I speak well?' to which the reply is 'Very nice: almost like a European'. Mr Nkuntee, proposing the health of the bridesmaids, continues 'My eyes are effusive of their joyful lacrimosity to perceive *coram* us this reception, and its bride and bridesmaids of amazing pulchritudity. I harbour expectation that they too will be espoused, and not recommend celibacy to young men, and will be led to the hymeneal altar' (1974: 99). The Best-man agrees that they 'will be conducted to the hymeneal altar with considerable éclat, and people will not be wanting to chant their epithalamium with becoming vociferosity' (1974: 99). Finally Mr Odzeikyir toasts the parents of the couple who have initiated the 'inosculation of *vinculum matrimonii*' (1974: 99). The Africans in the scene are comic in their enthralment to the alien language, but perhaps also admirable in their extraordinary creativity with it, and the off-stage Europeans can be read as mocked for their inherent, innate capacity to talk nonsense. Certainly the thrust of Sekyi's work as a whole was very critical of the colonial establishment, not least for the devastating effects that it had had on the self-respect of the indigenous people.

'The Anglo-Fanti' is a short story first published in serial form in *West Africa* magazine in 1918. Not an autobiography, because its subject is dead, it is not a conventional biography either, because of its exclusively present tense, its constant second-person address to the reader, and its unproblematic access to its subject's innermost thoughts. The duality of vision, identifying with the subject but maintaining a distance from him, gives the text a highly ironic charge, which is usually affectionate, and modulates on occasion into pathos; it reproduces the cultural rift which the text discerns in the Anglo-Fanti himself, in that he is growing up in a 'double environment' (1997: 179), a Christianized and Europeanized subject but also caught up in African traditions.

The 'Anglo-Fanti' of the title, Kwesi Onyidzin, has a name which translates as 'one without a name' (Osei-Nyame 1999: 140), which suggests an Everyman and quite possibly an Odysseus. The story of the small boy Kwesi takes him from childhood on the Gold Coast, son of a Christian and Europeanizing family, through school and high school, to legal training in England, and back to the Gold Coast. On his return from England he realizes that he must resist the Europeanizing that is rife around him, and the contradictions thus produced between his outlook and that of his family and friends eventually kill him.

How the narrative proceeds is by positing an 'ordinary little boy' (1997: 177), charming in his energy and fun, and then showing the specific tensions of his upbringing. As a Fanti, there are certain practices to which he must conform, but he is not allowed to be a Fanti unproblematically, because his family also identifies in many respects with the colonizers, embracing Christianity and classical education. The little boy is thus taught to look down on much that is African, and to prefer what is European, with the result that his whole life is distorted and eventually destroyed. With a form of double vision, showing how what is accepted and 'proper' is also deadly, the narrative ironizes all its characters and events, including Kwesi himself, who delights the reader at first but loses some of that sympathy as he progresses on his perverted Bildung. Newell correctly identifies this double vision as a combination of tragedy and comedy which points to the impossibility of combining 'Anglo' with 'Fanti' (2002: 172–5).[32]

The 'Anglo' part of Kwesi's life is often illogical and incomprehensible to the small boy, and it is shown to be a two-edged sword. If he enjoys some aspect of his Europeanized life, such as his English name and his English clothes, it invariably brings suffering, such as teasing, and the torture of woollen suits under a tropical sun. Yet the suffering must be endured in order that further rewards can be obtained; in the case of clothing, he valiantly wears his suits in order to be treated to European sweets (1997: 183). His development is in part an account of how he learns to trade more and more suffering for more and more rewards, and to value most the rewards that involve the greatest suffering, such as European schooling, until eventually the system collapses around him when he journeys to England. Here, the suffering ultimately outweighs the rewards as he finds it not at all the paradise he had been taught to expect. Within his training, Latin is one metonymy for the overall process of encountering European culture. It seems very attractive at first but hides impossible obstacles to his happiness (1997: 214):

> Fortunately, or unfortunately, for him, Greek is not compulsory for boys in his class and in two classes above his. Latin, however, he enjoys, because it consists for him mostly in learning declensions and declining Latin words. He finds it easy to work the simple exercises on the cases. He thinks Latin is very easy indeed. Even the conjugations have no terrors for him. But he soon begins to think that deponent and semi-deponent verbs are quite a nuisance, especially as regards the infinitive mood, and that irregularity and defectiveness in declensions are nowhere near such abnormalities in conjugations. The idea of the facility of Latin altogether disappears by the time he has gone beyond the stage of easy translations into and from Latin.

Latin appears, as often in schoolboy contexts, as a nonsensical and meaningless system, and here it signifies also Kwesi's alienation from his own Fanti culture. As with much in the story, moreover, the products of European civilization appear pleasant at first but have a fatal effect, or if truly worthwhile, are only attainable by an effort that is itself destructive.

On his deathbed (1997: 254), Kwesi complains that his life has been dogged by evil disguised in the shape of good. The duality can also be read in the first line of the above paragraph: 'Fortunately, or unfortunately, for him, Greek is not compulsory for boys in his class and in two classes above his'. The 'fortunately' is easy to grasp, in that Kwesi's confusion would be even more profound if he had to learn Greek with its new alphabet and greater quantity of declension and conjugation. So why the 'unfortunately'? There does not seem to be a simple answer, unless we suppose that in some way Greek would be 'better' for the schoolboy than Latin, perhaps even by giving access to the kind of proto-nationalist history that we have read in Horton and Blyden. As it is, the version of the classics encountered here is utterly pernicious, with no redeeming features, and to that extent creates a situation that is noticeably different either from the embrace of classical languages that we examined in the last chapter, or from the re-use of the classical repertoire that we investigate in this.

Ethiopia Unbound: Joseph Ephraim Casely Hayford

The classical repertoire is a minor if significant part of Sekyi's output, but it is important in the last of the nationalist texts that I shall examine here, *Ethiopia Unbound* by Joseph Casely Hayford (1911 [1969]). Like Blyden and Mensah Sarbah, Casely Hayford (1866–1930) was an educator, journalist, lawyer and politician, among the most prominent nationalists of the late nineteenth and early twentieth centuries. While he was an energetic agitator for West African political and cultural independence, founding the National Congress of British West Africa and writing several books on Gold Coast institutions, he was also a major player in the new pan-African movements, and attended Booker T. Washington's International Conference on the Negro in 1912. Overall, Casely Hayford subscribed to a version of Blyden's politics, advocating a society which could draw on Western accomplishments without rejecting traditional excellences, and certainly without descending to the Anglomania which Sekyi excoriates. Like Blyden, he had a substantial audience in West Africa.

The title of his book, which invokes Aeschylus' *Prometheus Bound*, Shelley's *Prometheus Unbound*, and the idealized 'Ethiopia' constructed from sources in the Bible and classical antiquity, strongly suggests the use of classical tropes to resist colonial incursions and to help in the elaboration of an African nationalist identity. Although the text has a good claim to be West Africa's first novel, its generic profile is complex and resists categorization – as Newell remarks, it is indeed 'unbound' (2002: 151).[33] Kwadwo Osei-Nyame links its form to its politics: 'The unrestricted discursive spaces and narrative forms which the novel accommodates [are] important to a work like *Ethiopia Unbound*, which speaks back to a Western tradition of colonial denigration of the African' (1999: 145). While there are two or three main storylines, which concern the nationalist leader Kwamankra, the Revd. Whiteley and Kwamankra's friend Tandor-Kuma, there are also numerous vignettes of other people and concerns. Towards the end of the text, as Newell comments, a series of lectures, speeches and letters to newspapers supervenes on the narrative structure, giving way in the last chapter to a potted history of the indigenous people of the Gold Coast (2002: 151).[34] Similarly, the texture of the narrative is sometimes realist and sometimes anything but, including scenes set in the Fanti afterlife, in a council of the gods, and in the imaginary Mfantsipim National University; Holden suggests that past, present, future and mythical time coexist (2008: 63). Finally, side by side with the 'supernatural' scenes, the scenes set in contemporary London or on the Gold Coast often have a very ironical, almost satirical cast which removes them to some extent from the requirements of realism. Such irony, which links this work to that of Sekyi, is, Newell suggests, 'one of the few discursive modes available to the truly self-conscious African who is, nevertheless, situated within the colonial language and culture' (2002: 151). Casely Hayford's deployment of classical tropes also shows him highly aware of the difficulties facing the cultural nationalists.

As all commentators point out, numerous different cultural and literary traditions are laid under contribution, but within the complex discursive structure of the novel, important roles are allotted to ancient Greece and Rome. In the first chapter of *Ethiopia Unbound*, the Gold Coast student in London, Kwamankra, browses second-hand bookshops with his British friend Whiteley and, having come across an edition of Marcus Aurelius, they discourse on the nature of divinity and the connections among Christ, the paganisms of the Fanti people and the paganism of classical antiquity (1969: 3).[35] Whereas Whiteley, who is due to be ordained, suddenly discloses doubt as to the godhead of Jesus (4), Kwamankra is comfortable with the notion of a common divinity underlying numerous different religions. As far as he is concerned, the pagan Romans learned from the Greeks, who learned from the Ethopians (5), and contemporary Westerners should learn again; 'We have caught His [Jesus's] Spirit and live; you follow the letter and are tossed hither and thither' (9). Over time Whiteley is convinced, and concludes 'as for the term "heathen", I think that it is arrogant for any devotee of any one sect to apply it to another. There is as much sense in it as the ancient Greeks dubbing all others barbarians' (26). If this aspect of the 'ancient Greeks' thus gives rise to the narrowness of contemporary Westerners, Kwamankra nonetheless judges that classical antiquity as a whole can show a series of figures, like Epictetus and Cleanthes, who together with others like Buddha Gautama (28) produce a wider tradition of human 'communion with God' (29). The two possibilities thus evidenced in the classical tradition correspond to the alternatives that Osei-Nyame has suggested for the novel as a whole: '*Ethiopia Unbound* does not make a sole claim to knowledge and civilization, since to do so would be to reproduce the tyranny of colonialist ideology. Instead, it provides an alternative thought system to Western systems of rationality which are pervaded with a sense of cultural superiority' (1999: 147). The classical tradition here can be aligned with the indigenous African system of thought in that both can provide alternatives to contemporary Western narrowness.

Kwamankra later claims to believe in 'the Father of all, call him Nyiakropon, Zeus, Ra, Jupiter, or by what name soever you please' (41), so that here the 'savage' and 'heathen' name of the African divinity is coupled with the gods of antiquity, implicitly correcting Western notions of a hierarchy among religions. Much later in the text, Casely Hayford does make a claim for the spiritual superiority of Africa, cast in the familiar terms of the likeness between native cloth and toga (197); the students in the text's imaginary university will be dressed 'not in top hat and broad cloth, but in the sober garb in which the Romans conquered the material world, and in which we [Africans] may conquer the spiritual world'. The conquering spirituality here draws on several compelling models, like those of Horton and Blyden, of the relations between the 'Ethiopians' and classical antiquity.

Kwamankra's notions of divinity are tested when his wife dies in childbirth, taking with her their daughter, and leaving him with their son to raise.[36] In a long central set-piece, however, he is able to journey to the afterlife, to meet his wife and daughter again, and to learn from them how mortals should live. As scholars regularly note, this part of the text invokes Bunyan's *Pilgrim's Progress*, with its shining city that may only be approached by a river crossed by means of faith (47). While much of the description of the afterlife is informed by Fanti conceptions, and much is idiosyncratic, other founding narratives of the journey are also legible, in particular those of Homer and Plato. Poignant moments in the Odyssean narrative are recalled when Kwamankra, unlike Odysseus in the Underworld, is able to embrace and kiss his family (52, 57), and the Platonic myth of Ur is perhaps invoked when Kwamankra feels that he is sent back from the afterlife 'on an errand to mortals' (53). The particular task laid on him by his wife, when he returns to ordinary life, is to 'testify against corruption and wrong in high places in the name of truth' (62), a duty that has obvious relevance for the nationalist opposition to colonialism.

After Kwamankra's journey, the second half of the novel, set on the Gold Coast, takes on a more incisively satiric accent. Many different scenes, most of them darkly comic, encompass the insidious moral corruption among the colonial civil servants, the encroaching racism among the European clergy (including, egregiously, Whiteley), the colonial establishment's hostility to Kwamankra's nationalist leadership, the failures of the water supply, the failures of the railway and the toxic effects of the liquor trade. Other more serious scenes show Kwamankra starting to teach his son about white people's conception of 'the yellow peril' (chapter 9) and 'the black peril' (chapter 10). The penultimate chapter, which is also a scene of teaching, elaborates the closest relation in the novel between the African and the classical tradition.

This important chapter is titled 'A Similitude: the Greek and the Fanti'. In it, Kwamankra's son is already 'grappling with the intricacies of Greek roots and Latin suffixes'; that is, he is following the normal disciplinary trajectory of the educated elite. The training involved is not only linguistic, because Kwamankra encourages him to draw comparisons between 'the mode of thought and the practice of the ancients; and he would insist that there was no better intellectual, moral, and national training for a young Fanti than such exercise involved' (199). Why this constitutes a 'national' training is made clear when Kwamankra asks his son to read to him from the English translation of *Odyssey* 6, and the son observes numerous similarities between the practices of the ancient Greeks and the traditional Fanti. The scene of Nausicaa's excursion 'looks very much like how the Fanti women prepare to do their washing in the brook, and it is curious the mention of the use of oil to anoint the body after a bath. Why, that's just what our people do' (201). Furthermore, 'Alcinoüs is described as a king. His daughter meets him as he is going to the Council with the chiefs of the land. There is something strikingly in accord with our own custom here – just what an *Omanhin* would do' (202). Marriage customs, hospitality, libations and sacrifice, and even the custom of counting a sneeze as a blessing, all ensure that 'the Fanti-born feels himself particularly at home with these Grecians' (203). The chapter ends with Kwamankra discoursing on the particularly striking similarities of the invocation of the deities in Greek and in Fanti, and the novel thus returns to its opening reflections on the nature of divinity. Perhaps answering Sekyi's novel, by offering ancient Greece as a means to African renewal, Kwamankra concludes that the Ethiopian 'gains vastly more in self-respect by intimate acquaintance with the ancient Greek than with the modern Saxon' (205).

The overall argument is kin to that of Blyden's address on liberal education, but we should note that the argument is now made within the domestic context, via a father's teaching to his son. The scene of domestic pedagogy perhaps addresses a few concerns, which may be understood also with reference to the preceding chapter, titled 'Race Emancipation – the crux'. In this preceding chapter, Kwamankra addresses a Pan-African conference and gives a speech which essentially ventriloquizes Blyden's politics, including his desire for a West African university. Kwamankra rejects the notion that educated Africans are necessarily separated from their own cultures, even though he agrees that Western methods of education 'denationalize' the African (192–3). Towards the end of this earlier chapter, Kwamankra meets Dr Blyden himself, who reminds him of the biblical prophecy that 'a little child shall lead them' and claims that the child 'is Africa' (197). The son in the penultimate chapter, then, who learns Latin and Greek and about Homeric society, can perhaps be understood in part as identified with that 'little child'. As such, he can suggest a future for West Africa which avoids the struggles of the contemporary, finding links between

Western tradition and indigenous African culture which validate them both, specifically in a version of ancient Greece. The domestic scene also suggests an advance on Blyden's rhetoric, making his arguments more familiar and appealing, thereby modelling perhaps the way in which the new self-respect can be disseminated among Africans.[37] If there is no contradiction between the Homeric and the Fanti, perhaps there is no contradiction in being a member of the educated elite and an advocate of traditional culture. The chapter confirms the thrust of Kwamankra/Blyden's rhetoric in the preceding chapter by pointing the way forward to a productive synthesis of cultures, instead of a conflict, and the educated African is shown to be still vitally connected to the ordinary people, rather than alienated.

The formal and generic peculiarities of this early novel may thus be partly accounted for in this Homeric chapter, in the scene of teaching. The final chapters of the novel abandon the earlier satirical narrative voice for a voice of explication and exhortation, so that readers of the novel can reproduce its teachings within themselves and for others.

In the late nineteenth and early twentieth centuries, cultural nationalists thus found various ways to use classical traditions in their political and cultural projects. The texts examined here display a range of positions: Sekyi uses classics to indict British colonialism for its undermining of West African culture and society, whereas Horton suggests that the classical tradition offers reasons for West African self-confidence and self-assertion. Blyden's dazzling erudition uses classics to help reimagine historical process and to build African independence politically, culturally and spiritually, but Casely Hayford adds a domestic, pedagogic dimension which is implicitly geared to spreading the cultural nationalists' appeal. As the twentieth century unfolded, however, classical education remained the source of acute debate and division, which are the subject of the next chapter.

Notes

1 Both these quotations are discussed in Echeruo 1974. Echeruo 1977: 9–10 has some other examples including the invocation of Quintilian, Vergil, Scylla and Charybdis in a dispute over the church organization of the Wesleyan Methodists.

2 See e.g. Ajayi (1965: 260–4) and Ayandele (1966: 246–8).

3 See Peel 2000: 279–83.

4 Hegel 1956: 99: 'Africa is entirely without history. Life there consists of a succession of contingent happenings and surprises. There is no aim or state there whose development could be followed; and there is no subjectivity, but merely a series of subjects who destroy one another'. On the early nationalists' work to overcome this assumption, see e.g. July's 'Introduction' to Sibthorpe 1970. On the loss of the memory of the early nationalists in subsequent West African culture, see Fyfe 1972: 157.

5 Aeschylus, Diodorus, Lucian, Hesiod and Ovid.

6 See Fyfe 1972: 71.

7 Spinoza Tract. Pol. c. 7, § 27.

8 The reference is to the Select Committee of 1865, with its cautious recommendation of preparation for independence.

In a similar rhetorical flourish, Mensah Sarbah ends an historical account of the relations between Britain and the Gold Coast with the words from Vergil's *Aeneid*, 'Forsan et haec olim meminisse juvabit', 'Perhaps one day it will be a pleasure to remember even this'. See De Graft Johnson 1971: 34.

9 Mazrui 1978 also argues for the influence of Egypt on ancient Greece and quotes Cheikh Anta Diop on the Egyptian roots of Greek culture, but does not discuss the use made by such as Horton and Blyden of this complex of relations.

10 Selden 1998 is a compelling account of the ways in which contemporary African-Americans too drew on classical literature in order to prove their rights to humanity and history, and conversely to dismantle the racist arguments of white supremacists. Selden makes the nice point that African-Americans never abandoned Bernal's 'ancient model', but continued throughout the nineteenth and twentieth centuries to insist on Greece's descent from Egypt. See also several of the essays in Orrells et al. 2011.

11 His views on people of mixed race were controversial at the time, in the context of Liberian politics, and are still troubling; see e.g. Gilroy 1993: 209–10.

12 Lynch 1967, and his introduction to Blyden 1978, remain important for our accounts of Blyden. For Blyden's identity as a 'colossus', if a complex one, see Ayandele 1971: 694 and 1979c. Mudimbe 1988: 98–134 investigates the contradictions in Blyden's texts and touches on the connections between his 'classical perspective' and his 'nationalist outlook' (123).

13 See Ronnick 1994 for an exception to this rule. Ronnick includes Blyden in her catalogue of African-American classicists, whereas this book claims him for West Africa; both are correct, and strategic. See also Ronnick 2004, 2004a and 2005. Blyden became a member of the APA in 1879.

14 The quotation comes from Horace *Odes* 3.30, and concerns the poet's claims to immortality. Horace was a favourite school text throughout the nineteenth century and beyond.

15 Blyden 1978: 150 (October 1873, to the Revd. John C. Lowrie, member, Presbyterian Board of Foreign Missions), 195 (17 December 1875, to the Revd. John D. Lowrie).

16 Blyden 1978: 24, 28 (31 December 1858, to the Revd. John L. Wilson, Secretary, Board of Foreign Missions of the Presbyterian Church, United States), 153 (October 1873, to the Revd. John D. Lowrie), 297 (15 February 1881, to J. C. Braman, Secretary, Trustees of Donation for Education in Liberia).

17 Blyden 1978: 29, to the Rt Hon W. E. Gladstone, British Chancellor of the Exchequer 1859–66.

18 Hair 1967: 434 has a more entertaining account of this letter: 'it begins splendidly, addressed from "a far-off and barbarous shore", continues with rich and speciously insincere adulation of the British statesman, throws in two quotations in Latin and one in Greek, and concludes as a begging letter with a numbered list of demands'.

19 Blyden 1978: 242 (to the Revd. John C. Lowrie), 500 (to R. C. Antrobus, Assistant Under-Secretary at the British Colonial Office).

20 See e.g. Mudimbe 1994: 27 on the confusion surrounding the meaning of the ancient Ethiopia.

21 'Ethiopianism' is also the name given to the movement for an independent African church, of which James Johnson was one of the leading lights. See e.g. Ayandele 1966, Ajayi 1998: 22–3. In the context of this enquiry it connotes a more general movement towards anti-colonial African independence.

22 The *Periplous of Hanno* is a short text which purports to be the record of a Carthaginian voyage down the coast of Africa. Blyden suggests that it shows that Sierra Leone was known to the ancients (1994: 217).

23 It came out in the respected *Methodist Quarterly*. According to Blyden, this pamphlet was later requested by Professor Edward Owen of the British Museum (Blyden 1978: 84, July 1871, to William Coppinger, Secretary of the American Colonization Society).

24 The anecdote is repeated in 1994: 176–7.

25 The quotation is footnoted 'Note issued for use of the troops by order of Sir Garnet Wolseley, Cape Coast Castle, December 20th 1873'.

26 The phrase describing the Cyclops is from Vergil, *Aeneid* 3.658. Blyden edited the *West African Reporter* and may well be quoting himself.

27 Blyden's conclusion, that the Sphinx must solve her own riddle, is picked up by other nationalist writers; see Zachernuk 2000: 70. On Niobe in the writings of African-American women, see Walters 2007.

28 See also 1994: 135, where Africa is the 'gateway to the loftiest and noblest traditions of the human race – of India, of Greece, of Rome'.

29 For his biography see Langley 1974.

30 On the phenomenon of pro-European cultural and literary clubs in West Africa, see Newell 2002.

31 Lang calls it a 'drawing-room comedy' and recounts that his friends likened Sekyi to Bernard Shaw (1986: 109). However, Abarry compares it both to English Restoration comedy and to the African story-telling tradition (1991: 158).

32 See Shaloff 1974: 595 on critics' views of the contradictions and doubleness in Sekyi's own life; he was a 'radical and a conservative', 'Christian and pagan', 'Akan traditionalist and Western progressive'. This duality was not a matter of the individual's moral ambiguity, as some critics seem to try to suggest, but symptomatic of the colonial situation in the Gold Coast. Osei-Nyame correctly reminds us of Sekyi's 'hybridity' (1999: 5).

33 Ofusu-Appiah notes that it is not a classic novel, because it is episodic, and in parts seems autobiographical (1975: 19–20). Holton links it to autobiography, and finds it formally postmodern (2008: 9).

34 See Wehrs 2008: 40 for a critique of this history, and of Casely Hayford's representation of Gold Coast society in general.

35 All references are to Casely Hayford 1969.

36 Holden 2008: 65 considers the text's attempts at remaking models of heroic masculinity within a modern African present.

37 See Holden 2008: 5, 68 on the nationalist autobiographies' desire to promote a collective response.

3

Twentieth-Century Struggles

In the early part of the twentieth century the contradictions surrounding West Africans' classical education became less and less manageable, and while the First World War brought about a major ideological shift, it did not solve all the conflicts. In this chapter we shall examine some of the major struggles in which classics became implicated. In the first half the focus will be on the trope of the 'educated African', which will connect to the study of the cultural nationalists undertaken by Chapter 2, and the second half will centre on the 1922 Report of the Phelps-Stokes Commission, and its consequences for classics.

During the first few decades of the twentieth century the governing framework of British imperialism in West Africa was the system of Indirect Rule, which had notable effects on the context of education. Although reasons of space prevent exhaustive detail here, a brief sketch is in order. 'Indirect Rule' named the system whereby the British governed via 'traditional chiefs' rather than by directly imposing their will on indigenous populations. The approach was devised, by Lord Lugard (1858–1945), to take account of the situation in Northern Nigeria, which was not 'pacified' until the early years of the twentieth century, and which presented the specific problem of a huge Muslim population both highly resistant to Christian conversion, and highly literate in Arabic and the Koran. According to Peter Burroughs, Lugard's formulation of Indirect Rule was a consequence of resistance to more interventionist policies, by both Africans and British 'merchants, moralists or sceptics', so that Burroughs can term it 'an elevation of expedient into principle', an 'idealization of pragmatism and rationalization of comparative impotence' (1999: 196). Once articulated, however, Indirect Rule became the method of choice for the rest of Britain's colonies, even though they might have very different local conditions, and once in place, the system quickly ossified to become more oppressive than Lugard may ever have envisaged.

Indirect Rule sometimes afforded to 'traditional chiefs' much more power than indigenous systems would normally have allowed them, and although the notion was that this preserved African forms, critics were quick to point out that in fact it preserved a form neither African nor British, because it allowed no change to the personnel of government, and was less consensual than many African norms. Furthermore, by appealing to British notions of Africa as primitive, unchanging and mysterious, it fed the myths which represented African cultures as fundamentally less worthy of respect.[1] As Ranger 1983 showed, with particular reference to East and Central Africa, the 'traditional' institutions of much of Africa were so ill suited to the ideology of Indirect Rule that other 'traditions' had to be invented with which it could work successfully.

Since those Africans who had secured a Westernized education were unlikely to be identified as traditional chiefs, and moreover may have ultimately descended from freed slaves and other more marginal members of society, Indirect Rule had the effect of keeping them from the positions of power which, as 'Black Victorians' or their descendants, they had come to see as their legitimate ambition. 'It had no role for educated Africans' (Cell 1999: 242). This effect, of excluding the educated elite, could even be represented as the aim of the system. Sivonen (1995: 39), paraphrasing Donald Cameron, the Governor of Tanganyika (modern Tanzania) in 1926, writes that 'The status given to the chiefs would construct a "bulwark" against political agitators. Such were Europeanised natives who might threaten the system in future by seeking political influence and attempting to rule the country in European style'. When schools were built by the government to educate the sons of 'traditional chiefs' and thus serve the purposes of Indirect Rule, they were likely to be very different from the schools which missions and independent Africans had already established, with their emphasis on the classical repertoire. Thus the Bo School in Sierra Leone, for instance, emphasized games, native dress, team spirit, inter-tribal friendship and character training, to the exclusion of much academic activity.[2] Even the location of this establishment was significant. Built in the Protectorate, the more rural 'hinterland' away from the coastal communities and the influence of Freetown, the school implicitly announced that the African beneficiaries of Indirect Rule were not to follow the career paths laid out by the likes of the Freetown-educated elite.

Yet Indirect Rule was regularly represented, especially by the British, in a very favourable light, as a means to preserve native African social forms rather than undermining them, and respectful of indigenous traditions rather than fostering the phenomenon that was called 'detribalization' or 'denationalization'. It was said to offer 'a humane and far-sighted alternative to either the policy of assimilation of the French and Portuguese or the doctrine of segregation in southern Africa' (Cell 1999: 241). 'Contrasts were drawn with the arbitrary brutality of German colonial practice and with the French program of "assimilation" whereby an elite cadre of Africans was educated to *become* Frenchmen in order to serve the empire' (Curtis 1996: 570).[3] In certain circumstances this virtuous version of Indirect Rule could be opposed to the role of the missions, which had often seen it as necessary to abolish indigenous customs in order to strengthen Christianity. Despite these claims, Indirect Rule can also be understood to link to the increasing racism of empire, in that it posited such fundamental differences between colonizer and colonized as would effectively stop the latter from acceding to real power. The ideology of Indirect Rule thus came into conflict with that dimension of mission education which had substantially invested in the educability of Africans, and had held out the promise of an existence fully modernized by literacy and Christianity. Even when the missions prioritized the role of the school as the 'nursery of the church',[4] more intent on producing converts than cultured individuals, they might clash with a government which often prioritized its own need for well-equipped clerks and engineers. Consequently, even without West Africans' commitment to the literary education already on offer in the secondary schools and Fourah Bay College, Indirect Rule might also contradict other strands of British imperialism itself. Apart from the general 'civilizing' mission of empire, the British also had an incentive to educate in order to serve the rapid commercial expansion of the various West African urban centres like Lagos, which required more than the basic education characteristic of Indirect Rule.

Insofar as Indirect Rule helped to make more acute the contradictions of empire, and in particular, made more difficult the position of the educated elite, official opinion came to see education as a kind of scapegoat for the dissatisfaction of that elite. Moreover, the educated also began to be perceived as responsible for their own unenviable position, because they embraced modernity and allegedly rejected traditional mores – including the power of the chiefly class from which they were largely excluded. The complaints about the educated African which emerge in the twentieth century are thus not altogether different from the distrust of the mission educated which we read in late-nineteenth-century sources, but they are conditioned by the new ideology of Indirect Rule as well as by the prejudices of the earlier period. Commentators like the prominent educationalist Victor Murray see very clearly that the educated African is a product of a contradictory system rather than himself (invariably 'him') generating the tensions for which he is then blamed (1935: 234–5).

Although contemporary contrasts were drawn between the British approach to indigenous institutions and the French goal of 'assimilation', or of producing Frenchmen in Africa, recent analyses suggest that French imperialism in West Africa was in fact embroiled in the same sorts of contradictions as British.[5] Conklin has analysed how French 'direct' rule was driven by the ideology of the 'mission civilisatrice' and a desire to impose authority on a variety of indigenous state structures (1997: 107–13), but also how the period after the First World War saw the development of the competing ideology of 'association', which tried to work with African institutions rather than endeavouring to eradicate them in the name of civilization. 'African societies would be allowed to evolve at their own pace and along their own lines, with the important proviso, of course, that their chosen path of evolution would not threaten French dominance' (Chafer 2002: 29–30). As was the case for the British Empire, the contradiction between the two systems persisted throughout the period.

In terms of our particular focus here, French colonialism tended to emphasize the teaching of French to the exclusion of other languages, and although Latin was important for the Catholic church, there were even fewer secondary schools in French West Africa than in the British colonies, and no degree-granting institutions until very late, so Latin did not have a very large purchase. Figures quoted by Crowder 1968: 375–77 show for 1934 fewer than 600 students in secondary schools throughout French West Africa, and fewer than 60, 000 in all schools together. Kelly (2000: 236–7) notes that there were no secondary schools in French West Africa in the interwar years; a lycée opened briefly (Kelly 2000: 191) in St Louis, but closed in 1921. However, Latin was occasionally learnt in St Louis, Senegal, in the late nineteenth century; in this context, Bouche (1975) notes how alarmed the French colonial establishment was in the mid-nineteenth century when the African Abbé Boilet preached that education would make all the colonial service open to Senegalese. 'Ainsi, les rudiments du Latin semblaient conduire directement aux professions libérales ou aux functions d'autorité, sans étape intermediaire' ('Thus, the rudiments of Latin seemed to lead directly to the liberal professions or the functions of authority, without an intermediate stage', Bouche 1975: 186). Despite the alleged differences between the British and French systems, the anxieties are shared, because structural.

In British colonies, Roman Catholic missions were slower than those in the Protestant tradition to found secondary schools and teach Latin, despite the requirements of the church service. Modupe Oduyoye claims that the Roman Catholics were determined not to give the literary education which, allegedly, would disqualify Africans from any useful pursuits and fit them only for government or commercial service (1982: 291). Donatus Ogado shows how the Roman Catholic mission in Nigeria, which arrived much later than the Protestant missions, determined on a High School in 1900 but did not get around to building it until 1928 (1988: 262). He also indicates that African assistants to Roman Catholic priests in Nigeria made use of a translated guide to the service, since it was not considered necessary for them to learn the language of the Mass (Ogado 1988: 101, 117, 130).

The educated African

One figure that we can use as a hermeneutic through the various strands of ideology that characterize this period is that of the 'educated African'. In the first part of this chapter I shall investigate this figure from the African and the European side, and show his relation to wider cultural and political shifts. With the Phelps-Stokes Commission into Education in Africa, in 1922, the various anxieties that feed the figure of the 'educated African' come to a head, and the Report of the Commission makes controversial recommendations in relation to Africans' classical education. Ultimately, however, responses to it in the schools indicate that not a great deal changes.

Throughout the period, the 'educated African' is a bogeyman and a figure of hate especially to Europeans, but in some ways to Africans too. How the trope of the 'educated African' works is to insist that whatever education

Africans gain is not real education, but equips them only with a simulacrum of learning, so that they become imitations of Europeans rather than authentic subjects. What distinguishes them further is an aversion to manual work, concomitant of 'book-learning', which sets them apart from 'ordinary' or 'genuine' Africans without positioning them for serious leadership. Such an education, furthermore, does not permit their escape from second-class status, and crucially, does not qualify them to make valid claims on their colonial masters. Instead it has but one outcome, to make the educated discontented with their lot. What the ideological sleight of hand is here, of course, is to suppose that Africans would have been contented, if uneducated, with the wholesale confiscation of their society and economy that was the fruit of imperialism. 'Education' is thus made the scapegoat for Africans' legitimate grievances against the European rulers, and the educated African is blamed for the flaws in the colonial system of which he is a product. Newell suggests that he is 'invoked by dominant power groups for seventy years or so, updated and upgraded with the passing years, revised to suit contemporary political controversies' (2002: 163). Within the trope of the educated African, all literary education – anything that goes beyond the three Rs – becomes questionable, but the classical languages are the object of particular suspicion, and make regular appearances both as a sign of African aspiration and as an index of how misguided those aspirations can be.

We have already seen, in the early missionary period, that Europeans like Townsend at Abeokuta in Nigeria and Kemp at Wesleyan Boys' High (Mfantsipim) in the Gold Coast discouraged Africans from literary and classical pursuits, and we can also note that although Africans' facility with classical languages was often praised by European commentators, it could also be denigrated as a superficial memorization, which did not ensure any real grasp. Educated Africans equipped with classical languages could thus be dismissed as not really educated at all. In 1842, when the Select Committee examined the Revd. J. F. Schön about the abilities of the children of liberated African slaves in Sierra Leone, at least one member of the Committee was rather suspicious of African achievements and asked: 'Do you find them to be as quick as whites in arithmetic?' (Sandon 1842: 461). To this, the Revd. Schön's answer was: 'I could not say as quick as whites; they do not exercise the power of thinking so much; they learn the rules very well, and can apply them'. When the questioner continued 'Do you think they have more capacity for the learning of languages than for the exact sciences?' the answer was 'I think they have. There are among the liberated Africans many who can speak three or four languages besides their own'. The conversation thus to an extent downplays the achievement of Africans in learning Greek and Latin because it assimilates this accomplishment to natural learning of African languages; and it also suggests that learning for Africans is not a matter of the intellect but of rote memorization. We might conclude that the learning of Samuel Crowther, whose educational trajectory is, as we have seen, often at stake in these exchanges, is especially censured. Considering that much contemporary education in Europe involved masses of rote learning, the statements in this report are perhaps rather tendentious, and we can recognize in them the reflex to downgrade the intellectual achievements of those to whom ideology would prefer to deny achievement. The reflex persisted throughout the early period, as when in 1878 the inspector of Mfantsipim wrote that the boys 'have a wonderful facility for committing anything to memory and get on with their Greek and Latin well but are easily thrown off their guard by questions which require thought' (Boahen 1996: 32).

On the other, African side of the debate, we can see someone like Blyden complaining in much the same terms about the limited nature of the education doled out to Africans, and welcoming efforts to improve it. Consider, for instance, a letter to the Revd. John Wilson, Corresponding Secretary, Boards of Foreign Missions of the Presbyterian Church, the United States. The first part of the quotation refers to the United States, but Blyden's main concern is with the 'Negroes' of Africa (Blyden 1978: 32, 9 June 1860):

> It has been common in the United States to believe that the colored man does not need any more than the elements of an education; and, accordingly, when he has acquired the ability to read and write fairly, a smattering of Latin and Greek, and possesses a rapid volubility, he is regarded in some sections of that country as a prodigy of learning. . . . There are efforts making by our real friends that look to the elevation of the standard of Negro Education.

Blyden's agitation for a West African University can similarly be represented in terms of correcting 'the artificial and superficial character of the attainments of the natives [of Sierra Leone]' (Blyden 1978: 145, 22 October 1873, in a letter to John Wodehouse, Earl of Kimberley, the British Colonial Secretary).

African commentators of the present day agree that the secondary education on offer to Africans in the early period often lacked quality, not to mention resources. Ajayi (1965: 154) proposes that the advanced school subjects were rarely taught in reality, and that the substance of the secondary education provided was advanced elementary instruction, with only a smattering of Latin and of Mathematics.[6] C. O. Taiwo (1975: 22) suggests that the wide range of secondary subjects available was not matched by any depth in the teaching, with textbooks either not available or not suitable.

Other types of critique are also legible in African-authored sources. Samuel Johnson's *History of the Yorubas* was completed in 1897, although not published until 1921; in his preface he uses the classical cultures to note the alienation of Westernized Africans from their own: 'Educated natives of Yoruba are well acquainted with the history of England and with that of Rome and Greece, but of the history of their own country they know nothing whatever' (1921: vii).[7] In the early years of the twentieth century the satirical work of Kobina Sekyi can be understood as an African attack on the educated African, as a product of the harmful education with which he has been provided, who attracts criticism because of his unquestioning admiration of all things English and his abandonment of things indigenous. In *The Blinkards*, furthermore, the education is shown to be only half an education, because the version of Englishness that the deluded Africans adopt is crude and not in the least aspirational.[8] Mimicry of the English, which was held to be a frequent outcome of Western education, is thus condemned both by the anti-colonial writers who advocate African self-confidence and cultural integrity, and by Europeans who belittle the 'mere carbon copy' (Milverton 1956: 184, cf. Macmillan 1934: 137).

African sources can show an acute sense of the nonsense produced by a 'smattering' of Latin and Greek. The autobiography of the Revd. W. E. Akinumi Pratt retails a story told against the highly educated citizens of Freetown (1973: 9). In the early years of the twentieth century the story circulated of the

> wonderful vote of thanks that the people of York [in Sierra Leone] gave once after a bram-bram meeting (Missionary Anniversary gathering). The people met and they said that when people from Freetown went and spoke to them, they always talked Latin and Greek, and they decided that in returning thanks this time, they themselves must put in a few Latin and Greek words. A small committee was formed and this vote of thanks was prepared and

> given: 'Mr Chairman and supporters, Christian friends, the vome-bomes, vamb-bams which you have just heard is the result of chemical actions. It has been truly and wisely said that mambo mambo et makanko, monkey banana three for penny which is to say, the Lord hath done great things for us whereof we are glad'.

Thunderous applause and hearty congratulations allegedly greeted this effusion, which digs effectively not only at the pretentious speech of Freetown, with its incomprehensible Latin and Greek, but also at the rhetoric of the church.

Latin and Greek are also tailor-made for the discourse on the educated African because they are often encountered in the short, memorable phrases dismissed in the term 'tags'. A secondary school education in West Africa would equip the scholar with a stock of such phrases, some of which we have encountered in the description of the founding of the CMS Grammar School at Ibadan. Numerous school mottoes, unlike that of Mfantsipim, are made of up such tags, like 'Non sibi sed aliis' ('Not for self but others', Fourah Bay College), 'Laboramus expectantes' ('We work and wait', Methodist Boys' High School), 'ut omnes unum sint' (So that all might be one, Achimota), and διώκω ('I pursue', CMS Grammar School, Freetown). Reminiscences of early-twentieth-century school-days by West Africans often mobilize such tags with a certain pleasure. Thus the Revd. Pratt, quoted above, dismisses those fellow-students who taunt him for his poor clothes with a phrase they had all learned, 'cuculus non monachum facit', the dress does not make the monk (1973: 10). Adegoke Olubummọ's maths teacher encouraged his students with 'magnum malum est ignorantia' ('ignorance is a great evil', 1980: 79). As late as 1961 the classics teacher L. M. Dolphin admits the pleasure of repeating 'tags' within the community of classicists, and calls them, with remarkable candour, 'our password, our old school tie, or our club membership card' (Dolphin 1961: 1). That the 'educated African' with his Latin phrases became a powerful and indeed indispensable figure in debates on education is indicated by a much later source, which criticizes twentieth-century education for its slavish adherence to the classics thus: 'An African who has received a European education often speaks and writes English with a partiality for long words and high-sounding phrases accompanied wherever possible by Latin tags which are not always strictly relevant' (Ukeje 1979: 80).

The Latin 'tag' has a venerable history in Europe as well as in West Africa, and although the discourse on the educated African is very dismissive of 'tags', Waquet, Stray and others have shown that classical education in Europe produced people with no better learning. That the role of the 'tag' was to differentiate by class and status, and that it succeeded very well, is demonstrated by Ronald Knox's *Let Dons Delight* (1939: 264):[9]

> God knows why it should be so, but as a matter of observation it seems to me quite certain that the whole legend of the 'English Gentleman' has been built upon Latin and Greek. A meets B on the steps of his club and says: 'Well, old man, *eheu fugaces*, what?' and B says '*Dulce et decorum est pro patria mori*', and the crossing-sweeper falls on his knees in adoration of the two men who can talk as learnedly as that.

In the West African context, 'tags' may on occasion be ridiculous, but it is also clear that once Africans can wield tags as effectively as 'English Gentlemen', the game is up for European preservation of class and status.

Latin and Greek thus lend themselves to the hostile discourse about the educated African for a multiplicity of usefully contradictory reasons. Since they do involve a great deal of rote memorization, they can indeed be easy at first, if the student has a suitable gift, as Kwesi finds in *The Anglo-Fanti*. If the demands of the later stages then turn out to be excessive, it is indeed possible to quit the study of the languages with only a 'parrot-like smattering', as the common critique had it.[10] Coupled with this idiosyncratic profile was the fact that the ancient languages were often publicly acknowledged as extraneous to the normal demands of daily life, and so could be ridiculed as decorative but useless accomplishments. Yet despite all this, Latin and Greek continued to wield huge cultural authority, as an indispensable part of any ambitious educational trajectory, and since they were necessary for practices like Law, where nationalists could successfully take on the colonial government, it was almost inevitable that the classical languages would constitute part of the critique directed against the 'educated African'. In the colonial context, Latin and Greek might have been the kind of cultural capital that would differentiate the European from the African, but since in the event they did so very imperfectly, they came under fire as threats to the proper working of colonial society.

The force of the European complaints against the educated African, as opposed to African suspicion of him, thus derives primarily from the possibility that African resistance to colonialism will be better equipped if better educated. Frederick, Lord Lugard, twice Governor of Nigeria, helpfully represents a range of European anxieties in his various writings. In a letter to his wife in 1912 he writes that he is: 'somewhat baffled as to how to get into touch with the educated native . . . To start with, I am not in sympathy with him. His loud and arrogant conceit are distasteful to me, the lack of natural dignity and courtesy antagonise me' (Perham 1960: 390). In a more public forum he combines almost all the publicly acceptable complaints (Perham 1960: 491, quoting the 1914 pamphlet 'Education in the Colony and Southern Provinces of Nigeria'):

> The primary function of education should in my judgement be to fit the ordinary individual to fill a useful part in his environment with happiness to himself, and to ensure that the exceptional individual shall use his abilities for the advancement of the community and not to its detriment, or to the subversion of constituted authority. The local press presumably writes what its readers demand and if it may therefore be taken as a criterion, we must admit that education has not brought happiness or contentment to the educated community of Nigeria. It should be the aim of our new system to train up a generation who should exchange this bitter hostility for an attitude of friendly co-operation, and who should be able to recognise and achieve ideals of their own, without a slavish imitation of the European, and be proud of a nationality with its own clear aims and future.

In 1922, in *The Dual Mandate*, he writes that educated Africans are (1926: 429):

> lacking in integrity, self-control and discipline . . . [with] no respect for authority . . . Education has brought to such men only discontent, suspicion of others, and bitterness, which masquerades as racial patriotism . . . As citizens they are unfitted to hold posts of trust and responsibility where integrity and loyalty are essential.

The overriding concern here seems to be that educated Africans are not automatically convinced of the rightness of European rule. Education is conversely seen to work properly when it obviates dissent, substituting 'friendly cooperation' for the 'subversion of constituted authority'.

Despite these sentiments, Lugard cooperated closely over a number of years with a very prominent 'educated African', Henry Carr (1863–1945). In 1892

Carr became the first African to hold the position of Inspector of Schools in Lagos, and he later achieved numerous other distinctions, while also encountering instances of prejudice that put obstacles in the way of his career (Taiwo 1975: 65). Schooled at Wesleyan Boys' High School, Freetown, Carr would have acquired Latin and Greek in the normal course of his education, but went on to express concern about their role in Nigerian education. Having passed the London Matriculation in 1878, he obtained a degree in Mathematics and Physics from Durham via Fourah Bay, in 1882, and, according to his biographer, was thereby rendered far too highly qualified for those posts in the colonial civil service which were open to Africans (Taiwo 1975: 7). He thus fell a victim to the racist tightening of the colonial service at the end of the century which saw high-level posts designated 'European', with better salaries, allowances, quarters, promotion prospects and medical facilities than were extended to the Africans in the clerical, subordinate and labour grades. After a spell teaching at the CMS Grammar School in Lagos, however, Carr was poached into government employment by Governor Moloney, who recognized his talents, and was moreover mindful of nationalist agitation for more Africans in responsible posts (Taiwo 1975: 129). Lugard was later to describe him as 'more like a very intelligent European' (Taiwo 1975: 79, quoting a private letter to Lady Lugard), but in a gesture quite uncharacteristic of the period, did promote him above Europeans (Perham 1960: 605). After his death in 1945 his library formed the nucleus of the University of Ibadan (Ayandele 1979b: 86).

Since Governor Moloney had prevailed upon Carr to leave teaching and enter the colonial service, it is clear that 'educated Africans' were critically needed by the colonial administration, and indeed a further complaint about education voiced by various sources throughout the period is that industry and commerce are so desperate for qualified personnel that they regularly poach boys out of school with minimal training (Perham 1960: 492). Concerned from a very early date (1897) about the effect of 'useless and premature' studies, and their 'distracting and enfeebling' effect (Taiwo 1975: 36–7), Carr wished students to confine themselves to English and the more technical subjects that would help to develop West Africa. His 1898 Report to the Legislative Council complained that boys studied Latin for 2 hours, 2 days of the week, whereas only 1 hour on 1 day was devoted to reading English, and only

90 minutes on 2 days to English grammar (Echeruo 1977: 61). He urged that the educational establishment 'guard against over-ambitious schemes of study', and suggested that Africans 'should, for the present at any rate, be content to instruct the children in such subjects as are likely to come before them in their ordinary life' (Taiwo 1975: 48). These strictures would exclude the higher secondary school subjects, including Latin, and indeed Lugard quotes Carr to the effect that 'he has found boys good at Greek and Latin who were wholly ungrounded in English' (Taiwo 1975: 88).[11] Carr also railed against what he saw as the materialism of students who wished to gain academic qualifications so as to work as clerks in the colonial administration rather than as farmers, as their fathers had done (Taiwo 1975: 37–8), and deplored the turning out of clerks in a situation where farmers, fishermen, carpenters and blacksmiths were needed (Taiwo 1975: 34). Even his biographer, who is eager to defend him from any criticism, sees that Carr decried the very means that Africans were using to advance themselves; had there been no Latin or Greek in West African secondary schools, there would have been no West African degreed professionals (Taiwo 1975: 77). So while 'literary education' as a whole might seem problematic, classical education provided a particular flashpoint.

Carr came under fire from both sides during his professional career. His work was attacked by Herbert Macaulay (son of the Macaulay who founded CMS Grammar School, Lagos) and other nationalists in the 1920s, as being ineffective in raising standards in Nigerian schools (Macaulay 1924). On the other hand, Hanns Vischer, the Director of Education for Northern Nigeria, complained earlier (1908) that the products of the Lagos schools were arrogant, addicted to European dress (which to him seemed a sign of over-weening ambition rather than of acquiescence in 'Christianity, commerce and civilisation') and spending too much time on Latin and Greek (Taiwo 1975: 75, 77, Graham 1966: 73–4).[12] Carr was closely involved in a project which endeavoured to square this particular circle, the foundation of King's College, Lagos. Lugard had long held that the cure for the 'educated African' was an education that would bring more of the public school ethos to West Africa, with an emphasis on moral development rather than on 'higher studies' (Tibenderana 2003: 29),[13] and King's College Lagos was designed precisely to correct the characteristic faults of the mission educators and to provide a new and improved version of the educated African.[14] Eschewing the familiar traits of discontent and self-importance, the students were to learn instead discipline, integrity and self-control (Taiwo 1975: 81).

F. O. Ogunlade gives a very detailed account of the ways in which plans for King's College were modified over time in Lagos and London, and predictably, the classics provided bones of contention. While the Nigerian Department of Education proposed that English, Elementary Mathematics and Latin should be made compulsory, Governor Egerton 'marginally commented against Latin being compulsory' (Ogunlade 1974: 331). The Principal, who was to be a European, was also to be the 'Professor' of English Language, literature and Latin, and Greek was present as an option, along with French, German and Arabic (Ogunlade 1974: 332–3). After the Lagos Board of Education, which included several African members, agreed that Latin would be compulsory, the proposal went to the Colonial Office in London, where officials promptly 'insisted on the removal of classics and European languages other than English from the syllabus . . . [they] strongly recommended a technical vocationally-oriented curriculum' (Ogunlade 1974: 336–9, Taiwo 1975: 88). Carr defended the more literary curriculum, but Ogunlade concludes that the new school did not completely fulfil the hopes of the Lagos educated elite, even though it also provoked great anxiety in London about the possibility that its new products would be politically disaffected.[15] According to Ogunlade, Governor Egerton was caught between the educated elite and the Colonial Office, trying simply to produce more qualified clerks for his administration (Ogunlade 1974: 343). The school did teach boys to Cambridge School Certificate examination standard, but even after its establishment Lugard's 1918 *Political Memorandum* on education held that 'Since English is itself a foreign language, it is probable that Latin Greek and French may with advantage be eliminated from the syllabus and treated as "special subjects"' (Lugard 1970: 133). According to his biographer, Margery Perham, Lugard won Colonial Office approval by cutting Latin, Chaucer and much English history from the King's College syllabus (1960: 507). Latin, and to a lesser extent Greek, provide the fulcrum on which the debate on the educated African turns, because they represent an aspirational education which will enable Africans to staff the colonial civil service rather than being confined to less powerful and less well-paid technical pursuits. Even when suspected by Africans of not being very useful to the development of their society, then, Latin and Greek have the distinction of being yet more politically suspect to the authorities in London.

As the twentieth century unfolded, some aspects of the discourse on the 'educated African' were modified, but before we examine this, we should note that as early as 1876, Edward Blyden had already deconstructed the entire manifold. In an article from *Fraser's Magazine* of 1876, on 'Christian Missions in West Africa', it is the European who is found to be insufficiently learned in the classical languages, as well as being arrogant and rude. Couched throughout in the rhetoric of the 'educated African', who thinks he knows but has only a superficial and mimetic understanding, Blyden's description of the encounter turns the stereotype on its head. He begins with the routine dismissal of the qualifications presented, and the humour generated by the mismatch between accomplishment and boast, but he is, exceptionally, an African making this judgement of a European, rather than the other way round (1994: 67):

> The more slender the outfit as to educational training and experience of those who come as instructors to the coast, the more supercilious – as, of course, must be the case – is their bearing. Many and amusing are the instances encountered by intelligent Africans of the very limited qualifications, coupled with large pretensions, of not a few who are sent to the coast as instructors.

Blyden then proceeds to further description of the European's limitations and pretensions, appropriating to himself the polished civility and understanding of manners which the European should have had:

> While sitting on the passengers' deck of one of the African mail steamers, a few years ago, we heard a young Englishman who had been engaged in educational work on the coast, and was returning home on leave, descanting upon the 'utter inferiority of the African' – and, by the way, these men who come to guide the 'benighted' seldom hesitate (such is their high breeding) to indulge in most contemptuous utterances about the race in the hearing of any member of it who may be a stranger to them. This young man . . . overflowing with erudition, and anxious to make known the extent of his researches in African philology, remarked to a comrade, 'The stolidity of these Africans is astonishing. Their words are mostly monosyllabic, and even those tribes whose vocabulary is the most copious possess no expressions for abstract ideas'. Attracted by the Johnsonese character of the sentence, we turned towards him and said, 'Sir, the words in the sentence which you just uttered, that convey any idea at all, are either Roman or Greek. All the purely English words you employed are monosyllabic, expressing no abstract thought.'

Blyden does indeed 'mimic' the European's utterance, repeating its crucial words, as if he were an 'educated African' parroting European culture, but for the reader, he has already signalled his superiority via the 'Johnsonese' and also, needless to say, via the immense insult that the 'signifying' speech delivers. The insult also, of course, turns on the relative facility of European and African with Latin and Greek. The European who speaks Latin and Greek as part of his immemorial heritage, has no understanding that this is what he is doing; the African, on the other hand, seizes the weapon of Latin and Greek to use in his struggle with the colonizer. The contest ends with the European still unable to recognize what he is up against:

> 'Oh,' he replied, with some surprise, 'but that only proves that we possessed the ability to appropriate and apply such foreign terms as we considered serviceable – a feat which your people are unable to achieve'. To this second outburst of almost pure Latin we made no reply, but turned away, leaving our learned pedagogue to enjoy the belief that, under the influence of his irresistible argument, we had succumbed; but we noticed that he took care during the remainder of the voyage to indulge, while in our hearing, in no more 'high falutin'.

As with some of the encounters examined by Greenwood 2010, this exchange inverts the roles of colonizer and colonized around their mastery of Latin and Greek. The European persists in thinking that the African can manage neither English, nor Latin and Greek, but the encounter has itself proved him wrong; Blyden's text closes in a welter of Latinate words which, however, give way at the end to the slang expression 'high falutin'. Blyden wins with language of whatever kind.

In the early twentieth century, the discourse on the educated African began to express less straightforward hostility to African achievements and more anxiety about the African's place in the modern world. The misfit between the educated African and his political and cultural environment became known as 'detribalization' or 'denationalization', terms which we encountered above in connection with Indirect Rule. While the naming of this phenomenon acknowledged the damage done by colonialism to African traditions, which had been undermined without being replaced with a full and satisfactory modern life, the discourse of the 'educated African' managed to continue to blame the victim for this state of affairs. As we have noted, he was accused of 'proud' separation from his ancestral community, and 'arrogant' refusal to submit to authorities either traditional or modern. Unsurprisingly, mission education continued as supplementary scapegoat, because missionaries on entering the country had avowedly designed to demolish much of indigenous culture among Africans in order to rid them of 'barbaric' practices. If the missionaries now were quite often those offering an education of high academic value to Africans, they could be arraigned not only for that but also for their earlier work of 'detribalization'.

By 1928, 'detribalization' is the main criticism which the nationalist J. W. De Graft Johnson feels required to address in his *Towards Nationhood in West Africa*, which contains a whole chapter on the 'Educated African' (1971: 42–50).[16] How he deals with the question is in part by dramatizing, in his rhetoric, a consummately classical education married to a determined defence of the ambitions of the West African nationalists, upholding both the parameters of traditional culture and the goal of self-determination. His frontispiece shows a white man in full colonial rig, with suit, tie, walking-stick and solar topee. By his side, yet slightly behind him, is an African man in traditional robes. The caption is 'in hoc signo', inviting the educated reader to complete the quotation with 'vinces' (Figure 3.1). 'In hoc signo vinces; In this sign you will conquer' is the motto which Constantine supposedly saw in the sky before a decisive battle, and which led to his conversion to Christianity. In the context of De Graft Johnson's frontispiece, the quotation is quite breathtakingly bold, combining as it does the classical tradition and the foundation of the Christian church in the West with the imperial ambitions of the British. The 'sign' via which conquest comes is no longer clear: is it the clothes of the white man, the clothes and posture of the black or the relation between the two that guarantees victory? Or is it simply the Latin 'tag' itself which will play the role of ultimate arbiter?

The chapters of *Towards Nationhood* are headed by epigraphs which derive from English literary classics and, more provocatively, from classical sources including Plutarch (on the first page), Cato, Plato and Sophocles, and as well as exempla from ancient history there are quotations embedded in the text, and discussed, from Thucydides, Aristotle and Tacitus. Latin tags are strictly absent. De Graft Johnson maintains the strategy, which we saw with Horton and Blyden, of using the empire's cherished cultural resources against itself, and to this end also discusses two modern commentators on the classics. In particular, he engages with Alfred Zimmern on Solon and with Gladstone on Palmerston's

[By kind permission.

IN HOC SIGNO

Figure 3.1 'In hoc signo', the frontispiece from Joseph William De Graft Johnson, *Towards Nationhood in West Africa: thoughts of young Africa addressed to young Britain* (London: Frank Cass, 1971, first published 1928). Reproduced with permission.

notion of Roman citizenship. In reference to Zimmern on Solon (1971: 116), De Graft Johnson equates West African legislators with the classical lawmaker because they are not faced with a 'clean slate', but with certain pre-existing conditions. In relation to Gladstone's exchange with Palmerston on the nature of the 'civis Romanus' (1971: 123), De Graft Johnson recruits the Grand Old Man to the nationalist cause; Gladstone had criticized Palmerston's position when the latter conceived of Britain's relations with the rest of the world as governed by 'the strong arm of power'. De Graft Johnson also points to the contemporary British fact that graduates of universities possessed two votes each (1971: 3), showing that the British distrust of the educated apparently did not extend to their own intelligentsia. Addressing head-on the question of colonial 'mimicry', he makes the point that it had been *Europe's* ambition 'largely to reproduce herself in Africa' (1971: 3), so that 'mimicry' becomes a two-edged sword, with any failings of West Africans laid clearly at the door of the colonizers.

To the issue of 'detribalization' De Graft Johnson devotes prolonged classicizing discussion. In particular, he compares British rule in Africa to Roman rule in Britain, a move which suggests again that cultural nationalists are inclined to invoke Rome rather than Greece when history and politics are at stake. Roman rule, he claims, never led to the 'denationalization' of Britons. The Britons 'spoke and wrote Latin and imitated Roman manners but they never became Romanised in nature. Race characteristics are not obliterated simply because a man becomes adapted to another civilisation' (1971: 1). While we might find this point debatable, in context it is significant in its equation of British and Africans as alike subjects of an alien power and alike resistant, ultimately, to acculturation; this is a different argument from, for instance, Horton's about the movement of civilization, because it responds more precisely to twentieth-century anxieties. Later on De Graft Johnson deals with the argument of George Townsend Warner, in *The Groundwork of British History* (London, 1912), which does claim that the British under Roman rule were uncannily like the educated Africans. According to Warner, the British copied the outward show but obtained none of the inner qualities that made Rome great, in the process losing their 'rough vigour' and 'love of independence' (1971: 99). De Graft Johnson concludes that it was only the immense length of the Roman occupation which makes this argument even plausible, a length which will not, he insists, be matched by the British occupation of West Africa. De Graft Johnson thus undermines the stereotype of the 'educated African' in his every classical reference, both by exhibiting thorough and detailed acquaintance with ancient texts and modern scholarship, and by ensuring that his analyses are not simply decorative tags, but serve the goal of African independence.

'Classics' versus 'Agriculture'

Given the overwhelming prejudice against the educated African, why did the British colonial establishment educate at all? De Graft Johnson even suggests that to be consistent, it should cease to do so (1971: 48), and to some extent this is exactly what happened. Although we have built up a quite ramified picture of provision of classical education to West Africans, the educated elite constituted only about 2 per cent of the population until after the First World War, and yet West Africa was much more lavishly supplied with secondary schools than were the British colonies in East and Central Africa.[17] It may only have been the avowed work of civilization, ostensible grounds for the British occupation in the first place, that prevented education from grinding to its logical halt. As Crowder pointed out, the administrations 'spent minute percentages of their annual budgets on the education of those whose occupation they had earlier undertaken on the declared grounds that they were going to bring them the fruits of western civilisation' (1968: 374). Reasons adduced to avoid the educated African included the examples of India and Egypt, where, allegedly, the policy of academic education had contributed to the 'Mutiny' and other forms of resistance to empire (Tibenderana 2003: 28, 33, 68, 94, cf. Wallbank 1934: 107, 116).[18] As the twentieth century wore on, there was added the fear that literate Africans would come under the influence of 'foreign agitators' like the Jamaican Marcus Garvey, or would travel to Moscow for higher education (Sivonen 1995: 227).[19] The pronouncements of colonial figures are sometimes remarkably frank. Sir Charles Temple, Lieutenant-Governor of Northern Nigeria, claimed in 1918 that European education should not be extended any further (1968: 220–1):

> I am not so bold, or presumptuous, as to suggest that we should close existing schools . . . the needs of commerce and government already created must be met. But I hotly oppose the extension of the system of European education to the great majority of natives who are still untouched, who I hold can, without dislocation or damage to anybody, be encouraged and assisted to develop on lines natural to them to become valuable members of the Empire.

European education is by implication corrupting, and it is unnatural, at least for Africans, who had best remain 'untouched'. Nine years later the Director of Native Education in Nyasaland (modern Malawi) wrote (quoted by Sivonen 1995: 93):

> Nor has the African escaped the machinations of the Marcus Garveys of the Negro World . . . Here in Africa we are dealing with an impressionable people already awakening to class-consciousness. We are forced to the conclusion that learning, unless most carefully handled, can become a very dangerous thing.

The modern critic Peter Tibenderana (2003) concludes that the authorities were afraid of any education which might bring Africans into contact with international currents of thought and thus contribute to their resistance to empire. Study of the history and literature of ancient Greece and Rome, with its constant scrutiny of power relations and its frequent encomia of liberty, would come under this heading even if Latin and Greek were not in themselves passports to further education. Of colonial India John Murdoch had written:

> We place in a boy's hands the histories of Greece and Rome, and hold up to his admiration the examples of those ancient patriots who had freed their country from domestic tyranny or a foreign yoke . . . Can we wonder, then, at the harvest which we too frequently reap . . .[20]

Although the Indian anxiety dated from an earlier period, the 1880s, the underlying ideological impulse was not exhausted by the time it reached West Africa. As we shall see later on, some nationalists identify their opposition to Britain firmly with the examples of ancient history, so the anxiety is not misplaced.

In this context, some schools identified themselves as offering an advanced education but reduced the likelihood of producing 'educated Africans' by refusing to provide Latin or Greek, as we have seen in the early period with Townsend at Abeokuta and in the struggle over the syllabus at King's College Lagos. This policy could run up against African resistance. When St Andrew's College moved from Lagos to Oyo, in the interior of Nigeria, it ceased to offer Latin, but a drop in enrolments meant that Latin was reinstated (Ogunkoya 1979: 19). As we shall see in more detail later, Wesley College Ibadan refused on principle to offer Latin to African boys until student agitation in the late 1930s brought about a change. At Government College Umuahuia, where 'no external examinations were taken because of Mr Fisher's strong conviction that they were entirely unsuited to the real education of the African student', half the boys left for other colleges because until 1938, they could not learn Latin (Hogarth 1944: 5).[21] At St Charles' College in Onitsha, Nigeria, a Roman Catholic teacher training college, Latin and other 'secondary subjects' were not taught, in order that students could not sit the Cambridge School Certificate; 'it was a common belief then [late 1930s] that if a teacher passed such examinations, he ran to the Civil Service for a more lucrative job' (Nnadozie 1965: 64). Even in the 1940s a student at a Teacher Training College in Tamale, in the Gold Coast, encountered opposition to Latin; he sent off for a correspondence course which would help him matriculate, and bought textbooks in Mathematics and Latin, including Cicero, in anticipation of the work. He was reported to the Senior Housemaster for ordering useless books, and since his correspondence course lessons never arrived, he suspected that they had been intercepted by the college authorities (Gandah 2004: 116).

As well as the simple withholding of Latin and Greek, another tactic was developed to keep Africans from academic education, via the examination system. All public exams were geared to failing large numbers of candidates and permitting only a very few to move up the educational ladder.[22] Kaduna College, for instance, would not increase its numbers to accommodate qualified students (Tibenderana 2003: 110). More restrictive still was the system devised at Yaba Higher College in Lagos, Nigeria, where there were no public exams but only a series of continual assessments by staff which revolved around 'character' as much as academic ability (Tibenderana 2003: 109–16). Rather than producing leaders, the college turned out 'well-trained assistants' for the British colonial services, and, moreover, only as many passes were permitted as there were relevant vacancies in government offices. Successful candidates went into the available posts no matter what their personal inclinations or preparations might have been (Ajayi and Tamuno 1973: 12–14, Otegbeye 1995: 73). Unsurprisingly, even though the entrance standards were very high and the drop-out rate among the highest in the world (Fafunwa 1974: 144), Latin was not required as part of the entrance exam to Yaba (Elliot 1945: 35). Since the exams in some Nigerian secondary schools were designed only to send boys to Yaba, rather than to other institutions of higher education like Fourah Bay, or abroad, boys would be trapped within a system that permitted no objective measurement of their talents (Aluko 1979: 33). Where public examinations were well established, for instance in Sierra Leone, the colonial government nonetheless planned, in the 1920s, to abolish such exams and bring in others which would be more 'suited to local conditions'. The result of this plan, which was defeated by Sierra Leonean protests, would have been to curb the educational ambitions of many Sierra Leonean students.[23]

Possibly the most powerful tactic developed to combat the evil of the 'educated African', and to downplay literary and classical pursuits, was the emphasis on 'agricultural' education. Successive government initiatives from the late nineteenth century tried to encourage what might variously be called 'agricultural', 'practical', 'vocational', 'manual', 'technical' or 'industrial' education, and these efforts came to a head in the 1920s. Even at the beginning of the period under investigation, it was a matter for official regret that Sierra Leoneans preferred to trade rather than to farm, and this despite the acknowledged poverty of much Sierra Leonean land (Rowan and Wellington 1827: 6, 11, 33, Wyse 1989: 5–7).[24] Later on, as we have seen, the growth of the colonial civil service made clerical occupations rewarding and attractive. Yet even the task of supplying clerks and engineers became fraught with contradiction, when someone like Henry Carr could regret the desire of students for clerical work in towns instead of time-honoured labour in ancestral fields or workshops. Although these predilections for modern occupations over farming were often attributed to the culpable materialism of Africans, some commentators were aware that Africans were simply making rational choices within the new socio-economic conditions. 'It is difficult to expect any enthusiasm for a Back-to-the-Land movement when a bush farmer working in a primitive manner can apparently expect to earn something like 5d. and a clerk something like 50s. a week' (Brown 1964: 373, quoting the Superintendent of Education at Warri, Nigeria, in 1934). Modern commentators agree that Africans' choice of the classics over agriculture showed them to be, not helpless in the face of an alien culture, but adept at manipulating the hostile circumstances of colonialism.[25]

The emphasis on 'agricultural' education thus ignored many of the real demands of the colonial administration, as well as the active choices made by Africans. That it was largely determined by ideological preferences for certain kinds of African identity, rather than by acknowledgement of historical conditions, is suggested by one of the major strands of the discourse on the educated African. This was that academic education was producing a population of young men who could find no employment in government or mercantile offices, because there were too many of them. This discourse of the discontented unemployed persisted throughout the period even when it was clear that Nigeria, for instance, suffered from a shortage of literate manpower and was forced to import clerks from Sierra Leone and the Gold Coast (Ogunlade 1974: 328), and when boys with minimal education were snapped up by government and mercantile offices because of the shortage of them.[26]

That so many contradictory complaints could be voiced simultaneously points to the overpowering force of the ideologies that were being wielded rather than to the actual parameters of a historical situation.

Agricultural and manual education for Africans might strike some as a strange notion, given the often peasant economy of African communities and the prevalence of skilled crafts that predated the European incursions. One explanation for the apparent mismatch was that such education was designed not so much to teach *ab initio* as to counter the European influences that had earlier detached Africans from their traditional skills.[27] It was also often designed to teach agriculture informed and driven by capital, and by profit rather than self-sufficiency.[28] Another very important task of such education, however, was to confirm Africa in Europe's view of it as, precisely, rural and traditional, even when tradition was now undermined on all sides by modernity, and when agricultural activity was being transformed by European determination to extract the continent's mineral wealth. The idealized virtues of 'Christian ruralism' that Europeans wished to attribute to Africans could thus prove more compelling than any lived historical circumstances (Tibenderana 2003: 79, Sivonen 1995: 133–9, 242–4). In many early sources the 'educated' African is unfavourably compared to the 'authentic', 'genuine' article who is necessarily a peasant farmer. Quite how the peasant farmer is to remain genuine, yet benefit from the twentieth-century civilization that the empire claims to confer, is left unanalysed.[29] Disregarding the many crucial changes that had already come about and that would develop further, and driven by the multiple other contradictions attendant on colonialism, the emphasis on agricultural education bore many ideological resemblances to Indirect Rule.[30]

Quite often, the schools themselves undermined any positive result that might have emerged from agricultural education. While such education was meant to inculcate the dignity of labour which academically educated Africans allegedly rejected, and thus cure the Africans of their allegedly ingrained idleness, the schools seem sometimes to have perceived it as a way to exploit pupils' unpaid work (Berman 1974: 534, Osuntokun 1984: 5, 6).[31] Memoirs of interwar education always include the cleaning of buildings and the cutting of grass, ostensibly as part of character-formation, but also inflicted as punishment, thereby making quite clear what the official view of agriculture and manual work in fact was (Olubummọ 1980: 29–32, Aluko 1979: 12).[32] Critics did not overlook the fact that agriculture was shunned by the educational establishment in Britain (Njoku 1969: 95), and that leaders of African descent elsewhere, such as Booker T. Washington, had certainly not been produced by vocational training (Murray 1929: 305–6).

The ideology of 'agricultural' education received a shot in the arm in the interwar years, as a result of the prolonged debates on the future of African colonies consequent on the First World War. After the war, the British authorities, guided by American emphasis on 'self-determination', committed themselves to the eventual independence of their African colonies and undertook to prepare Africans for self-rule. What was not articulated was the timeframe for these developments, and throughout the first half of the century colonial officials regularly discussed independence in terms of decades, and even 'generations or centuries'.[33] The nature of the imperial project was now described in new ways, in terms of Africa as a 'sacred trust' and of Britain's 'mandate' to govern,[34] but as Murray 1929: 259 recognized, 'the idea of mandates raised the whole question of the purpose of the European nations in Africa and presented a writ of quo warranto [by what authority] to all of them'. Since the First World War had also demonstrated the dependence of the imperial powers on their colonial possessions, Lugard's notion of the 'dual mandate' provided a useful coordination of the protection and development of Africans with access for the rest of the world to Africa's riches.[35] The war also produced a new humility about the right of the 'advanced' peoples of the world to rule, consequent on the remarkable barbarity they had recently displayed, and by the same token colonial subjects were able to be much more critical of their masters.[36] Within the new political context, the new language of responsibility came to mean that much greater efforts had to be made towards the education of Africans. Although this did not ensure a system of universal free primary education, or anything remotely approaching it, there was a definite increase in educational activity and perhaps even more so in pronouncements about it. Since so many of the lines of force converged on the figure of classical education, that remained a focus as the early twentieth century unfolded, and reached new heights of controversy with the Report of the Phelps-Stokes Commission.

The Phelps-Stokes Commission: classics as educational slavery

The Phelps-Stokes Commission on Education in Africa was set up by the Phelps-Stokes Trust, which was a charitable foundation devoted to the education of those whom it called Negroes, mainly in America but also in Africa. In 1920 the members of its African Education Commission visited West, Central and Southern Africa, and a Report was published in 1922, as *Education in Africa*. Without any African members domiciled in Africa, and headed by the Revd. Thomas Jesse Jones (1873–1950), who had recently completed a report on Negro education in the United States, the Commission in West Africa found against the classics at every level. Instead, it came down firmly on the side of agriculture, hygiene, sanitation, carpentry and housecraft, and moral education. The conclusion of the Report was that the imposition of the classics on West Africans had distorted their educational opportunities and abilities, with the consequence that they were excluded from productive engagement with the arts and sciences of the modern world. Since the classics thus constituted a sign of the lack of appropriate development to which British colonies had been condemned, the colonies still suffered from a form of slavery. The Report claims that (Jones 1922: 26):

> Educational slavery has been painfully apparent both in the retention of certain conventional subjects that have excluded others much more applicable to life, and in the teaching of a subject content that should long ago have given way to results of modern research related to the life of the pupils. . . . The excessive emphasis on classical languages has excluded proper provision in physical science, social studies, and other phases of modern research.

Modern subjects, the Report urged, should now be included in the curriculum even at the expense of classical subjects: 'How much time can be spared for Latin when the pupil has not a respectable knowledge of the principles of sanitation? Can time be given to Greek when the pupil is ignorant of the elements of physics or chemistry?' (1922: 66). The Report thus represents itself as the bearer of modernity, even though it does acknowledge the important roles played by the classics at earlier junctures (1922: 76):

> Unfortunately the college curriculum has only recently begun to change the traditional character of the subjects taught. The large place given to the classical languages has limited or excluded the necessary time for social and physical science, sometimes even for history.... Many European and American supporters of classical learning now concede that the effective study of social and physical science results in equal culture and character with the additional important result of capacity to serve society along some of the definite lines of its modern requirements. All will readily grant that the classics have made a vital contribution to the development of humanity, but this recognition of the classics is in no respect antagonistic to the conviction that culture, character and useful human service can be attained by the recognition of the results of modern scientific research . . . The influence of the classical requirements of some European universities is distorting many phases of education in African schools . . . New degrees, such as Bachelor of Science, have been introduced which require no Greek and little or no Latin [and this kind of provision should be extended to Africa].

Classical education is thus seen to be responsible for Africans' exclusion from modernity, and certainly does not represent access to higher education, professional careers or the ability to resist British colonialism.

Although the Commission does respect the role of Latin in public exams, noting that 'The claims of Latin will require special consideration in behalf of the few who are compelled to pass the conventional tests of European universities' (1922: 66), it tends to subscribe to the deadly stereotype of the 'educated African' when it remarks that (1922: 76) 'Africans have too readily believed that the culture and character of Oxford University graduates can be realized most successfully through the study of the classical languages'. This looks uncomfortably like the African who knows only the surface accomplishments of Western civilization and cannot reach its profounder depths. The Commission also quotes approvingly a 1920 statement from Governor Clifford of Nigeria (Jones 1922: 175) that:[37]

> there is throughout the southern provinces an abundance of schools but very little genuine education; that the children are themselves curiously eager to attend school, but are much less willing to remain there long enough to acquire any real and useful knowledge; and that too many of them, no matter how imperfectly educated they may be, thereafter regard themselves as superior to agricultural pursuits, and prefer to pick up a precarious and

> demoralizing living by writing more or less unintelligible letters for persons whose ignorance is even deeper than their own.

Despite the Commission's rhetoric of departures from the accepted norms, such pronouncements duly recycle European fears about the 'educated African'.

Even those aspects of the classics which were not linguistically based came in for censure. The Report claims that 'History, too, must answer the test of good citizenship . . . In this spirit recent history is more important than that of ancient times; the history of our own country than that of foreign lands; the record of our own institutions and activities than that of strangers; the labours and plans of the multitude than the pleasures and desires of the few' (1922: 67). In this context, 'the teacher will not be content to deliver lectures of abstract wisdom based on ancient civilization' (1922: 68) but will be an integral part of the community and linked to it by multiple modes of interchange. In many ways these strictures were very progressive, potentially affording value to African histories and cultures in a way that could only be celebrated, and they address concerns which are recognizable today in the educational systems of many countries. Certainly the Commission found aspects of classical education which might give even supporters pause. In many secondary schools preparation for public exams determined all the students' activities, so that any talents other than the purely academic remained underdeveloped. The problems attendant on this system were sometimes recognized; at Fourah Bay, alumni had given money to establish the teaching of science, indicating African awareness of other needs (1922: 48).

An extreme case of overemphasis on classical languages could be found in East Africa, object of a separate later Phelps-Stokes Commission, where students might study Latin for 17 years as preparation for the ministry (Jones 1925: 161) and seminaries run by the Catholic White Fathers used Latin as a medium of instruction (161–2, 214). The Commission notes that this situation is 'strangely in contrast with other education in Africa' and has about it feelings that are at the very least mixed. 'When . . . the visitor asked the pupils what they knew of St Francis of Assisi, one of the 14 boys who held up their hands gave in fluent Latin and without any trace of hesitation a perfect history of the life, his work and the influence this had on the church' (Jones 1925: 161).[38] The Principal of the Little Seminary at Bukalasa is quoted (161):

> The science to be acquired is, of course, mostly of a clerical nature, Latin being foremost . . . The sixth form (first year) is the foundation stone. The students do not begin Latin, but are taught, in the vernacular, grammar, arithmetic, geography, history. They learn to reflect and to think by parsing and analysis. Teaching of Latin includes Morphology (fifth form), Syntaxis of words (fourth form), Syntaxis of sentences (third form), Revision of the whole grammar (sixth form), Rhetoric (first form), with numberless exercises. Manual training and athletics are provided every day.

In a comparable (though earlier) document (Bishop of North Victoria Nyanza 1905: 192), the White Fathers explain that

> In a little seminary we could not omit the language of the church . . . [Kiswahili] is mere child's play for Baganda of a studious disposition. Latin and English are of course much more difficult for them, but they display considerable taste for them; some pupils even become troublesome in their demand to be taught new words and expressions.

Although there is a quantity of Latin on offer, there is no plan to enter students for public examinations or to afford them the opportunity of further study; the education is geared to religious practice and is not 'liberal' or pre-professional in the sense which we have seen in the West African colonies.

What alternatives did the West African Commission offer in place of education with a classical bias? While it advocated education in modern science, it also stressed broader principles of 'adaptation' whereby Africans would learn, for instance, history and botany via African examples instead of English. 'Adaptation' would also include lessons in sanitation and hygiene, in agriculture, as being the likely career destination of many Africans, and in the elusive entity known as 'character'. 'Character training' was presented as a means to fit the African for the demands of modernity, including eventual political independence, but it also had in view the correction of sexual indulgence (1922: 25) and what the Report calls 'the emotional activities characteristic of the African people'. For these would be substituted qualities the Report lists such as cleanliness, punctuality, thrift, temperance and self-control (1922: 27).

These conclusions were predictably controversial. The Commission was quickly seen to have its own agenda, which might not intersect with that of the Africans who were its ostensible objects of enquiry. That agenda seemed to many to stem from the situation in the United States.[39] Since he had just completed the compendious report on 'Negro' education in the United States (Jones 1917), the head of the American philanthropic body, the Revd. Thomas Jesse Jones, although of European descent, had seemed to his peers eminently qualified for the African task. Unfortunately, the education of African-Americans was itself no simple issue. Jones' earlier report had found that the historically black, academic colleges, like Fisk and Howard, were not serving the contemporary needs of the Negro, and that what worked were places like Booker T. Washington's Tuskegee Institute and the Hampton Institute, where Negroes learned to advance in industry by means of training in occupational crafts and skills, improved farming methods, and moral uplift.[40] The emphasis was precisely *not* on aspiration or competition with white scholarly achievement. Predictably, then, Jones' report on Negro education was criticized by black leaders of other ideological persuasions such as W. E. B. Du Bois, a consequence which was not stressed by the British colonial officials who greeted the new African Report. The reception of Jones' *Education in Africa* in 1922, then, may plausibly be said to be driven by many different considerations, of which impartial judgement was only one. Polarized by its findings, the educational establishment in West Africa continued to respond to it throughout the interwar period.

Education in Africa was welcomed with open arms by some of the colonial authorities, as demonstrated by Governor Guggisberg of Ghana, in 1925, recommending its policies without reservation. Sivonen paraphrases thus (Sivonen 1995: 86):

> Africa would be given wider opportunities than ever before and their country would be freed from the greatest evil which had ever confronted it . . . an unsuitable educational system which produced only a large number of literate unemployed, half African and half European. Their education up till then had provided a glimpse of the highest notions of western civilization, but was still insufficient to help them to grasp these ideas or to apply them to practical conditions. In other words, the school system of that moment was denationalising Africans. . . .

While Guggisberg was known as one of the more enlightened colonial officials, some other favourable responses to *Education in Africa* rather too obviously foregrounded the interests of the colonial powers over those of the Africans. One correspondent wrote to the Revd. Jones that: 'I believe you have here the very best chance in the whole of Africa of educating an intelligent, cheerful, self-respecting, and generally docile and willing-to-learn African native on simple, straightforward and satisfying lines to the benefit of himself and the whole country . . .'[41] The rhetoric perhaps gives the game away; the African product of adaptation is not here expected to be scientifically enquiring, equipped with the benefits of modern sociological research as he moves purposefully towards independence, but should instead remain 'cheerful' and 'docile' within a 'simple' education. If the point here is, as it seems to be, to educate in such a way that Africans do not question the dispensation under which they are educated, then it is hardly surprising that *Education in Africa* attracted very mixed responses overall.

In London, the Report issued forth in, among other things, the founding of the Advisory Committee on Native Education, later called Advisory Committee on Education in the Colonies. There were no African members on this Committee. Its Memorandum on Education Policy in British Tropical Africa of 1925 follows the overall precepts of the Phelps-Stokes Report and foregrounds the concept of 'adaptation', which became as much of a watchword as 'agricultural education':

> Education should be adapted to the mentality, aptitudes, occupations and traditions of the various peoples, conserving as far as possible all sound and healthy elements in the fabric of their social life; adapting them where necessary to changed circumstances and progressive ideas as an agent of natural growth and evolution. Its aim should be to render the individual more efficient in his or her condition of life, whatever it may be, and to promote the advancement of the community as a whole through the improvement of agriculture, the development of native industries, the improvement of health, the training of the people in the management of their own affairs and the inculcation of true ideals of citizenship and service. It must include the raising up of capable, trustworthy, public-spirited leaders of the people, belonging to their own races. Thus defined it will narrow the hiatus between the educated class and the rest of the community . . .

The issue of 'adaptation', larger than that of agricultural education but connected to it, addressed some notable failures in European education as purveyed in British West Africa. Many thoughtful authorities lamented the necessity for African students to learn via examples that were alien and more or less meaningless. Another, later educational commission, noted that (Pickard-Cambridge 1940: 146):

> It should be a commonplace that 'history' and kindred subjects for the African should imply first of all a study not of the Roman Republic or the Wars of the Roses, but of the history, political structure, social and economic conditions and geography of his own country; that his botany and zoology, even if the elementary principles are the same for all the world, should take for its typical examples the plants and animals of his own region of Africa. What do we find? In some sets of papers which it was proposed to set in examinations for scholarships, there was scarcely anything that bore on African life even remotely, but questions on the geography mainly of America and India, on the ridge-and-furrow system of cultivation, on the groundsel and the bog-bean, and on the papering of walls.

This report was authored by A. W. Pickard-Cambridge, the prominent classical scholar.

The paradigmatic example of non-adaptation is always laid at the door of the French, who taught their African colonial students that 'Our ancestors were the Gauls. They had blue eyes and fair hair'.[42] But the British were equally culpable in omitting an African dimension from formal education; memoirs such as those of Olubummọ from the thirties regret the absence of, for instance, African music amid the well-loved hymns (1980: 125–6).[43] Genuine adaptation did begin to take place in education, and most relevantly for our inquiry, in 1938 the University of London altered its matriculation requirements for West Africans. The Report of the Gold Coast Education Department for 1938–9 explains (34):

> Almost all the Gold Coast students who proceed to University courses qualify to do so by obtaining exemption from the Matriculation Examination of the University of London through securing the requisite number of 'credit' marks in prescribed subjects in the School Certificate Examination. Undoubtedly, such a system is liable to have a narrowing influence on the curriculum of secondary schools. In 1938 however some relief was given by the introduction by the University of London of a new regulation to the effect that a West African candidate for the Matriculation Examination, or for exemption from it, whose native language is not English, need not offer any language other than English. In future, therefore, the secondary school course need not necessarily embrace the study of two foreign languages in deference to the needs of pupils who desire to proceed to university studies.

The 'two foreign languages' would necessarily have included Latin in earlier years, and in fact the Report goes on to note:

> But for the Intermediate Arts Exam of the University of London, Greek or Latin remain as compulsory subjects. In actual fact, these subjects attract many Gold Coast pupils and considerable success is achieved in the study of them.

In a similar move, in 1934 Twi, Fanti, Ga and Ewe had obtained acceptance as examination subjects by the Cambridge University Local Examinations Syndicate, and the first three of these vernaculars were 'accepted by the University of London as a subject included in those which counted towards exemption from its Matriculation Examination'.[44] Hausa and Yoruba had been accepted as 'optional special languages' for the University entrance qualifying examinations of the University of London in 1922 (Omulewa 2006: 272). Even at an advanced level, then, there was some 'adaptation' in the sense of taking account of particular West African circumstances, but classical languages were still present at the threshold of higher education.

Twelve years after the 1925 Memorandum from the Advisory Committee, Mumford and Parker (1937) could report on favourable responses to Phelps-Stokes throughout the educational establishment. The mission schools, which provided a great deal of the unadapted academic curriculum, including classical languages, were prepared to admit some failings in the past but also to resist the vocational imperative. Since they acknowledged the importance of 'character-building', and dreaded the production of 'proud' Africans, they were prepared to admit some agriculture (more often, simply gardening), hygiene and nature study to their curricula, but they continued largely to found the same sorts of schools as before.[45] Ajayi writes that even when, as it were, they 'smote their breasts and pleaded guilty to the sins of their predecessors in fostering an allegedly idle middle class with no roots in and no love for their own country, good for nothing except imitating European vices', they continued to found literary schools and sometimes even decreased the emphasis on industrial and technical education which they had included earlier (1965: 270–1). W. Carson Ryan, a prominent educator, wrote from the point of view of mission schools addressing the Commission that (1923: 281):

> You shook us up, you made us think; and though at first we were wrestling, I feel all the same that we are making the ideals you held up to our gaze

> increasingly our own. In our own school our study of history has become a study of the growth and development of the British Empire with Crown Colony and West Africa emphasis – replacing the detailed study of the History of England; our study of geography is of the world with West Africa as the home center instead of the British Isles. We give physiology and hygiene a much larger place in our curriculum, and hope to introduce the study of physical or chemical science at an early date, though this may have to put out our beloved Latin in order to find room for itself . . .

Here as elsewhere the sciences are the hardest to introduce to the curriculum, not only because they make huge demands on equipment and facilities, but also because they go head to head with Latin, which puts up commensurate resistance.

While colonial authorities, and many schools, welcomed the conclusions of *Education in Africa* and the 1925 Memorandum from the Advisory Committee on Education in the Colonies, nonetheless substantial critiques were voiced from the moment of publication. One of the other members of the Commission, in fact, wrote to Jones immediately that 'the whole tenor of the report runs counter to their [Africans'] own methods and aims . . . To a man they are convinced that the teaching of the Classics is a sine qua non of higher education.'[46] The Assistant Director of Education in Ghana is reported to have greeted the Commission's recommendations with the dismissive 'it's much too late for this kind of thing in the Gold Coast' (Collins 1996: 207). Whatever the innate virtues of adaptation and agricultural education might have been, in the colonial context it was inescapable that Africans should assume they were being fobbed off with a second-class education, training them to be hewers of wood and drawers of water, and little else. The *Gold Coast Leader* accused the Report of 'trying to make the African fit in with the European's scheme of exploitation and control',[47] and Mayhew saw the problem clearly (1938: 49):

> Those who urge that a child should learn only what is useful are usually those who want a perpetual supply of cheap labour. They hope that the child who learns only to dig or hoe will never want to do anything else. It is not the business of the schools to feed the labour market. It is their business to help pupils, not only to live, but to live well.[48]

Where reforms were carried out, it was usually without appropriate funds, so that although science was recommended, the money necessary for well-equipped laboratories was rarely forthcoming. In the absence of cash, subjects like Latin, which required only a room, a board and a teacher, continued to press their claims. In the absence of science, the recommendations of Phelps-Stokes were watered down to consist of education in sanitation, agriculture and character training, which were then interpreted as excuses for making pupils work in school buildings and gardens, and for teaching them proper deference. The overall effect, or rather lack of effect, of Phelps-Stokes may be summed up by noting that in the first half of the twentieth century, nationalist opinion rejected the principles of 'adaptation' and sought academic and literary education above all. Only later in the twentieth century did there emerge a comparable demand for technical education (Boahen 1996: 292).

Phelps-Stokes thus mounts a particular targeted attack on West African practice, but in many other parts of the continent, classical education was distinguished by its absence. A brief review of other colonial situations will help to set Phelps-Stokes' strictures in wider context. In the British colonies of East Africa, for instance, where as we have seen the White Fathers used Latin as a language of instruction in their seminary, and published a Latin-Luganda dictionary and grammar (Jones 1925: 161–2, 214), the educational scene was otherwise, the later Phelps-Stokes Commission found, completely bereft of secondary schools (Jones 1925: 43).[49] According to Bassey 1999a: 34–5, Africans in the Portuguese and German colonies were trained only for roles as peasants and artisans, and even with unambitious schools, high fees and huge failure rates kept students out. In Belgian colonies, the seminaries of the White Fathers might teach Latin (Jones 1915: 291, Manning 1998: 165), but the Belgians neglected post-primary education to such an extent that in 1951, there were 30,000 school students of whom none qualified for university education (Bassey 1999a: 35).[50] Belgium became notorious for the miniscule number of university graduates available on the eve of independence, which is tallied at between 17 and 39.[51]

For South Africa, with its particular racial conflicts, Lambert's crucial study (2011) rehearses the struggles at Lovedale and other prominent missionary establishments over the teaching of Latin and Greek to 'natives' in his chapter 'The Classics and Black South African Identities'. From the 1840s till the 1870s, Lovedale purveyed a classical education to South African blacks, but the ideology changed in the late nineteenth century, in a pattern that is recognizable from the present study, and the education became more vocational. While much of the rhetoric is very similar to that employed in the West African context, the political environment is notably different, both because South Africa was educating white as well as black children, and because South African whites were determined to keep blacks unable to compete with whites in any field, even in technical or vocational pursuits.[52] By contrast, the authorities in West Africa often acknowledged that Africans should take on much of the responsibility of serving the colonial administration as missionaries, teachers, clerks, engineers and medical assistants, even while they remained in subjection to the British empire. In South Africa the authorities were explicit that Africans should remain 'hewers of wood and drawers of water' (Bassey 1999: 33, quoting a 1912 letter to the *Rhodesia Herald*) and to that end they eventually used the Bantu Education Act to close down Lovedale and comparable institutions. Because of the apartheid policy of 'separate but equal', however, Latin and New Testament Greek were then offered at the ethnically organized 'homeland' universities, and most famously at the University of Fort Hare. This latter institution had served the black population of East, Central and Southern Africa, since 1916, rather as Fourah Bay did for West Africa – with the proviso that East, Central and Southern Africa were all settler colonies where most educational resources were directed to the children of white colonists.

Debates about classical education for those of African descent often took similarly impassioned yet perverted forms in other contexts. Kenneth Goings and Eugene O'Connor 2011 have demonstrated how knowledge of Latin and Greek was sometimes withheld from African-American students in the United States, provoking them to resist both publicly and also by continuing to study in secret. Racial segregation, of course, gave a particular slant both to the desires of African-Americans to acquire a classical education and to the reluctance of white authorities to comply.[53] A representation which is different in certain notable respects is offered by Greenwood 2010 for the Anglophone Caribbean, in the chapter 'Classics as School of Empire'. As in West Africa, classics was entrenched in the elite secondary schools and had a major role in securing professional advancement, but classics does not appear in Greenwood's text as a sign of black 'educability' or a touchstone of black achievement. Greenwood relays no sense that the colonial authorities were troubled by black acquisition of Latin and Greek or that the contrary pressures towards 'agriculture' and its ilk were directed specifically towards black students; one possible explanation lies in the particular contours of the history of education in the Caribbean, where elite schools were founded for the children of white settlers but gradually became available to the children of 'coloured' or black parents.[54] Where classics is embroiled in the toxic pressures of colonial culture, in Greenwood's analysis, is in the anguish caused by the ruthless system of examinations for 'island scholarships' to Britain, and in the alienation that results when the classically educated 'native' is at home neither in the Caribbean surroundings nor in the imperial culture which he has acquired. Certain moments in Greenwood's study do correspond very clearly to the West African context. Caribbean students are just as pleased as West African when boys from the islands outperform British boys in public examinations (2010: 89), and Eric Williams' correction of a supercilious Oxford student resonates with Blyden's demolition of the 'educated European'. The Englishman expresses surprise at Williams' being able to speak English, but after a Latin test at which Williams proves effortlessly superior, he is able to explain that 'we speak Latin in Trinidad' (Greenwood 2010: 88).

Responses in the schools

In the West African colonies, the Phelps-Stokes Report dominated discussion of classics for the next decade, but its recommendations were never fulfilled in any straightforward way. Although the Commission had no members who were native Africans living in Africa, it did include the prominent American educator James Emman Kwegyir Aggrey (1875–1927), later known as 'Aggrey of Africa' or 'Aggrey of Achimota', who had been born in the Gold Coast and had emigrated to the United States when a young man. To Aggrey and his particular personal influence was attributed much of any success that the Commission enjoyed, and having impressed numerous audiences both black and white during the Commission's tours of Africa, he went on to become a crucial part of Achimota School, which was itself one of the most important results of the Phelps-Stokes Commission. Because Aggrey combined classical and 'adapted' education in compelling ways, and had a great effect on many of the contemporary nationalists, he forms part of the account of classics in the British colonies of West Africa.

Son of the interpreter of a Gold Coast chief, Aggrey was educated at Mfantsipim in academic subjects, including Latin and Greek at which he excelled, but he went on to study and teach in the United States, where he lived for over 20 years, and to acquire degrees in medical sciences as well as further qualifications in classics and theology. Only his premature death prevented his obtaining a PhD from Columbia University. On his death his extensive library, including Gibbon and other histories of Rome and Greece, formed the basis of the library at Achimota School (Newell 2002: 19). From an early date he seems to have represented his identity as bound up with his success in classics; for instance, he allegedly explained part of his long Ghanaian name as translated by 'wide-ruling Agamemnon' (Macartney 1949: 18). According to his first biographer, he wrote to his nephew in 1912 pointing out that when he was being trained for the ministry he ranked 'first in Greek, in Latin, in Bible history, in Logic, in Exegesis, yes, first in everything' (Smith 1932: 46).[55] At slight provocation, or none, he would quote long passages from Latin and Greek authors', and in later life, his conversation with his wife was allegedly punctuated by classical literary discussions (Smith 1932: 6, 73). Apparently he even read Horace in Latin to his unborn child (Macartney 1949: 36). Interestingly, his biographer flirts with the construct of the 'educated African' when he notes that Aggrey loved the roll of long, sonorous words, using them to impress, and inventing Latinate neologisms (like the Africans in *The Blinkards*, perhaps) such as 'tantabulator' to describe himself as a drummer (Smith 1932: 46). Smith also notes that (1932: 45) 'Of all Latin tags he loved best Caesar's Veni, vidi, vici . . . he was himself in a hurry to conquer the world', and another commentator claims that he held his classes spellbound with expositions of the classics (Macartney 1949: 26).

Having obtained further qualifications in the United States, graduating from Livingstone College with gold medals and delivering Latin and Greek orations on the occasion, Aggrey became the pastor to two very poor African-American communities in the South. At this stage, he is represented as regretting some of his classical education, insofar as it was not at all relevant to the needs of his neighbours in Miller's Chapel and Sandy Ridge. With his ability to quote Hebrew, Latin and Greek, he was, he said, as if 'in an aeroplane' in relation to his congregation (Macartney 1949: 39), a situation he addressed by teaching them improved methods of cultivation and housekeeping instead. In later years he is recorded as having spoken on this misfit to audiences in South Africa (Smith 1932: 87, 176), saying that 'Neither Latin nor Greek can save us, nor even mathematics – only Jesus can do it' (Macartney 1949: 76). Later too, he is represented as having urged West Africans to turn their classical learning to better effect: 'We of West Africa have proven that we can get the classics, theology and philosophy. We are past-masters in jurisprudence and dialectic. The question is, can we turn such knowledge more and more into service for the common weal?' (Smith 1932: 266). In representations such as these Aggrey sidesteps the legacy of the 'educated African', by acknowledging West Africans' great intellectual strengths, and does not simply advocate agricultural or industrial training as the alternative.

Aggrey was a gift to the Phelps-Stokes Commission in that he was an immensely learned African who apparently wished to move beyond the classics and saw the value to Africans of the other useful arts. In his own person he combined, perhaps even reconciled, the claims of the literary and the practical. Dr C. T. Loram, an Inspector of Native Education and member of the Native Affairs Commission in South Africa, wrote to Revd. Jones of the Phelps-Stokes Commission in 1921 that 'Surely he is the best answer to your opposition to the classics! His Latin and Greek have coloured his thinking, but he has still found time for sociology, economics and politics' (Smith 1932: 171).[56] Furthermore, Aggrey's politics were also directed towards reconciliation, in that he espoused the cause of harmonious cooperation between the races. To this end he apparently never took offence at the numerous institutional insults dealt out to him, as a black man, in the United States or in Africa.[57] Instead, he garnered repeated praise for his ability to interpret different racial communities to one another;[58] his message of tolerance and cooperation was epitomized in the image of the piano, with its black and white keys, both of which are required for the best music. Although such praise was perhaps chiefly drawn from white audiences, his speeches were directed towards a renewal of black self-confidence, as in the famous image of the eagle who has come to believe itself a chicken, but discovers that it can still fly.[59] Another of his sayings was that 'Only the best is good enough for Africa' (Smith 1932: 198), and indeed his conviction that Africans should gain access to the best of European civilization, without losing what was precious in African culture, made him valuable to the Phelps-Stokes Commission as an exponent of 'adaptation' in education. Crucially, of course, he was a black man recommending 'adaptation' and 'agricultural education' to other black people, rather than a white man imposing it. That he was well aware of these considerations is suggested by another famous utterance: 'In Africa it is not what is said that matters, nor even how it is said; what matters is, who says it.'[60] If a white were to indicate that a 'full-orbed' education was preferable to Caesar's Gallic Wars, he would not be believed, whereas Aggrey could, allegedly, persuade his audiences to leave 'Virgil, Livy and Demosthenes' and raise chickens instead (Macartney 1949: 56). Unsurprisingly, given the assimilationist slant of his politics, Aggrey condemned the aims and methods of Marcus Garvey (King 1969: 519, Roberts 1990: 259) and was criticized in his turn by Garvey (Macartney 1949: 76), by W. E. B. Du Bois (Jacobs 1996: 48), and by Africans in Africa who thought he had been bought off by the white establishment (Macartney 1949: 56).

By those who approved him, Aggrey was remembered chiefly as a spell-binding orator. Sources agree that it was difficult to explain how exactly his appeal worked, and they suggest that it was partly a question of his personality, his gestures and the music of his speech as much as the content of his speeches, which were apparently only rarely committed to writing or print (King 1969: 512). Intriguingly, he compared African civilization itself to non-literary figures from history: 'Like Socrates, the intellectual father of Plato, like the lowly Nazarene who has thrilled the world, the West African never wrote a line since he left his native heath . . .' (quoted in Smith 1932: 84).[61] Part of the effect that he exerted may perhaps be attributed to his premature death, which removed the possibility of any failure, and part perhaps to the desperate need in the post-war period, as the contradictions of empire multiplied, for a figure who would attempt a work of reconciliation between the races. King (1969: 526) calls him 'mythical', and confronts head-on the paradox that he appealed equally to black and white audiences – each saw in him what they needed. King concludes that Aggrey succeeded for reasons that he himself did not fully understand, particularly insofar as he did not realize that his appeal to black audiences lay in, precisely, his significance as an African with a higher education. As Gray 1986: 189 puts it:

> Dr Aggrey as a central figure in the Phelps-Stokes Commission might advocate rural adaptation and racial moderation, but, quoting Latin tags at Fourah Bay, feted by Guggisberg, welcomed as an equal by missionaries

> and liberals throughout the continent, he symbolised for his countrymen in the Gold Coast and for the thousands of Africans who saw and heard him elsewhere, the successful seizure from the whites of the advantages of their classical education.

King shows how young Africans who heard him, including the nationalists Azikiwe and Nkrumah, were inspired not to improve themselves by farming, but to leave for an advanced education in the United States (1969: 527–8). Meanwhile, white commentators dreamed that adapted education would produce more leaders like Aggrey (King 1969: 524), presumably not noticing that he had been produced by a completely different system.

As interpreter and mediator, and reconciler of conflicting kinds of education, Aggrey was crucial to perhaps the most significant and lasting consequence of the Phelps-Stokes Commission, which was Achimota School and College in Accra. In that it deliberately set out to combine the best of European education, including prominently Latin and Greek, with the best of African culture, this school represented a completely new direction for the education of Africans. Devised by Governor Guggisberg and founded in 1924, it had as first Principal A. G. Fraser, who insisted on Aggrey as Assistant Vice-Principal – and by the same token Aggrey refused to work with anyone but him (Simpson 1995: 87). The school eventually comprised numerous institutions for different ages, from a kindergarten to a University degree course, and broke the mould in various other ways including that it was co-educational from the start, and non-denominational, albeit with an acknowledged Christian ethos. As a purpose-built establishment with lavish facilities, it represented a far greater investment in West African education than the British government was wont to make. Most radically, however, even though it was a government foundation, the school was run not by government but by a council which had always to draw half its members from the native African population, and this innovative constitution was explicitly designed as a step on the road to African self-determination. Since the leading teachers were not all Europeans, but were drawn from throughout the Empire, the staffing policies too were radical. Some teachers had lived or taught in south-east Asia, so that as C. Kingsley Williams, an early Principal, explains (1962: 27), 'a large number had actually been in close contact with a high non-European civilization, and a culture which was ancient when the culture of Britain was more like the culture of West Africa than the modern white man likes to remember'.

What was the role of classics in this new foundation? Predictably, it was contradictory, pointing towards the difficulty of the Achimota enterprise as a whole. We should note first of all that the ethos of the school was not designed to be overwhelmingly academic; hobbies of all kinds were regularly promoted, and music and art, including African traditions, were as important as more academic subjects. The goals of the school were what we should nowadays call holistic, involving social service as well as practical and even experimental work on the school farm. The Report of 1932 states (Mayhew 1938: 165–6):

> Achimota hopes to produce a type of student who is 'western' in his intellectual attitude towards life, with a respect for science and capacity for systematic thought, but who remains African in sympathy and desirous of preserving and developing what is deserving of respect in tribal life, custom, rule and law . . .

In this context the classics stood ready to represent the best of the West, and ideally to be integrated with the best of Africa. The students usually took Latin, except when they were enrolled on the commercial course or for teacher training (Report of the Department of Education, Gold Coast, 1937–8: 39, Agbodeka 1977: 59). Although the only full degree that students could study for was Engineering, they could take the BA Intermediate Arts exam of the University of London, which required Latin (Agbodeka 1977: 61). True to form, Latin could be a cause of comment, favourable or otherwise. In 1932 the Report of the Committee appointed by the Governor of the Gold Coast finds the inclusion of Latin 'a little surprising', given that the students are already learning one foreign language, namely English; the Committee concludes that African parents are possibly 'under the mistaken opinion that it [Latin] is learnt more universally in England than is actually the case' (Achimota College 1932: 54). As so often, Latin is cited as a point of misunderstanding between Africans and the colonial establishment. Wallbank similarly situates Latin as a sign of African input into the school's curriculum, while reserving judgement as to its wisdom (1935: 240):

> In addition to studying English, the secondary pupil continues his vernacular studies and what must seem surprising to many, Latin is taught to all. This has been included because of the insistence of Gold Coast opinion which evidently regards it as a fundamental hallmark of an educated man.

But 'undoubtedly some observers will be dubious regarding the emphasis upon religion; and to others, including the author, the inclusion of Latin for all secondary students is difficult to justify' (1935: 245). By other commentators, as with other schools, Achimota was praised for its students' prowess in Latin. The Report of 1932 is cheered (Achimota College 1932: 54):

> To those of us who have been accustomed to see many English boys weary of Latin and uncertain of its constructions after years of teaching, it was refreshing to note the enthusiasm of the teachers and the courage with which the pupils tackle the difficulties.

Williams (1962: 147) quotes Charles Roden Buxton MP who had visited the school:

> There at last and there alone we are doing something handsomely and wholeheartedly, something of the kind we would wish to do for our own rising generation. We are handling the question of African education, not on the cheap, as a thing to be dealt out grudgingly to people inferior to ourselves, but on a great scale.
>
> The impressions that stand out most at the present time are (a) the hard and strenuous work put in by the staff; (b) the delightful relations of European, African and Indian on the staff; (c) the high standard of manners through the school; (d) the high standard in the various classes I attended, among which the Latin perhaps impressed me the most.[62]

We might also measure the prominence of Latin at Achimota by the existence of the multilingual play written by two staff members (Williams 1962: 62), in which Julius Caesar discovers Achimota. One of the two authors recorded that it was performed (Marshall 1981: 33–4):

> by the members of Guggisberg and Lugard Houses, the houses under the charge of the two members of staff who taught Latin, viz, H. C. Neill and the present writer. Based on Caesar's account of his first invasion of Britain it purported to describe an invasion of the Gold Coast of those days by Caesar and his legions. The dialogue was entirely in Latin save for Galasenno who spoke French as a Gaul – and very good French, too, as there is no such thing as 'pidgin' French – and two of the Gold Coast 'natives' who could make nothing of Volusenus's questions and kept answering in their own vernacular – Fanti. Caesar was supposed to have founded Achimota, and the play ended with him paying a second visit to see how the College was progressing. . . . It was enthusiastically received.[63]

The play demonstrates some of the contradictions surrounding Latin in the colonial context in that the language is domesticated and almost naturalized at Achimota, to the extent of the school's claiming direct descent from Caesar; yet the play also registers the dynamics of conquest, and stages 'natives' who may either be too uncivilized to reply in Latin, or too smart to collaborate with the invader.

Latin was also caught up in various foreseeable struggles over the future of Achimota. While the Principal of Achimota might consider that 'the Latin syllabus has little cultural value for West African students' (Elliot 1945: 44), Gold Coast parents were quite likely to want a prestigious school to focus far more on European subjects than on African traditions (Murray 1929: 330). In 1938, the Report of the Achimota Committee represents the parents in rather patronizing fashion when it notes that 'it has been argued that Latin is out of place in an African school, and that as it is no longer necessary for London Matriculation, it might make room for other studies. But it is clear that there is at present a real demand for it on the part of pupils and parents, who regard it as one of the distinctive elements in the English education which they desire to imitate' (Achimota College 1938: 91).[64] Correspondingly, nationalists such as J. B. Danquah and Nnamdi Azikiwe were opposed to Achimota as a colonial institution, despite its more liberal ideals (Jenkins 1994, Newell 2002: 209). The colonial administration could conversely find it quite 'subversive', given its claims to be 'liberal, multicultural, Africa-centered, anti-racist, and (in some respects) anticolonial' (Jenkins 1994: 178), and it garnered resentment among other institutions which were considerably less well funded (Ward 1965: 185, Bartels 2003: 99). Commentators could be sceptical of the idealistic rhetoric of the founders and conclude that Guggisberg was simply trying to fill the higher levels of the colonial civil service, enabled by the unexpectedly large revenue from the newly established trade in cocoa (Ward 1965: 163). On the other hand, Francis Agbodeka, one of the first generation of historians of Africa, shows how the 'holistic' ambitions of Achimota, undermined by the familiar contradictions of colonial education, were gradually abandoned in favour of a curriculum geared to academic success, with 'adaptation' abandoned by the 1950s (1977: 138). For Agbodeka, the presence of Latin at Achimota retains an overall negative valence, indicating that after the war at least, the school became completely part of the colonial establishment without the ability to challenge received wisdom (1977: 157).

The histories of other prominent West African schools after Phelps-Stokes illustrate a range of responses to the new imperatives. Mfantsipim had reorganized its curriculum in the early years of the century, giving first place to 'liberal education' and second to 'sound useful knowledge' (Boahen 1996: 147), and it consolidated its academic, traditional, classical identity under Lockhart, the Principal in the 1930s. According to Agbodeka, other Gold Coast schools followed its prestigious lead.[65] In his annual reports, published in the *Mfantsipim Magazine*, Lockhart indicates that 'adaptation' was tried and found wanting. For instance, in 1931 the employment of a new teacher enabled the school to offer commercial subjects for the first time, but no parents enrolled their son in the new course. Lockhart's response is short and to the point (*Mfantsipim Magazine*, Bu Ber 1931: 5, Boahen 1996: 291): 'Critics . . . from time to time ask why we are not teaching these subjects . . . The answer is now known; parents wish their boys to learn Latin, and we presume that at present that is the end of the matter'. Throughout the late 1920s and 1930s Lockhart's reports regularly acclaim the examination successes of his students, noting that they often exceed the performance of English boys, especially in Latin, and regularly gain exemption from the matriculation for the University of London by their performance at School Certificate level (Bartels 1965: 302–6). This emphasis on examination success, Boahen concludes, gave confidence to African students, even if it had deleterious effects on their overall notion of education (1996: 309–10). In the Speech Day report of 1934 Lockhart himself was explicit (Boahen 1996: 309):

> There are eminent men in Africa today who are engaged in measuring the Negro's skull to try to determine his capabilities. In a humble way and with a thankful heart, we would advise these earnest enquirers that their quest had already been determined. The African has, in this and other schools, shown what he can do and to what extent he can profit. No case has been made for a type of education different from that which is given in Europe.

Lockhart also worked to counter the stereotype of the 'educated African', particularly by noting that his students, while very educated, were always in demand for employment (*Mfantsipim Magazine*, Bu Ber 1931: 4).

Another Gold Coast secondary school with a strong classical tradition was Adisadel College, founded in 1910 by the Anglican Church,[66] where in the 1930s Latin was compulsory and Greek optional; there does not seem to have been even lip service paid to the notion of adaptation, far less agricultural education. Adisadel had a tradition of students and teachers studying privately for University degrees; in the 1930s, Albert Hammond became the first student in the Gold Coast to obtain the (external) London University BA Honours degree in Classics entirely by private study (Amissah 1980: 6). In the 1940s Henry van Hain Sekyi took First Class BA Honours in Classics at Legon, the first student to do so, and went on to take First Class Honours in Part 1 of the Classical Tripos at the University of Cambridge (Amissah 1980: 64). Reports of the Education Department in the Gold Coast regularly note events at Adisadel, particularly the productions of Greek drama, of which more later. In 1933 'the study of Greek and Latin has in the last few years notably increased in popularity and improved in efficiency – interest being stimulated in 1932 by the production of the Antigone' (36). In 1935, 'a classical bias has been given to the curriculum at St Nicholas and Latin has been made compulsory, Greek being optional. In 1934 the school most successfully produced the Antigone of Sophocles' (39). And in 1936, after a production of *Agamemnon*, 'This school is earning a reputation for the production of Greek plays – a feature of the school life which has resulted from the school's attitude to the humanities' (32). Greek was not abolished until the 1960s, making way, perhaps belatedly, for science; the Hamlyn Greek Prize and Hare's Classics Prize, which had been awarded for decades, were replaced by prizes for Science and French.

Two boys drew on their facility with the classics to advance themselves considerably. One boy who was so keen to attend the school that he sat on the floor until a desk could be provided for him, went on to win the Hamlyn Greek Prize and the Hare's Classics Prize in one year, 1946 (Amissah 1980: 1949). The school's historian himself, G. Maclean Amissah, failed his Fanti paper because, having been brought up in Northern Nigeria, he actually spoke Hausa better than his 'mother' tongue; the ethos of the school ensured that he concentrated on Latin and Greek more than on the African language, and he got through Junior Cambridge (the School Certificate) on the strength of his Latin (Amissah 1980: 41).

A different ethos ruled at Wesley College, Ibadan, founded in 1905. Latin was eschewed, as part of inculcating pride in the African heritage, but also, it appears, in order to prevent boys undertaking further study abroad, rather than staying in Nigeria and serving the church there. J. O. Ajibola, 'the first person from Wesley College Ibadan to take a foreign examination and pass it' (Ajibola 1985: 70), gives a detailed account of the ways in which, he claims, he forced the Principal (1920–35), the Revd. E. G. Nightingale, to put Latin on the curriculum. At that time, before the reform of 1938, the Cambridge School Certificate required passes in: English Language and prescribed books in English Literature; Mathematics, including Arithmetic, Algebra and Geometry; Latin or Greek; and two other subjects. Nightingale planned to set a final test in Geometry and if students did not pass it, to drop Geometry from the school syllabus, which would have rendered it impossible for any student to sit the Cambridge School Certificate. Ajibola, by his own account, coached the students to revise Geometry all night, while the Principal was asleep, in order to pass (1985: 71).

Ten years later, as a teacher at the College, Ajibola took on the issue of Latin too. According to him, a scholarship was offered to a student who had matriculated – but no current Wesley College Ibadan student could matriculate, because of the absence of Latin or Greek from the curriculum. Ajibola's account shows an immediate polarization between the European headmaster, who seems to be included in the term 'our colonial masters', and the largely African Synod (1985: 71–2):

> I started to be a member of the Synod, Western Nigeria District as from 1923 and I seemed to have been a thorn in the flesh of our colonial masters because I would always speak out my mind frankly and politely without the fear of any consequence. In the Synod of 1931, the Board of Governors of the Methodist Boys' High School Lagos brought to the Synod a motion that that School was prepared to offer a scholarship to any teacher who had passed either Durham or London Matriculation so that such a Nigerian could become the Vice-Principal of the Methodist Boys' High School, Lagos. As a matter of fact, I was the only teacher in the Methodist Church then who had passed one of the two matriculations mentioned in their proposal. When the matter got to the hands of our colonial masters, they added two other conditions which would eliminate me as a candidate. The two conditions added were:

1 Such a candidate must be unmarried.
2 He must not be above twenty-five years of age.

> The Synod, ignorant of what we suffered at Wesley College Ibadan acclaimed the proposal. Knowing that the two conditions were aimed at eliminating me, I refrained from speaking about No. 1, but based my argument on No. 2 stating that the proposal was not meant for the present generation because Wesley College Ibadan could not produce any teacher of 25 years of age who could have passed either Durham or London Matriculation, and also that Methodist Boys' High School Lagos, which then did not go beyond Junior Cambridge could not produce such a candidate. As soon as I finished speaking, the Principal of Wesley College Ibadan got up and said that the last speaker (me) had posed as if he knew more than the Principal of Wesley College Ibadan because the average age of the students who left the College the previous year was 22 years and if a student left the College at the age of 22 and could not pass either Durham or London Matriculation within three years, he doubted whether such a person could obtain a degree if sent abroad for further education. I got up again and stated that Latin or Greek was a compulsory subject for the Matriculation and neither was being taught at Wesley College Ibadan. The eyes of the members of the Synod were then open as to what went on at Wesley College and immediately passed a motion that Latin or Greek must be taught at Wesley College. . . .
>
> At the Synod of January 1932, the late Rev. E. E. Williams asked whether Latin or Greek had started to be taught at Wesley College Ibadan. The Principal's reply to it so annoyed the reverend minister that he spoke vehemently that Wesley College, being in Nigeria should be handed over to the Nigerians so that we could teach our boys what we liked. He was supported by other African members of the Synod. No sooner had we returned from that Synod that the Principal included Latin as a subject in the College Syllabus. It was in June of that year 1932 that I tendered my resignation from the College so that I was not one of those who taught Latin at Wesley College Ibadan.

The conflict over the teaching of Latin is here represented very clearly as part of the anti-colonial struggle.

Such accounts suggest that Africans are ready to take control over their education as much as they can, and that when they do, they demand education in classical languages, not least because that is the quickest route to their own advancement. 'Adaptation' at Wesley College had consisted in the absence of the much-criticized literary education, in order that boys could concentrate on different strengths, but this proved not adapted, in any other sense, to Africans' needs and desires. The African resistance to the withholding of Latin is compounded by distrust of the European Principal who is taking decisions on their behalf. Ajibola sums up on Nightingale thus (1985: 73):

> If the Rev. E. G. Nightingale had not been a negrophobist, he would almost have been idolised as the Principal of Wesley College because he was a man of sterling qualities . . . But however much he might love a person, as soon as that person began to aspire to go abroad for further education, he became his enemy.

This judgement is seconded by that of Falade (1985: 45):

> Up to and including the time of Mr R. Hughes as principal, it was a sacrilege, if not a sin, to surreptitiously or clandestinely take any public examination as a student. If one unwittingly took such an examination and the authorities knew about it, it would fetch one a summary dismissal from the college.

The notion of 'unwittingly' taking a public exam suggests the very wry way that some Africans learned to see their situation.

The Revd. Nightingale, however, appears in very different guise elsewhere, stressing the vernacular, over against Latin, to foster the confidence of Africans in their own culture and heritage. He stresses not only the Yoruba language but also Nigerian dress (Olubummọ 1980: 91). Olubummọ begins his account of student life at Wesley College Ibadan as follows (1980: 1):

> Every generation of Wesley College students knew the story of the student from a Lagos secondary school who on his first visit to Wesley College stopped at the main gate and read the motto as Bai e-nai-tai n-se i-ran-se. He soon realised that this was not Latin in which he was well versed – he knew all about Non sibi sed aliis, per ardua ad astra, Domini opera pro bono publico.[67] So he decided it must be Greek, which, fortunately, he also knew reasonably well. The story goes on that he took two steps backwards to have a good look and, scratching the part of his head in which he stored his Greek vocabulary, went on 'Bai, yes, two, e-nai-tai . . .' But that is as far as there is agreement . . .

Olubummọ (1980: 3) goes on to explain that there are two endings to the story:

> Some people complete by saying that the student was so shocked when he realized how inadequate the classical education given by his school was, that he applied for admission to Wesley College. Another version says that a Wesley College student who happened to be passing just then saw the difficulty of the Lagos scholar and said 'BÍ ẸNITÍ ŃṢE ÌRAŃṢẸ – as one that serveth!' One might add that even if our Lagos friend had known that

> the motto was in Yoruba, there was no guarantee that he would have been able to read it.

The Yoruba motto is preferred, as Fanti was at Mfantsipim, in a gesture of opposition to the traditional school motto in Latin or at best in English. The imaginary student from Lagos is an example of the 'educated African', cut off from his own heritage because he does not recognize Yoruba, and with an imperfect classical education that largely consists of memorized tags.

Latin was, however, downgraded in other ways too. Olubummọ distinguishes Latin, in the familiar gesture, as one of the few subjects, along with Mathematics and Science, that makes secondary education truly secondary (1980: 80), but agrees that at Wesley College the attempts to teach Latin and Mathematics were 'half-hearted' (1980: 8–9), compared to the teaching of General Elementary Science, and confined to the first two years (1980: 72). The students were not enthusiastic about Latin, and dropped it as soon as they could, although the teacher wisely warned them that without Latin, they could not pass the London Matriculation (1980: 74). The author regrets, later on in the account (1980: 125) that it was not made more clear to the boys that without Latin and the London Matriculation, 'one could not make much progress academically' (1980: 125). In fact another alumnus of Wesley College, Obafemi Awolowo, later Premier of Western Nigeria, taught himself Latin after he had left the college, in order to be able to move to the next educational step (1960: 74). Similarly when Kwame Nkrumah, later the first President of independent Ghana, attended Achimota in the late twenties for teacher training, he thought himself fortunate to be learning alongside secondary school students, from whom he hoped 'to pick up a little Latin and higher mathematics in the hope of being able to sit for the London matriculation examination later on . . .' (1973: 13). This was never an easy option; as head teacher of the Roman Catholic Junior School at Axim, he took a private course to prepare for London Matriculation, but failed in Latin and in Mathematics.

The classics kept another prominent place in West African education during the 1920s and 1930s, despite the efforts of Phelps-Stokes and the agricultural lobby. Mythical narratives from classical antiquity featured in various educational contexts, the heroic tales possessing an inherent interest as well as the aura of long-lasting European favour. 1920s school texts such as 'My Duties' involved the stories of Hercules, Regulus, Socrates and Leonidas as well as those of Isaac Newton's dog, John Howard and Florence Nightingale (Murray 1929: 177).

Elementary readers advertised in the pages of *Nigeria Magazine*, the successor to *Nigerian Teacher*, were regularly based on classical myths as well as on Shakespeare stories,[68] and while the prized narratives of English literature were always more popular than those of Greece or Rome, the latter did command a sustained interest. From Achimota, Williams reported that books on mythology were very popular in the school library (1962: 54), and Newell that the school printing press produced a Fante *Odyssey* (Newell 2002: 77, citing *Achimota Review* 1937: 95).[69] In 1937 E. F. Andrews-Ayeh, house master and Twi master at Adisadel College, published a Twi translation of Charles Kingsley's *Heroes*, including the stories of Perseus, Jason and Theseus, with a foreword by the Headmaster of Adisadel.[70] A book of children's stories in the Longman's Twi series, written by W. D. Wadley of the Gold Coast Education Department and published in 1938, contains versions of *The Merchant of Venice*, the *Arabian Nights* and Apuleius' *Golden Ass*, while in 1948 M. B. Walton published a Fanti translation of M. R. Pease's *Stories from the Latin Poets*, with selections from Ovid and the *Aeneid*. Such initiatives suggest that any perceived contradiction between African schools and the classics could be successfully managed.

The activity surrounding classics in the 1930s suggests the range of responses to the Phelps-Stokes Report, but indicates that the Commission was not ultimately successful in eradicating the classics from West African syllabi and substituting adapted, technical, practical, vocational, manual or agricultural education. After the war familiar attitudes, on the part of both Africans and colonial authorities, continued in operation. In 1947, for instance, the Bo School in Sierra Leone requested to be allowed to teach Greek. Bo School, founded in 1906, was a showcase for how Britain was handling the education of the sons of native chiefs who would, under Indirect Rule, form the buffer class between the British and the ordinary Sierra Leoneans. Since the native chiefs were not to become 'educated Africans', Bo School, as we saw earlier, emphasized qualities other than academic achievement. Consequently, the request for Greek flew in the face of its ostensible ideology, and was perhaps even more disturbing in that it coincided with the year, 1947, in which the practice and ideology of Indirect Rule were officially abandoned. The Report of the Department of Education is predictably disapproving (1948: 4):

> At the Protectorate Assembly in August, 1947, a member made the request that Greek should be included in the curriculum of the Bo School. No

> possible advantage would be gained by such a step. The pupils would not reach the stage where they could obtain a useful knowledge of Greek life and thought, matters which may be studied much more easily in the many excellent English translations of the classical authors. Its introduction would undoubtedly overload the curriculum to a degree which could only result in the pupil's progress in essential subjects being retarded . . .

Much of the rest of the Report plays variations on the theme of paper qualification versus character-formation, the very theme that had largely operated to deprive Africans of the education they chose.

What is relevant to our enquiry is that even after the Second World War Africans continued to identify secondary education with attainment in the classics, and therefore to demand classical teaching. Some schools might respond to such demands quite eagerly; in 1951 Oron Boys' High School in Nigeria, which had been founded in 1905, hired as Principal Mr U. U. Okure, who made it possible for boys to begin Latin in the middle and upper classes (Wiles 1955: 12). Such an opportunity was not to be missed. The first African headmaster of Mfantsipim in the Gold Coast, F. L. Bartels, reintroduced Greek to the school in 1954, after a hiatus of 38 years (Boahen 1996: 421).[71] At this point, there was no practical need for Latin and Greek in order to pass Cambridge School Certificate at the level required for matriculation, because of the adjustment to the language regulations in 1938. But the classics were too entrenched as a component of certain kinds of West African identity to be eradicated from secondary schools; too much was at stake, both where the classics were already available and where they were not.

Notes

1 Contemporary critiques of Indirect Rule, especially in relation to education, can be found in Murray 1929: 270–90 and 1935, and Mayhew 1938: 108–12. Good modern analyses include that of Sivonen 1995; see also Burroughs 1999 and Cell 1999.

2 See Corby 1981 and 1990. Sumner notes that the absence of subjects such as Latin or Chemistry meant that the boys could not move to higher education (1963: 383).

3 Ginio 2006: 93–5 restates the opposition and goes on to complicate it.

4 A few authorities dispute the honour of coining this phrase. See Bartels 1965: 89 on William West, Chairman of the Methodist church.

5 See also Mazrui 1978: 10–13 on the (alleged) differences between French 'cultural arrogance' and British 'racial arrogance'.

6 See Egerton 1908: 17, and Report of the Education Department, Gold Coast, 1925: 18, for similar diagnoses from the contemporary European side. In 1887 the *Lagos Record* claimed that Lagos secondary schools taught Latin, Greek, Hebrew, French and other modern languages, geometry, trigonometry, book-keeping, drawing, rhetoric and logic, moral philosophy and political economy, Roman and ancient histories, mythology and antiquities, natural philosophy in its various branches, astronomy, chemistry, physiology, geology and botany (Echeruo 1977: 58). Echeruo is not alone in his scepticism about this syllabus.

7 Johnson goes on to compare Ifa divination to the oracle at Delphi, and the kings' ballad singers to 'the rhapsodists of the Homeric age' (1921: 125), thus foreshadowing some of the work of Casely Hayford.

8 See Newell 2002: 163–4.

9 See Harrison 2007: 208. A says 'Alas for the swiftly passing years' and B answers 'It is sweet and fitting to die for the homeland'.

10 E.g. the comments of Governor Macdonald noted in Chapter 1 (Macdonald 1852: 183).

11 Echeruo 1977: 66 adds that Carr was disturbed by Lagos students leaving school 'still ignorant of English, but with their memory stored with disjointed fragments of Latin declensions and conjugations'.

12 On the politics of dress in Africa see Allman 2004 and Ross 2008.

13 See Ranger 1983: 221 on the ways in which the 'public school ethos' helpfully provided for a harmony between rulers and ruled.

14 See Ogunlade 1974 for the background to this foundation in the rapid economic and commercial expansion of Lagos, and in the increasing demand for colonial clerks.

15 See also Ajayi and Tamuno 1973: 9.

16 De Graft Johnson became a founder member of J. B. Danquah's United Gold Coast Convention, and later a prominent educator.

17 The statistic is given by De Graft Johnson 1971: 48, Crowder 1968: 374 and Ohaegbulam 2002: 223.

18 On this issue see also Seth 2007.

19 For an account of Garvey from within classical reception studies see Shilliam 2011.

20 John Murdoch, *Education in India* (Madras: SCKS Press, Vepery, 1881) p. 17, quoted in Viswanathan 1989: 133.

21 Hogarth 1944 goes on to note that when external examinations were introduced, in 1940, all the 13 boys who were entered managed to pass. In the 1940s, the fourth form spent a year on Greek history, which was received 'with keen interest'. Umuahuia is about 100 kilometres north east from the Delta.

22 See e.g. Otegbeye 1995: 74 for the subjective view of the situation; critical discussions include Tibenderana 2003: 92, 109–10, Omulewa 1980, Ajayi and Tamuno 1973: 12–15.

23 See Cole 1960: 185. Sumner 1963 does not provide independent confirmation of this, but does show a lot of discussion and planning of education in the early 1920s, including the abolition of certain exams (181).

24 Paracka 2003: 14 makes the point that Sierra Leonean land was unsuited to Western cash crops.

25 Foster 1965 and Sumner 1963 were especially instrumental in developing this interpretation.

26 On Carr's diagnoses of the situation, see Taiwo 1975: 34, 50, 88. On the fiction of the unemployable see Tibenderana 2003, e.g. 105.

27 Murray 1929: 50–2 discusses the undermining of traditional skills by colonial enterprise, and at 221–2 the stimulation of such skills in schools. See also Ayandele 1979b: 99–100 on the contradiction whereby Africans were taught handicrafts to produce objects which could be more cheaply imported.

28 For instance, at Achimota in the Gold Coast the 'agriculture' taught largely concerned cacao, the cash crop that helped to transform the region. See e.g. Wallbank 1935: 240. On agriculture as the teacher of virtuous labour see e.g. Mayhew 1938: 132–3, 141. A critic of much colonial ideology and practice, Mayhew was nonetheless enthusiastic about this dimension of agriculture, because 'Left to himself, the African is not an ideal wage-earning employee . . . he regards it as far more pleasant to cultivate at his own time just what he needs for his own food, and to enjoy the abundant leisure that this sole occupation leaves him'.

29 See the various critiques of Murray 1929: 324–5, Crowder 1968: 398, Newell 2002: 164.

30 Azikiwe 1934 is a thorough critique of education industrial and agricultural.

31 See also Jones 1922: 157, which is quite open about requiring girls in girls' schools to do the necessary domestic work of the establishment.

32 Some students such as Otegbeye (1995: 51) enjoyed the escape from the school buildings.

33 Donald Cameron, as Governor of Nigeria, used this phrase in an Address in Lagos in 1933; see Wallbank 1935: 239.

34 Cf. the use of 'stewardship' (18) and 'trusteeship' (23) in Mumford and Parker 1937, an article about progress in education.

35 The Phelps-Stokes Report was remarkably candid about this. See e.g. Jones 1922: 2, on Africa as an 'undeveloped treasure-house', and 1922: 9, 'civilization . . . looks to African to replenish its resources'.

36 See Manela 2007 on Woodrow Wilson, self-determination and the importance this concept had for colonized societies.

37 Given his other pronouncements, this may be thought uncharacteristic of Clifford. See Cookey 1980.

38 Murray 1929: 133 further records that in one agricultural college, at Tsolo in the Transkei, Xenophon's *Oikonomikos* was used to instruct in composition.
39 See Musgrove 1952 on the narrow limits set itself by the Commission and the way its questions predetermined its answers.
40 On the classical education of African-Americans, and the Phelps-Stokes Report on Negro Education, see most recently Goings and O'Connor 2011. The racist claims that African-American command of the classics was either a deception, or a case of the parrot, are analogous to how West Africans' classical learning was often received.
41 Letter, Edward B. Denham to Jones, 4 June 1924. Quoted in Berman 1971: 142. Denham was the Colonial Secretary of Kenya.
42 On this famous phrase see e.g. Zachernuk 1998: 496.
43 Olubummọ later acquired a BA from Fourah Bay and a PhD from Durham, and became a prominent mathematician.
44 Report of the Education Department of the Government of the Gold Coast, 1934–5: 39.
45 See e.g. Parsons 1963: 125–6.
46 Letter, Arthur Wilkie [one of the commissioners] to Jones, 20 January 1923, Phelps-Stokes Fund file A-22 (3), quoted in Berman 1971: 138.
47 Quoted in Brown 1964: 373.
48 I can hardly resist pointing out how revolutionary these last two sentences sound in Britain in 2012. But I must.
49 In 1937 there were still no secondary schools in Kenya, Nyasaland, Northern Rhodesia, or Zanzibar (Ashby 1966: 199). The Headmaster of one of Uganda's foremost schools, King's College Budo (founded 1906), fought to prevent the introduction of Latin, against the wishes of his African governing body. The latter acquiesced only when he threatened to resign (Castle 1972: 72).
50 Ashby 1966: 358 dilates on the consequent shock of independence to a system which had nurtured no Europeanized cadre of leaders. He goes on to point out that the university education eventually provided, at Lovanium, required quantities of Latin and other humanities, and was more demanding than English degree programmes.
51 See Mazrui 1978: 53, Ashby 1966: 233
52 For the latter point see e.g. Lambert 2011: 107. It was recognized at the time too, e.g. Fraser 1927: 134, 148. On university education in South Africa see Lulat 2005: 283–305.
53 See also Selden 1998, Keita 2011 and Malamud 2011.
54 Bacchus 1994 and Campbell 1996 offer detailed accounts which show how secondary schools arose in the crucible of multiple shifting lines of demarcation among white, coloured, black, and upper, middle and lower class. Both point out that there was rarely an explicit colour bar in place in secondary schools, but that they only became permeable to coloured and black students as the families of the latter moved into the middle class.

55 Cf. Greenwood 2010: 86 on Eric Williams: 'his aptitude for Latin was an inalienable part of his intellectual persona'. See also on Joseph Appiah in the next chapter.

56 Hans Vischer wrote that one of the members of the Commission 'suffers impatience and sums up the position in Latin, which makes Jones climb walls' (quoted in Parkinson 1998: 17), which perhaps helps to shed light on the Revd. Jones' opposition to classical education for Africans.

57 Ward (1965: 184) suggests that Achimota garnered some of the support it did because its European Principal Fraser, and Governor Guggisberg, refused to countenance any discrimination against Aggrey.

58 See e.g. Ward 1965: 186.

59 One version of this story can be found in Macartney 1949: 42. Allegedly Aggrey never wrote it down, and it circulated in many versions.

60 Quoted in Brown 1964: 26.

61 The 'native heath' here, rather confusingly perhaps, is Egypt or Ethiopia.

62 Roden's wife was the niece of the great classicist Jebb.

63 Williams (1962: 62) calls the play 'Caesaris Incursio in Oram Auream', and says that it was written in Twi, Fante, Ga, Latin and French.

64 The Report goes on to note that students evidently study Latin for its own sake too, and thereby form 'mental habits of permanent value' (91). It also suggests that while the removal of Latin from London Matriculation might mean that Latin lessons can give way to increased teaching in English, 'a good Latin lesson is almost as much a lesson in English as in Latin' (92).

65 Agbodeka 1977: 138 lists Accra Academy, Wesley Grammar School, Ghana National School and Tamale Secondary School as among those which adopted the practices of Mfantsipim rather than, with Achimota, trying to combine the academic with the practical.

66 Earlier on, Adisadel had been St Nicholas' Grammar School and earlier still S. P. G. Grammar School.

67 'Not for self but others'; 'by hard work to the stars'; 'the Lord's work for the public good'. These are all 'tags' and also school mottoes.

68 E.g. 1938: xiv, vi, 253.

69 The Report of the Gold Coast Educational Department of the Gold Coast for 1935 mentions a translation of Book 9 of the *Odyssey* by H. C. Neill and others, which may be the book to which Newell refers.

70 Nnamdi Azikiwe, the Nigerian nationalist and first premier of the Eastern Region, studied *The Heroes* by Charles Kingsley at Hope Waddell Training Institute in Calabar in 1920 (1970: 73).

71 Bartels was himself an impressive classical scholar at school, winning several prizes; he obtained a Maths degree in 1935.

4

Classics and West African Modernity

Classical education is a contested topic throughout the period under consideration; it can act as a barrier to African achievement or as an incentive, and it is repeatedly mobilized as metaphor or metonymy for the overall failings – or successes – of colonial education in British West Africa. In the early period, classical studies were simply imposed on selected African students, first as part of the route to church leadership and secondly as part of the normative curriculum at secondary level. In both these contexts classical education contributed to the making of the new 'elite' or 'middle class' which was one of the fruits of European imperialism. West African responses to classical education ranged from resistance to wholesale acceptance, and subsequently, if classical education was deliberately denied, it was often energetically pursued. At the same time classical languages functioned constantly as a test of Africans, whether recognizing their achievements and positioning them to reap the fruits of Western culture, including higher education, or, just as frequently, disqualifying them or showing them up as misguided in their assessment of what was worthwhile and what was not.

The Report of the Phelps-Stokes Commission summed up this latter trend by denying that classics had any place in West African modernity, but the educational choices made by West Africans continued to align classics firmly with a concern for the appropriate development of their societies. While educational choices are never free, but are conditioned by multiple social, cultural and political factors, they remain relevant to an investigation of the cultural dynamics of colonialism. Since the change of 1938 meant that Latin or Greek was no longer necessary for the Cambridge School Certificate and the associated possibilities of matriculation for a British degree, we may conclude that the purely instrumental dimension of classical education became less important. In the run-up to independence, however, classics continued to be significant in other ways, to the extent that when new University Colleges were founded in Nigeria and the Gold Coast, Classics was among the first Honours degrees offered there, just as it was at Fourah Bay College in 1876. The identification of classical education with modernity was thus sealed in the years after the Second World War – although in the years after West African independence, in the 1960s, new university foundations rarely offered Classics among their degrees, schools began to phase out the language teaching (Thompson 1966: 54), and the discipline correspondingly lost ground.[1]

After the Second World War, the educational landscape changed in response to the conflict and the new ideological formations which it had thrown up. The defeat of the Nazi project meant that the principles of racism were discredited, if not eradicated, and the new emphasis on self-determination for states helped to crystallize the resistance to colonialism in Africa and elsewhere. There was also a repeat of the effect of the First World War, in that ordinary Africans had learned yet more, firsthand, about the shortcomings of Europeans. Given these factors, and the explicit anti-imperialism of the United States, it became highly unlikely that Britain would be allowed to hang on to her colonies indefinitely. Realistic plans for the end of empire and the departure of the colonial authorities had thus to be made, and these entailed not only elements of African representation in colonial governance, but also viable schemes for the expansion of education at all levels, just as West Africans had been advocating for many years. As late as 1939 Lord Hailey could write 'British policy as yet exhibits no clear view of the future of the educated African' (Collins 1996: 203) but only a few years later the Elliot Commission of 1945 was investigating the possibilities of establishing a university in one or more West African colonies, thereby again coinciding with plans urged by Africans in the previous century. These pressures resulted in the opening of several new secondary schools, by the colonial government, often in partnership with African representatives, by missionary bodies, or by independent African enterprises.[2] Sixth forms and pre-University preparation classes also began to embed themselves (Bartels 1965: 276). The schools often included Latin among the subjects designed to prepare African students for their roles in a changing world. How exactly Latin would accomplish this task, is a matter that we can look into more closely at this juncture.

The account of classics in these developments is part of the story of secondary and higher education generally, as it was in the previous chapter, but the specificities of the role of classics still merit comment and analysis, particularly since African-authored sources now contribute much more to the story. This chapter will consider the roles of classics in the secondary schools and universities as they prepared for independence, and examine two autobiographies by prominent West Africans, in which classical languages can be read to play an important role in subject- and class-formation, as well as in the self-representation of the autobiographical persona. The chapter concludes with a discussion of the short story, 'The Devil at Yolahun Bridge', which is paradigmatic in its use of classical references to mount a critique of colonialism.

Technologies of the self

We have seen that Latin and the classics were of practical use to aspiring West Africans because they facilitated higher education at Fourah Bay College or abroad. Moreover, they added to the prestige of schools, not least by proving students' ability via external exams which were not susceptible to many forms of 'adaptation'. In the Ibadan Grammar School, we have seen that Latin and Greek afforded students the opportunity to speak in an exclusive code, and other sources, including autobiographical ones, can suggest that Latin and the classics could help to articulate the collective identity of the boys in a school. Philip Holden, in his study of colonial autobiography, suggests a related set of considerations. His overall argument is that 'nationalist leaders . . . all wrote autobiographies in which the growth of an individual implicitly identified as a national father explicitly parallels the growth of national consciousness and, frequently proleptically, the achievement of an independent nation-state' (2008: 5).[3] Within such autobiographies, the 'school-day reminiscences' can have a particular role, which is to prefigure the community of the incipient nation by means of the collective of boys. In addition, the boys' community can be represented as elaborating a masculine identification that is otherwise liable to be undermined by the authoritarian practices of colonialism. Holden suggests that such masculine self-fashioning is promoted by networks characterized by vertical filiation, within hierarchies such as those of patriarchy, or horizontal fraternity, among groups who are more or less equal (2008: 5). At the end of his study, Holden concludes that colonial education is represented, by such autobiographies, in more positive ways than might be expected, and that the reasons are its enabling of an awareness of community, and its promotion of the boys' autonomy (within limits) via self-regulation (2008: 129). Such regulation is offered by a series of disciplines or Foucauldian 'technologies of the self' (2008: 24) which can be seen retrospectively to prepare the autobiography's subject for the political struggle ahead.

With these parameters in mind, I should like to examine some of the roles that Latin and the classics may have played in forging the West African identities that emerged into independence. The schools at issue are largely elite foundations with substantial traditions – they have in fact achieved Lugard's dream of establishing the English public school ethos in Africa, but have combined it with Latin – but because they operate in the colonial context, the ideology which they purvey to their students is rarely straightforward. When forming masculine gendered subjectivities, for instance, the schools may not have operated in ways very different from schools in Europe, but other dimensions of subject-formation were caught in the colonial contradictions which classical education was primed to address. In the texts that I shall examine, Latin and the classics serve the project of incipient nationalism not only by their gendered identifications but because they can signify discipline, work, control, rationality (Holden 2008: 33) and, of course, the overcoming of difficulties placed in one's path by the colonial power structures. They are thus on track to foster the 'middle-class' ethos and ideology which was examined in Chapter 1, and some commentators have indicted the products of the elite secondary schools as distanced from many of the realities of West African life. This is in fact a criticism which both the autobiographies examined later in the chapter partly address.

In the school context, Latin may be represented as a threshold that the child must cross in order to begin the process of maturation.[4] The boy from Lagos who tried to enter Wesley College Ibadan, only to be thrown by the Yoruba epigraph on the gate, had the correct expectation of a test to be passed before he enters the school, even though he mistook its exact nature (Olubummọ 1980: 1). *Kossoh Town Boy*, by Robert Wellesley Cole (1907–95), describes how the narrator, unusually, started Latin in primary school, with a feeling of excitement at the new stage broached (1960: 147–8):

> It was with this same excitement that we received the news that we were to start Latin that year. It was not part of the normal syllabus but as luck would have it, that year the Rev. W. T. Thomas, MA, was acting principal and he felt it would be a great asset to the boys in our class who were due to go to a secondary school. We jumped at it, and I can recall with what thrill I went through the conjugation of my first Latin verb, amo, and my first Latin declension of mensa.

About to enter Mfantsipim, the youthful Joseph Appiah discusses with his friend the subjects that will now be required of them, perhaps with slightly less enthusiasm (1990: 30): 'in addition to science there were subjects like algebra, geometry, trigonometry, British Empire history, Latin and Roman history and other completely new subjects'. The adult Appiah who writes the autobiography distances himself from the child in terms of Latin (1990: 27): 'if I had known any Latin then, [on arrival at school] I should have consoled myself with "Tempora mutantur et nos in illis mutamur"' (Times change and we are changed in them). His accurate diagnosis of the situation is suggested by the vignettes in *Mfantsipim*, the termly magazine of the school, of new boys, called 'greenhorns', who prepare for their initiation ceremonies by practising their Latin (*Mfantsipim Magazine,* Bu Bir 1944: 5, cf. Adow Bir 1945: 19): 'Greenhorns . . . have gone to the extent of surveying some of the most snug nooks and corners for repeating "amo" for hours on end and learning notes by rote'.

Latin could serve as a metonymy for the transition to more demanding schooling not only because the subject really was new to the child but also because Latin was customarily taught in ways that were dull, alienating and meaningless; it thus figures the necessity of enduring and surviving unpleasant experiences that has for so long been one of the hallmarks of formal education. The locus classicus is perhaps the autobiographical account of the young Winston Churchill, set to learn the singular of the first declension on his first day at prep school: 'What on earth did it mean? Where was the sense in it? It seemed absolute rigmarole to me' (1960: 17). Among West African autobiographies, that of Robert Wellesley Cole is pertinent, although his strictures would definitely apply beyond the educational system of Sierra Leone. He is clear about the shortcomings of the teaching (1960: 164–5):

> As for Latin and Greek, there were no introductory talks on life in ancient Rome and Greece, which would have made us realise that the books we

> were trying to translate were the letters, writings, diaries or compositions of actual people, who had the same peculiarities as people living in our time … We would have realised that the writings of such authors as Horace, Caesar, Livy, Virgil, Tacitus, Pliny or Juvenal were expressions of different kinds of personalities … In the absence of this guide we saw their works as so many pieces of literature which somehow we had to translate and memorise in parts. So many exercises in mental dexterity in fact . . . we missed much of the inner meaning and beauty of what we read … Our text-books were too often full of scientific minutiae which now in retrospect seem of minor importance compared with the fire and inspiration of the author.

As Stray puts it (1998: 280) this is 'Latin without the literature, without the Romans, in fact without anything except the grind which promised to make the learner disciplined and middle-class'. What does set Cole's indictment apart, and make it resonate within the colonial context, is that the teaching consists of surface without depth, exactly what African boys were routinely accused of when they were termed 'educated Africans'. While the difficulty and indeed incomprehensibility of Latin is recognized in a host of Western school reminiscences, it perhaps takes on a more pointed or even sinister cast in the colonial situation, which here enables Cole's heroic self-representation as one who can excel at Latin, and Greek too, despite the drawbacks of the educational methods, and can also appreciate the literary culture of the texts that he is set. We might contrast Cole, as represented in his autobiographical text, with the little Kwesi of Kobina Sekyi's *Anglo-Fanti*, who could not cope at all with the ever-increasing demands of Latin.

Because of its forbidding inherent qualities, Latin often appears under the sign of a technology of the self which will eventually discipline that self and render it better at managing other challenges. While this is a highly recognizable way of representing Latin in European culture, as a powerful means to intellectual training, it sometimes appears within West African sources in particularly heightened contexts. In *Mfantsipim Magazine* for Bu Bir term 1936, an article about the worth of learning Latin stresses, like many such articles, the value of its mental discipline and the access it affords to English vocabulary, but also suggests connections between Latin and African languages (*Mfantisipim*, Bu Bir 1936: 20–1). Subsequently, Latin is sometimes represented as a self-conscious part of the route to independence. As recorded in *Mfantsipim Magazine* of Bu Bir term 1948, K. A. Busia, later to become

President of Ghana, gave the Speech Day address and to his own (alleged) surprise, cast it all in terms of the classics (9):

> I did not know, until I began to think of what to say tonight, which subject was most closely associated in my mind with Mfantsipim; to my surprise, I discovered it to be Latin, for whole chunks of Latin passages, memorized and forgotten long ago, rushed into my head from I don't know where . . . from this slender store of my classical knowledge, anxious to display itself, I have chosen, contrary to all precedents, a text. It is a passage from Cicero's Pro Marcello. Don't worry, for I am not going to inflict chunks of Latin on you. Here is a translation of the passage: Sixth formers, listen carefully, you never know where your unseen is going to come from . . .

All of the passages which Busia goes on to cite, which include Socrates and Pericles in Thucydides as well as the Cicero, inculcate the value of patriotism, but he reads them in the context of the boys' need to develop as citizens of a new country rather than of one secure in its own traditions. In order to build that new country, the older man invites the boys to form a particular kind of community with him, which is mediated by the demanding traditions of the school, here represented by Latin and its unseens. A few years later David Balme, then the Principal of the new University College of the Gold Coast, which went on to become the University of Ghana, drew on Latin in a different but related way (*Mfantsipim Magazine,* Bu Bir 1952: 24–6). Obviously well aware of the persistent discourse which aligned 'Latin' against other pursuits, such as sport or agriculture, which were alleged to train character, he posits Latin as the best discipline of the self, because it requires the 'moment of truth'. He cites himself as a tyro translator, guessing at the correct solution rather than being able to understand it, and embarrassed by the critical scrutiny of the Latin master who saw through his success. Latin is thus represented as a crucial test of character, more searching than practical or vocational pursuits, which insists that we be able to 'know why we say what we say and think what we think' (26). Its practice may be understood to constitute preparation for the independence to come.

Despite the prominence of Latin in these two speeches, by men who were part of Ghana's transition to independence, the elite secondary school Mfantsipim does also relay, through its magazine, the sense of tensions surrounding Latin and the classics as the school moves towards independence. In 1950, as Boahen remarks (1996: 432), the Adow Bir term edition is suddenly much bigger than earlier issues, and contains more material by boys. A Latin society is formed with 45 boys (20), but this is perhaps in part at least a response to the ground that 'science' is gaining in the school. For instance, there is a long autobiographical fragment by 'Aristotle' (28–31), who turns out to be a scientist discovering new elements and exposing the anti-progressive politics of the literary 'pen-pushers'. He tells how Henry the Navigator has sailed to West Africa and found a school with 'eager boys delving into the mysteries of the universe', while in another 'small, bare room' were the tattered remnants of a Latin book. Latin is thus symbolically opposed to science, with the latter proving much more attractive to the boys. In the face of this multiply difficult situation the Latin club seems to expire after a couple of terms; it seems to return in 1955–6, however, and its discussions are quite often about classical models of politics as well as about the more straightforward virtues of learning the languages (Eso Bir 21, Bu Bir 33.)

In a very different move, in 1950 the first African headmaster, F. L. Bartels, instituted a new subject, 'Current Affairs', for which boys attended talks by prominent people designed to enable them to understand the complexity of their emergent nation. Tellingly, 'Current Affairs' appears in *Mfantsipim Magazine* in a Latin translation, 'currentes res', during the first few years of its existence, as if the startling modernity of Bartels' innovation had to be circumscribed by the ancient language with which much of Mfantsipim's history had successfully identified. In 1955 the headmaster's Speech Day speech is devoted to encouraging boys, and parents, to value intellectual activity outside the remit of exams, and in this connection 'simple courses on Christianity and science, and the story of Greek thought, given during the year, are attempts in that direction' (*Mfantsipim Magazine*, Bur Bir 1955-Adow Bir 1956: 10). Another perhaps even greater innovation is the African Studies group, which does not start up until 1958, just after Independence, and which in 1959 is celebrated in Latin: 'utinam studii in rebus Africanis diu vivant et bene eveniant!' ('let's hope that African Studies lasts long and turns out well!' Adow Bir 1959: 21). This idiosyncratic utterance again perhaps suggests a tension between the school's customary identifications and its new role within an independent Ghana.

Overall, of course, independence was not conducive to the prominence of Latin. In 1956 it is openly acknowledged that upper forms hate classics

(*Mfantsipim Magazine*, Bu Bir 1956: 33). Even at Achimota its decline was felt, as in a series of documents which were produced by an informal staff discussion group, and which were successively titled 'Quo Vadimus, Gold Coast Future' (1940), 'Pointers of Progress' (1942), and 'Towards National Development' (1945) (Addae 2004: 107, cf. Bartels 2003: 81–2). From Latin to the language of independence is a short but precipitous route. Also at Achimota, Agbodeka records that Latin paradoxically 'led the way', in the 1950s, introducing a more light-hearted attitude to studies, and got (Agbodeka 1977: 164):

> many a hardworking and serious student jokingly repeating 'Lupus flabat et flabat, sed frustra' [The wolf huffed and puffed, but to no avail] or 'The women of Alba Longa are of tantalizing beauty'. This classroom relaxation developed with the activities of amusingly eccentric Latin teachers, one of whom even got the name 'Lupus'.

Why Latin is singled out is presumably because of its special role at Achimota, which we investigated in the previous chapter, and here it signals the paradox of academic rigidity combined with sudden camaraderie[5] – perhaps it is no accident that the atmosphere in the classroom mellows as it becomes more obvious that Achimota students will be among the first leaders of an independent Ghana.

Kossoh Town Boy: Latin and Greek, Father and Nation

As a technology of the self which inculcated discipline and fortitude, Latin had long been invoked in the West African tradition as in the European. But as independence approached, its role could become quite complex – necessary for building up the boys who would lead the new society, but threatened by various manifestations of modernity. In this section, I examine autobiographies from two men who were prominent mid-century nationalists, and thus went to school in the earlier decades of the twentieth century, when the role of Latin and the classics in the formation of gendered or politicized identities was perhaps under less pressure. While schools sometimes encountered difficulty preparing boys for political roles, writings by men who attended prominent secondary schools take gender inculcation almost for granted; masters and boys are both engaged in the work of 'making men'.[6] The masculinity involved displays recognizable parameters of endurance and self-reliance, even though such qualities sometimes come into implicit conflict with the subordinate status of all Africans under British colonialism.[7]

Writers can represent their younger selves as highly aware of the girls in the corresponding girls' schools, and these 'sisters' often play quite a large role in reminiscences. On occasion, Latin and the classics are involved in the relationship between boys and their 'sisters'. Thus Olubummọ, who started at Wesley College in 1938, describes how boys could put to use the very limited vocabulary of the first Latin declension (1980: 73). As some will recall, the first declension in Latin used often to be illustrated with mensa, a table, and the student would have to learn the various cases of the noun. Since the translation of the vocative case of mensa is 'o table', the textbook here would offer the novice a truly bizarre scenario of interspecies address. Olubummọ cites the famous passage from Winston Churchill's autobiography, already noted above, on his mystification when asked to talk to a table (1960: 18):

> 'Mensa means a table,' he [the teacher] answered.
>
> 'Then why does mensa also mean O table,' I enquired, 'and what does O table mean?' . . .
>
> 'O table, – you would use that in addressing a table, in invoking a table.'
>
> 'But I never do,' I blurted out in honest amazement.

The Nigerian student goes one better than the British statesman, and actually finds a use for the alien tongue (1980: 73).

> Winston Churchill was said to have asked under what circumstances he would be called upon to address a table. How naive! Did he not realize that under 'mensa' hides 'puella'? After two or three lessons, one could take a few tentative but purposeful steps with puellam amo or Oh, puella bona! Da mihi rosam.[8]

With this kind of instruction Latin could appear as 'a welcome diversion from English Grammar, Geography or Arithmetic' (1980: 73), and Olubummọ states that he went on to study Greek privately with the Revd. Soremekun (1980: 72). The space devoted to Latin in Olubummọ's memoir is itself quite striking, given that he went on to become one of Nigeria's first research mathematicians.

Further humour lurks in this account insofar as any real girls thus addressed were highly unlikely to be learning Latin themselves. In the first decades of the century, Latin divided male from female in British-ruled West Africa as effectively as it did anywhere else, which was one of the factors that made Achimota such a potentially revolutionary institution, because it demanded Latin of girls as well as boys.[9] *Kossoh Town Boy*, by Robert Wellesley Cole, describes the schooldays of a young Freetown boy in the 1920s and extends the scene of the address in Latin thus (1960: 183–4):

> As for the Annie Walsh [Memorial Girls' High School], it was the practice among the senior boys of our school to write to the senior girls of that school, expressing the warmest sentiments for some particular girl or other, and asking to be accepted as her special friend . . . The letters which we wrote were penned with great care and in lofty imagery. They were often embellished with Greek and Latin quotations, although interestingly enough none of the girls' schools did Latin or Greek. But that did not deter us from baring our souls in the assumed light of the classical masters.

A later version of the autobiography, *An Innocent in Britain*, which takes the story into adulthood, adds the vignette of the narrator's father's amusement at the incongruous attempts at communication (1988: 16):

> As Grammar School boys, we paid our compliments to them [the girls of the Annie Walsh] in letters quoting Greek and Latin posted by the hand of a younger sister or brother or friend of the selected queen. . . . his [the writer's father's] humour could not resist the fact that here I was quoting the classics here and there, whereas the girls, our dear sisters of the Annie Walsh, knew neither Latin nor Greek.

The father's amusement perhaps seals the equation in which masculinity is aligned with classical languages and femininity with their absence, particularly since he himself has learned Latin and Greek. Insofar as the narrator's identity as a classicist is enforced on many levels by his father, Holden's model of vertical filiation seems highly pertinent, and Holden's analysis of the individual male autobiography offering the contours of the incipient nation is also relevant. We might compare the relationship between Eric Williams, first prime minister of Trinidad, and his father, as represented in his autobiography; on the occasion of his first Latin lesson he 'walked up and down the house, reciting all the tenses, my father beaming indulgently all the while' (Greenwood 2010: 86–7).[10] The narrator of *Kossoh Town Boy* often claims a particularly strong relationship with the father, and his father in turn, in ways that I shall shortly explore, offers a particular kind of identification with the nation.

At its very beginning, the text proclaims itself as the story not only of 'a little boy' (1960: 11) but also of the social class to which he belonged, and it is strongly conscious of the ways in which its subject's Krio culture makes him a 'Black Victorian', identified with Britain, Christianity, education, work and sobriety. The narrative thus constructs relationships for the 'little boy' which will form him as a man and as a Sierra Leonean, and both these identities are mediated by the classical languages and by success in them. Latin and Greek, in turn, are the occasions of much work and suffering, but at the same time are represented as part of the subject's normative culture. Perhaps they might be thought of as a further dimension of the Anglo-African hybridity that characterizes the Krio.[11]

What achieves and maintains the identification with the father is a potent combination of repeated physical punishment and rewarding paternal approval (1960: 104–7). Since the narrator claims to love and respect his father throughout and also to find in him, when adult, a trusted companion and confidante (1960: 110), the combination is represented as working extremely well. Chief among the father's designs for the son, which he has to inculcate with such energetic discipline, is to excel at school, and the father speaks very early on to the son of going to the Grammar School, where he himself went, and perhaps even studying in England. When the son reaches the age of 9, the plan shows a gendered dimension, since the young Ageh (his African name) is prevented from helping his mother with domestic tasks, or trading for his grandmother, as he has enjoyed doing, in order that he may concentrate on his studies (120–2). Formal education thus takes him away from 'female' activities and also from activities, like market trading, which might be accounted more African than European. Further reinforcement occurs when Ageh is punished when he comes fifth in class (118), and by his own account he never comes below second again.

Cole attended the Government Model Primary School, where as we saw above he was, exceptionally, able to take Latin in his final year, and we learn later on in his text that this school had been founded only a year before he began to attend it, in 1914 (1960: 112, 155). This coincidence between the life of the autobiography's subject and the life of his nation is a theme that becomes more insistent as the narrative develops. Although Ageh is first intended for the CMS Grammar School, when the time comes he is sent instead to the newly founded Prince of Wales School, the first secondary school in Sierra Leone to be opened by the British government (in 1919). Despite the prospect of his son's disappointment, Cole senior has made a political decision to throw in his lot with the government foundation and thus to be part of Sierra Leone's history in the making, as he acknowledges explicitly himself (154). This decision may have been quite remarkable in that it went against the suspicious 'caution' of Krio parents who normally wanted the 'cachet' of a mission grammar school (156).

Although Robert Cole was not at a mission grammar school, he was learning Latin, as we saw above, and his father arranged for him to take private tuition in Greek (beginning in 1921, 168). By his own account, Cole was well disposed to the new language, partly because of its similarity to Krio (168):[12]

> I liked Greek even before I started it, just as I liked the idea of studying Latin. I was soon intrigued by its alphabet and its euphonic sounds. The Greek accents and conjunction also reminded me of our own Krio language in which accented pronunciation played such an important part.

Nonetheless, Greek was the occasion of a frightful failure, akin to coming fifth in class, which represented a historic turning point for the autobiography's subject. During his first year at Prince of Wales, he claims, discipline was lax because the school had no tradition and sense of identity to help keep the boys in line. Cole did not resist the downward trend (168): 'With the general slackening of the work at school I became lazy, and soon I began to be careless even with the study of Greek, a subject which needs detailed application'. When the moment came for his father, as was his habit, to ask him what he had been learning, and to quiz him on the topic, he was unable to respond in a satisfactory manner. His father asked him the principal parts of λαμβάνω but received no reply; he asked the principal parts of ἐλαύνω, which had allegedly been studied that very day.[13] 'Again Ageh was dumb: he could not answer' (169):

> Without a word father went out of the room, down the stairs, out into the garden and the night, and came back presently with the freshly cut twigs of the guava tree, whose strokes are more biting by far than an ordinary cane. For about the only time in his life that I can remember he thrashed me with emotion, that is as mother did, without pausing to count the strokes, and only ceasing when he had got over his anger.

Since Cole has devoted a few pages earlier in the text (104–7) to explaining his father's dispassionate and rational way of punishing his children (contrasted, as here, with that of his mother), this display of emotion centred on the learning of Greek is very striking, and it invites the interpretation that it is via Latin and Greek especially that the son is to be formed into a worthy successor to the father. This is the last time the subject is beaten by either parent (169), so it is in several ways a historic moment.

The father's demands are seen to be appropriate, rather than excessive, a few years later, when Cole's mastery of Latin and Greek is, according to his text, put to an extreme test which has serious repercussions for all Sierra Leone. In 1922 – in the year of the Phelps-Stokes Report – the British colonial government allegedly proposed that Sierra Leoneans should no longer sit the external exams of the Cambridge Local Examinations Syndicate, because these 'dealt with matters foreign to African children, and threw too great a strain on their minds' (185). When this proposal was met with determined and vocal opposition in Sierra Leone, the government eventually devised a compromise, whereby the exams would be offered one more time and if the candidates did not acquit themselves well, the exams would then be withdrawn.[14] As *Kossoh Town Boy* tells it, the students who sat the exams at the end of 1922 were well aware that the destiny of their country rode on their performance. For a people who considered themselves bound to Britain by numerous historical ties, the external exams administered from the colonial centre represented the validity of their culture and their hopes. The text is moved, by the exam crisis, to acknowledge the colonial situation more explicitly than it ever does elsewhere (186): 'We were a subject people, and our only chance of survival lay in maintaining these contacts with Cambridge and with Oxford, London and Durham'.

Cole's success in the Senior Cambridge exams of 1922, then, can be understood to ratify possibilities for his country as well as for himself. He recounts that he gained first-class honours in the History paper, and four distinctions overall, including in Latin and Greek. A boy from India gained four distinctions also, and one boy from England gained six (187). After this triumph, his father insisted that he not move immediately to a degree, but rest, and in the unfolding of the autobiographical narrative, we next hear the father's story, which is one of repeated breakdowns of health that prevented him from studying Medicine in England, or for the ministry in Sierra Leone, so that he finally decided to attend a technical college and become a water engineer (188). In his insistence on his son's effort and achievement, then, we are invited to read the trace of his own disappointment, and we can conclude too that the son is further burdened with the duty of maintaining the family's claim to be 'middle-class'. Although the father is a qualified engineer and Superintendent of the Freetown Water Works, which Cole rightly remarks was almost unheard of for an African in the early twentieth century, he had not made it into one of the truly commanding professions such as the ministry, Law or Medicine, and he is represented as waging a constant battle to preserve social distinction in the polyglot and socially promiscuous culture of Freetown (128). His son's training in Latin and Greek, then, resonates on several levels, including the personal, the social and the national. The model of identity held out to the autobiographical subject, with classics as a prominent component, is concerned with effort, endurance and achievement, and these are signs of masculinity, of class alignment and of national identity.

Joe Appiah and the ghost

Another autobiography that weaves Latin and the classics into an elite, masculine subjectivity, poised for independence, is that of the Ghanaian Joseph Appiah (1918–90). I have already drawn on this text in order to discuss Latin as a marker of the threshold of secondary school, but it is paradigmatic in other ways of a mid-century West African identity produced by the interpenetration of indigenous and colonial cultures. Whereas this combination might in other circumstances prove a difficult contradiction, Appiah's text works to make it into a seemingly effortless triumph. Latin and the classics help to signify various important aspects of the subject's persona, including his flexibility, persistence and natural gift for leadership.

Joseph Appiah was born in 1918 in the Ashanti region of the Gold Coast, into a family which was related to Ashanti royalty on both sides and also contained 'some of the first Westernised middle-class Ghanaians' (Gates 1990: ix). He became a nationalist lawyer and politician, but also joined the English aristocracy when he married Peggy, the daughter of Sir Stafford Cripps.

During the years before 1954 he studied and worked in London, campaigning for independence as president of the West African Students' Union; once back in Ghana he fell foul of Nkrumah's regime and was imprisoned by him. After the 1966 coup that deposed Nkrumah, he continued in politics, working for the Supreme Military Council under General Acheampong and later, imprisoned by Jerry Rawlings. He survived the political and social upheavals of postcolonial Ghana, retiring from public life in the late 1970s, and he represents himself, by the end of the autobiography, as battle-scarred but now above the fray. The subject of the autobiography is represented throughout as an attractive mixture of commitment to traditional African virtues and facility with Western systems, and the classics, invoked in various ways, form a significant part of the projection of this persona.

One small example is Appiah's design for the names of his first son; although 'As a Saturday's male child, his first name was automatically KWAME' (1990: 230), Appiah also apparently planned for 'Socrates' to feature among the names, and was only deterred by his wife's insistence that this would be a burden for the child.[15] This duality of heritage, European and African, is legible throughout the text on several levels. For instance, the title of the autobiography is *Joe Appiah: Autobiography of an African Patriot*, but the author's name appears as Joseph Appiah. This intimation of a difference between 'Joe' and 'Joseph', or between different possible identities and roles, is not coincidental, and the difference pervades the text, although it is, I suggest, almost always skilfully managed. For instance, although Appiah becomes a lay preacher in the Methodist church, he claims to believe in reincarnation and to consult regularly the 'little people' or 'mmoatia' of traditional Ashanti belief (of which more later). Moreover, Appiah's career not only spans Ghanaian and Western traditions but also noble lineage and democratic commitment. Born into a wealthy and aristocratic Ashanti family, he was the beneficiary of an elite education at Mfantsipim, and claims towards the close of his text that because of generous support from his family, he was not required actually to earn a living as a lawyer, and thus could take what cases he wanted to and preserve a measure of independence from other pressures (1990: 329). Despite his wealth and status, however, the 'Joe' of the text is a thoroughly demotic character, at home among all classes, fluent in Creole and pidgin as well as in formal English, and adaptable to all circumstances including prison. The moments when he speaks Creole or pidgin are represented as well-received by their audiences (1990: 306, 325–6, 323),[16] and when incarcerated by his political opponents, he claims to act as an older brother figure, 'experienced prison graduate and lay-preacher' (1990: 323), assisting his fellow-prisoners to understand and manage the routines.[17]

We might note here that Robert Wellesley Cole has some similarly bilingual moments, when he 'forgets' his middle-class identity, but they are accompanied with more anxiety. In one encounter he meets his European Headmaster, who asks him where he is going. Cole accidentally speaks Krio in his reply – 'Papa sen me, sir' – but on the Headmaster's further query, in 'terrible tones', Cole has quickly to correct himself to English – 'I am on an errand for my father, sir' (1960: 150). In this meeting at least Cole is seen as less able than Appiah to answer the conflicting demands of an identity formed in colonialism.

Appiah's text thus has to manage potential disjunctions in class roles, represented by different linguistic registers, but also a further tension, which is in the move from 'fiery' nationalist and anti-colonialist politician and orator, to elder statesman who explicitly denies having harboured ambitions towards high office (1990: 329). Furthermore, the very fact of survival, as a politician, during Ghana's turbulent post-independence period, might suggest compromises or at least a flexibility that might trouble a stance of moral authority. I shall suggest that classical references offer a framework within which to manage some of these tensions.

There are moments in the book where the classical references might be categorized as simple 'tags', as when an attractive acquaintance is compared to Helen of Troy – one who, incidentally, unlike the original, did not get the chance to derail the protagonist's other plans (136). The text offers several almost throwaway classical references, such as 'crossing the Rubicon' (217) for the action of getting married, in a manner that could be described as urbane and slightly ironic.[18] The text often wants to insist on a distance between Appiah's subjectivity and the tumultuous events in which he is immersed – wants to insist, in fact, that he kept his cool (300) – and the cosmopolitanism of the classical references, even if (or, especially) in slightly incongruous situations, aids this stance.[19] Part of this stance of knowing urbanity is that classical quotations are sometimes translated, but never explained further, implicitly thus addressing an educated audience rather than the ordinary people of Ghana with whom the text's subject often nonetheless claims an understanding.[20]

Many uses of classical reference are more pointed than 'tags'. For instance, Peggy Appiah's first visit to Ghana is acclaimed: 'Peggy, like Caesar, could proudly say "Veni, vidi, vici"' (206), while the triumph of an anti-Nkrumah candidate in an election is described with the words 'Not even Caesar, on his triumphal return to Rome from his Gallic wars, fared better' (244), and on Appiah's release from prison he himself is greeted with 'a hero's welcome, fit for a Caesar returning in triumph from the wars to Rome' (268). There is thus, as it were, a crescendo of Caesars. The classical repertoire is often invoked, contrastingly, to characterize the subject's opponents. This is not a simple gesture of vituperation, because to use the repertoire in this way also suggests that the subject has access to a greater cultural vocabulary than his opponents, and correspondingly a longer historical perspective. One particular example coordinates literary and political command in the sudden shift of register from high classical to corporeal; the break with Nkrumah and the Convention People's Party is represented thus (243):

> This was a very sad but very necessary break with friends of yesteryear; the ancient Romans had a more appropriate word for our relationship, now broken – '*Amicitia*' not '*Amici*'. '*Amicitia*' was friendship in the fullest sense; '*Amicus*' was merely a person who voted on one's side of the House. Nkrumah and I had stood in the same bath and used the same water and one towel; I had cut his hair many, many times; I had cooked for him; in London, I had inserted into his rectum native suppositories from his dear mother and held his legs against the wall for a minute, as instructed, before releasing him to go to the lavatory. He had become a friend in the fullest and truest sense; but when he saw what was wrong and refused to put it right, he ceased to be a moral being and a friend.

The text here represents Appiah as a friend prepared to go to many lengths, but also as a principled politician equipped with a wide cultural reference which will help him avoid Nkrumah's mistakes.

The *Autobiography* sometimes draws on the symbolic repertoire of the classics to discuss Ghana and its history, in a way that might seem reminiscent of the work of the early nationalists such as Horton and Blyden. Other modern histories, such as that of the French Revolution, which might have seemed apposite, do not appear at all within the *Autobiography*. While the quotations are sometimes ironically dismissive – three members of a despised commission are a 'triumvirate' and Nkrumah's office is a Sanctum Sanctorum (253) – they can also be highly memorable. When Appiah returns home from imprisonment under Nkrumah, the text invokes Tacitus (269): 'Men and women of Ghana could no longer think as they liked nor speak what they thought. I recalled to mind the awful truth of Tacitus' words: "*Rare* [*sic*] *temporum felicitate, ubi sentire quae velis et quae sentias dicere licet*" ([in the] rare felicity of the times when you can think what you like and speak what you think)'. The *Autobiography* here performs the important task of joining its subject to the mass of Ghanaians, the 'men and women of Ghana', while also evoking his superior political wisdom via the classical quotation.[21] This wisdom can be read even when the contrastingly unwise person is a colleague; General Acheampong was alerted to the coming coup by many people including 'a seer in Europe', but 'the old boy' had ignored the warnings (299–300): 'Strange as it may seem, this seer had gone to the extent of mentioning the names of those who were playing the roles of "Cassius" and "Casca" and "Trebonius" and "Ligarius" et alia and yet, as if ordained, the chairman [Acheampong] brushed it all aside even as Julius Caesar had done before'. After Acheampong is deposed, Appiah, as a prominent politician, is invited to meet the conspirators, who respectfully address him as 'Papa Joe' (301). According to his own account, he 'stared at each of them . . . "Et tu Brute", I thought in silence as I turned my gaze on each of the dramatis personae, for I knew that it was the man they had deposed who had made them what they were' (301). Again the classical (and Shakespearean) reference operates as a claim to political (and here, moral) superiority and a correspondingly long perspective, which, we are invited to conclude, helped the historical Appiah to survive when others did not. The *Autobiography*'s persona is simultaneously in the thick of Ghanaian politics *and* at a distance which is both enabled and validated by his classical learning.

In less personal contexts, the text can draw on classical antiquity as a trope which signifies immortality almost as effectively as does Christian eschatology, so that specific actions can be placed within a resonant frame. Thus in the text's account of Appiah's visit to Carthage, after the 1951 Nationalist and Trade Union Congress held in Tunisia (179), the ruins of Carthage are described as

> immortalised by Cato at the beginning and end of every speech that he made in the Roman Senate of his day: 'Delenda est Carthago!' I found a tooth and a Roman coin lying side by side when I scratched the ground where I had

> stood contemplating the past. These finds and the ring and handworked tray presented to me by my hosts still remain as eternal reminder [sic] of that Congress in Tunis.

Two things are 'immortal' or 'eternal', here, Carthage and the Congress, and there is also perhaps an incipient meditation on both time and change, since the tooth (presumably not Roman) and the coin could symbolize decay and persistence, while the destruction of Carthage may equally well call to mind the long-lasting empire of Rome. The end of empires is also, of course, a suitable meditation for an African nationalist in 1951. Appiah travelled on to Rome after the Congress but describes it largely in terms of a visit to the Vatican (180–1).

Towards the end of the autobiographical text, the highly dramatic and exciting political narrative fades out and instead, a series of short chapters offers more philosophical reflection and prescription. Here particularly, the autobiography's persona is removed from the hurly-burly of political strife, and comments from what claims to be a higher plane. As well as the Christian faith, Rome and Athens are invoked to contribute to a moralizing political discourse in which, as with the early nationalists, African states and the cities of antiquity are unproblematically equated. The search for individual power and prosperity is condemned:

> It seems that Africa today is faced with the platonic problem of making men fit for power. The consuming quest for individual greatness among those in power is as alarming as it is disastrous, for history teaches that it was this same quest for individual greatness that was the triumph and tragedy of ancient Rome. (343)
>
> Our youth yearn for the good things of life without regard to the means by which the good life may be attained. They may do well to consider the reply to the question put to the Delphic oracle nearly three thousand years ago by the Athenian fathers at the height of their prosperity: '"Can anything ever destroy Athenian prosperity?" Thrice they asked and thrice the same answer came: "Too much prosperity will destroy Athenian prosperity."' (349)

While the equation between Rome and Ghana may not be as arresting as it was in the texts of Horton and Blyden, it is still important that the text both inserts Ghana's history into a classical tradition and simultaneously modifies the tradition by the accession of the African republic. The *Autobiography* shows

J. B. Danquah, 'doyen' of Ghanaian politics, making a similar move when he reminds Nkrumah, in his last letter from prison, of the difference between the legal position of Paul, who claimed 'Civis Romanus sum', and himself, who could only claim the much more precarious status of a 'Civis Ghaniensis' (345). Danquah posed the question 'Is Ghana worth dying for?' which Appiah addresses via a substantial disquisition on not only the women of Battista's Cuba, but also on the deaths of Socrates, Cicero and Jesus (346).

In the second, politically active and philosophically reflective part of the *Autobiography*, then, classical references play a relatively familiar role in attesting to the subject's wisdom, perspective and success, as well as helping to heighten the resonance of certain dramatic events. In the first half of the text, narrating the youth of the subject, the classics appear in a different guise in that Latin, and a particular Latin teacher, play a large role in the account of Appiah's schooldays. Within the narrative, the classical references can be read in the terms suggested by Holden, in which the new nation is figured by the community of the school. The horizontal, fraternal identification suggested by Holden is perhaps more important than the vertical filiation with the father which was so significant for Cole. Classical references in the account of Mfantsipim show the young Appiah both combating the illegitimate authority of the colonial power and recognizing the legitimate authority of those figures and institutions which are genuinely worthy of respect. In this process, he is shown to become a figure of legitimate authority himself, and his great triumph, the Mfantsipim strike of 1936, is clearly a rehearsal for his adult anti-colonial activity.[22]

Latin, as we have seen, is an important part of what awaits the young Appiah and his friends in the elite secondary school of Mfantsipim, as a test, of course, but one that within the context of the school they are expected to pass. The Latin master, E. N. Agbettor, features prominently in this part of the autobiography; he is the 'one and only senior Latin master' who joined the school on graduation, 20 years earlier (35), and according to Principal Lockhart, writing in *Mfantsipim Magazine* (Bu Ber 1931: 5) 'Mr Agbettor has been the means of getting more boys through Matric Latin than any other teacher'. Appropriately demanding, Agbettor also takes pains to interest the boys in their lessons, even from the first day (unlike Robert Cole's teachers). 'Dear Old Agbet', as he is often termed, begins the school year with a lecture on the virtues of being able to read Horace, Cicero, Virgil, Caesar and Livy, on the help that Latin will give with English study, and finally on the story of Romulus and Remus and the founding of Rome. 'Here, indeed, was a teacher who could engage the interest of the biggest dunce in any difficult subject with ease' (36). The teacher has the additional interest of a physical tic that makes him confuse his 'l's and 'r's, while still requiring the boys to pronounce all their Latin correctly (35). 'Dear Old Agbet could see the mote in the eyes of others but was never conscious of the beam in his own'; the narrator represents himself as both excited by the possibilities of the new subject and well able to judge the teacher of it.

The issue of genuine authority, its nature and its provenance, often involves the figure of the Latin master. As a senior boy, Appiah reflects on the three previous years and concludes that 'Of the entire staff I liked only two and loved only one, whom I considered as a father – Old Agbet' (60). However, when the class is working towards Senior Cambridge exams, Appiah as form monitor manages to pass a 'crib' or 'key' from one student to another, so that Agbettor is deludedly pleased with the class's excellent translations. The crib finally discovered, Agbettor storms out of the class, whereupon Appiah plays the statesmanlike part and seeks him out to apologize on behalf of all and to raise 'three cheers for Old Agbet, the best Latin master that ever was' (76). When Appiah takes on his own mantle of legitimate authority by becoming Senior Prefect, he extemporises a 'Ciceronian' speech (80), and is particularly reassured to see the smiling paterfamilias, Old Agbet, as he enters on the duties of his office. Realizing that he must now say the school's grace, six times a day, he decides to maintain the tradition of saying it in Latin 'if only to assure Old Agbet that I had not forgotten [my Latin]' (82).

According to the autobiography's narrative, Appiah as Senior Prefect did not only conform to traditional authority, but also challenged it. In particular, he led the strike of 1936, when the boys protested en masse against new regimes of food and medicine which they found to be highly unsympathetic. Their grievances went unheard until they took direct action, driving out the masters and later, even the police (89–90). Although the grounds of the strike might seem very specific, the *Autobiography* clearly interprets them in terms of the whole colonial struggle: 'the gathering storm that was to wipe from the faces of the authorities the complacency of more than half a century' (89). The authorities also seem to understand the dispute in this way, for they finally send a deputation to meet Appiah, who clinches his personal victory and that of the boys by meeting 'the whole power structure of Cape Coast . . . the provincial commissioner, the High Court judge . . . the senior medical officer . . . .' while sitting in bed in his pyjamas (93). However, Appiah's defiant attitude does not extend to Agbettor. During one morning, the striking boys meet Old Agbet, who rails at them that they should be preparing their Latin rather than 'fooling around' on strike. 'This was the one person in the world to whom we could never show the slightest semblance of disrespect. I called for "three lusty cheers for Old Agbet, the finest gentleman and Latin master in the world"' (91). Appiah's proper respect for true authority is allegedly returned with interest: 'I heard later that he [Agbettor] considered our attitude of deference to him on that day as the greatest honour bestowed on him in all his life' (91).

During the part of the autobiography set at Mfantsipim, the text constructs its subject, Joe Appiah, as a figure worthy of respect in two main ways. He is represented as a revolutionary nationalist in the making in that he is impatient of the constituted powers, but his respect for proper authorities, those recommended by their lasting qualities, shows him to be qualified as a leader and not just a revolutionary. We may be invited here to draw a comparison with Nkrumah. The constituted powers are identified with the colonial government and much of the school; the proper authorities include, prominently, the classics, which are, of course, inculcated by the school.[23] Appiah's political education includes Roman history, and he represents himself using the classics, especially Cicero, to help form himself as a lawyer who will take on the might of the British empire. 'As a budding lawyer, Cicero, then, was ever to remain my ideal' (61). Defending himself against a charge of infringing discipline, he quotes 'the Acts of the Apostles and Cicero's In Catilinam and Pro Milone' (48), and as Senior Prefect, as we have seen, extemporizes a speech 'in true Ciceronian style' (81). Much later in the *Autobiography*, Cicero is still invoked in different ways (143, 329).

Appiah's text thus successfully inserts him into a classical tradition distinguished by its recognition of true worth and its coordination of legitimate authority with appropriate obedience. This, as a lawyer in the making, he can use against the illegitimate powers of the British Empire, combining the antiquity of the classics with the innovation of the anti-colonial movement. At the close of the *Autobiography*, in fact, Appiah squares the circle by crediting his classical education with the inspiration for his anti-colonial activity (340):

> Four factors were responsible for this enlightenment [about British colonial rule]: the first was the teaching of English and British Empire history; the second was the teaching of Latin side by side with Roman history; the third was the school's possession of a good library and the fourth and greatest blessing of all was the gift of an Irish headmaster who shared and nursed a feeling similar to mine.[24]

That this was not an unmanageable paradox may be suggested by the fact that Robert Wellesley Cole's autobiography makes a similar equation; it is through Roman history, especially that of the wars with Carthage, as taught at the colonial school, that he experiences 'the first stirrings of nationalism. To me the Carthaginians were fellow-Africans' (1960: 176).[25] Other texts offer analogous perceptions; at Government College Ibadan, Tunji Otegbeye found it ironic that boys were encouraged to read about the gladiators and the revolt of Spartacus (1995: 60), and Wyse claims the direct relevance of Homer and other poetry 'to people who were later to articulate the aspirations of their compatriots' (1990: 9). Appiah's coordination of apparently contradictory traditions is, in his account, rewarded by a new tradition in the future, which he describes in the context of planning his career after Mfantsipim: 'in all my crowded plans, Latin . . . held a pride of place. How pleased I was later, when my son, with the same enjoyment, won prizes in Latin oratory and continued to make it a hobby . . .' (61). The classics here may also be understood as part of the gendering of the subject via filiation, as we saw with the autobiography of Robert Wellesley Cole.

At the end of the account of Mfantsipim school days, the *Autobiography* pulls off a particularly brilliant combination of the classical and the Ghanaian. Throughout the narrative of youth, the text represents its subject as a confirmed Christian, but also one who investigates the traditional Akan spirit world with its population of 'mmoatia' or 'little people'. He holds regular meetings with these spirits, including Mame Wata, the water spirit or 'mermaid' (47), and we may note that he invokes them in a form of Latin (46) – although he claims that their language is initially 'all Greek to me' (65). Although consultations with these 'friends' punctuate the later life as well, when he reflects on his school career, investigations into the 'invisible' world rank of equal importance with his enjoyment of Cicero, Caesar and Vergil (61), and it is this combination which launches the young Appiah firmly on his successful path, by enabling a triumph in the Senior Cambridge exams. The death of a school friend, Asamoah, shortly before the exams, is followed by his reappearance in Appiah's room as a spirit or ghost. What is more astonishing than his reappearance, however, is his message. He tells Appiah how to pass the coming exam, in particular what passage of the Latin unseen will need attention (98–9):

> It was about midnight; I had just retired to bed after the usual nightly revision. Sleep had not yet overtaken me; I was ruminating over what I had revised that night. Suddenly, I sensed his presence in the room . . . 'Well, Joe, it's a pity that now even my best friends appear to be frightened of me.... Why not rest your weary soul and leave those books alone? Only two things require to be revised – proof of Pythagoras's theorem and a certain Latin "unseen"' . . . There followed, a few weeks later, the Cambridge exams and the final parting for those of the sixth form. Both the proof of Pythagoras's theorem and the particular Latin unseen adverted to by Asamoah had turned up.

It is perhaps not a coincidence that Asamoah was the student earlier discovered with the 'crib'. The effortless combination of the Western and classical with indigenous traditions, represented as an important aspect of Appiah's success, is here deepened by the fact that the scene replays the conventions of ghostly visitations as elaborated in classical epic.[26]

Classical education is thus shown to help develop a character which is well suited to the independence struggle, and in another phase, to frame political and philosophical reflections which help to place the autobiography's subject in an authoritative position 'above the fray'. Since Appiah had not ever actually led his country, this philosophical detachment could also serve as a consolation. Throughout the text, classical reference is also a sign of elite status and of superior attitude, whether it be leading the revolution at school or 'keeping his cool' in prison. To that extent, the classics also operate within the text to distance Appiah from the ordinary people of Ghana whom he tried to serve, and the text's claims to a kind of transcendence may even be considered undermined by the precise cultural form in which they are often cast.

Despite their instrumental role in opening further educational possibilities to boys, the roles of Latin and the classics in twentieth-century schools were not simply practical. As well as the various cultural tasks which they fulfilled in terms of patrolling the structures of colonial authority and power, they could also contribute to the formation of specific kinds of subjectivity. Within the autobiographies that record such schooling, they show prominently that the colonial subjects could master whatever colonial society threw at them. In these various ways Latin and the classics helped not simply to forge the mind-manacles on which colonialism depended, but crucially to enable, for the colonized, representation of autonomy and success, within the colonial system but also as a way of dismantling it. As the bearer of this fruitful contradiction Latin, and the classics generally, found a significant role in the new mid-century universities. Here they also came under scrutiny as representatives of 'Western' culture and tradition.

Classics and 'Western' culture

In 1947 Indirect Rule was abolished, and commentators suggest that with this political and cultural shift, the UK government began to take into partnership the 'educated elite' rather than the 'traditional chiefs', seeking collaborators with a working knowledge of, and sympathy with, the traditions of Western civilization, who would maintain the cultural ties between the new African states and the metropolis.[27] Since classical education was already entrenched in West Africa in various ways, it was at hand to supply a version of such traditions; thus ancient Greece and Rome were called upon in certain European-authored texts to offer a humanist, inclusive orientation that would link Europeans and Africans and would, crucially, help to ground the shared project of founding the new universities. In the early years of European colonialism, as we have seen, colonial discourse could understand African and European as linked by the possibilities of Christianity; in the early twentieth century they could be represented as separated, educationally, along the faultline of classics, as part of the attempt to suppress African aspirations and prolong European imperial control. When the empire looked instead to be running up against its limits, African and European had to be represented again as in important respects alike. Since those important respects were often identified in terms set by Europeans rather than Africans, the classical heritage came in handy again as a way to represent that likeness. Inasmuch as West Africans had developed an indigenous tradition of classical education and reference, however, which even offered a version of ancient Greece as conditioned by African cultures, British invocation of the classical heritage can also be understood as a response to African pressure.

In some ways, this task of developing a discourse of shared culture could have been accomplished by English literature, which was taught much more widely than was Latin, Greek or classics in general.[28] But classics was available to be represented as not-English in a way that escaped English itself, as when Blyden pointed to the classical languages as a resource untainted by racism. Arnold Bradshaw, writing in the centenary celebration volume for Fourah Bay College, remarks that West African students were aware that Latin and Greek represented a high culture which precisely was not that of England (Bradshaw 1977: 22). So, the trope of sharing the classical heritage, which is prominent in some of the mid-twentieth-century texts, is itself complicated by the question whether that heritage is shared *with* Africa *by* Europe, or emerges from a third source to be available to both. In either case we can also read independent African claims to the classical heritage as exerting pressure on the European discourse. In response, some of the European discourse about classics works to build a 'Black Aegean' of creative negotiation among ancient Greece, Africa and the imperial powers.

In the last year of the war two reports were published which envisaged the university education of Africans, the Report of the Commission on Higher Education in the Colonies (Cmd 6647, Asquith Report), and the Report of the Commission on Higher Education in West Africa (Cmd 6655, Elliot Report). The latter became controversial when it issued *two* reports, a majority and a minority; the former recommended three university colleges, one in each of Sierra Leone, the Gold Coast and Nigeria, while the minority report argued for a single university-level college at Ibadan in Nigeria, with three feeder colleges at Achimota, Fourah Bay and a new Nigerian location. Although the Labour government first signed up for the minority report, West African agitation and protest was such that the majority recommendation was eventually adopted. Relevant for our purposes here are the rhetorical moves that the Elliot Report makes, especially with reference to the classics. Ashby 1966: 219 suggests that parts 'are written with an eloquence which merits their inclusion in any anthology of writing about Africa' and also points out that the Elliot Commission, unlike the Asquith, had three Africans on its board. They were K. O. Korsah of the Gold Coast, I. O. Ransome-Kuti of Nigeria and E. H. Taylor-Cummings of Sierra Leone (Ajayi and Tamuno 1973: 18). The African members all voted with the majority (Ajayi et al. 1996: 56).[29]

The opening pages of the Report are distinguished by an interest in the possibilities of the classical heritage as something which links Europe and Africa. Quite early on, it features a comparison between some varieties of indigenous African education and that dished out to Spartan boys (Elliot 1945: 8): 'The initiation of the youths into manhood, for instance, involved, till very recently, tests of endurance of a most searching kind. The flogging of the [Fulani] youths by the elders in the presence of the tribe recalls the tales of initiation of the Spartans'. Such a comparison had been made earlier by the novelist D. O. Fagunwa in an article for *Nigeria Magazine*, tracing the idea of 'discipline' from Sparta to the present day (Fagunwa 1939: 363–4),[30] and it may be thought to construct a link between Africans and Greeks that can be understood to the Africans' advantage, inserting them into a tradition which otherwise might have been identified only with the white West. The Report then moves away from this position, implicitly critiquing the Fulani instead, when it continues (8): 'The qualification of one's dairyman by public beatings administered by his seniors, and pushed almost to the point of death, exemplifies one of the difficulties in interchanging African and European values.' The paradox that the European values are, allegedly, informed by the classical heritage which includes the bizarre Spartan practices, here escapes the authors of the Report.

The African student appears in different guises elsewhere in the Report, being adept at classical languages and comparing favourably to English school boys.[31] Although we have seen African students characterized in these ways in earlier sources, absent from the Report is the tired reflex which describes African students as having facility with the surface accomplishments of the Western tradition but no access to its 'depths'. Since the Report is anxious to construct an African who is ready for university education and to inhabit a fully realized modernity, no such gesture would be admissible. The African may even be thought to surpass the English boy in that he can manage being taught Latin via English; 'as though we should all find ourselves being taught

Greek in Arabic' (Elliot 1945: 11).[32] The fact that African students sometimes come to school equipped with several African languages is not, as it could be in the nineteenth century, an excuse for denigrating their achievement with Latin or Greek, but instead locates the African student in a position of some privilege with respect to the ancient languages (Elliot 1945: 12):

> this multiplicity of tongues . . . gives the African scholar an outlook on languages differing altogether from that of his schoolboy British contemporary. Latin is simply one more language. Greek, to the Africans who reach Greek, is simply another . . . Greek thought, Greek settings, Greek wars, Greek rituals would be much more familiar and recognisable to him, once the initial unfamiliarity had been overcome, than the ideas that he will eventually find in English. Compare, for instance, the mental adjustment required to read and understand the trial and death of Socrates, with that necessary to master the Gold Standard or the workings of the Liverpool Cotton Exchange.

That the African student is better equipped to understand classical narratives than the workings of some iconic institutions of the twentieth century can also be construed now not as a mark of inadequacy, but as testimony to the common humanity which the Report is busy building in the face of colonialism's end.[33]

In yet other parts of the Report the African student retains the connection to the classical past that can render him kin to the Europeans. Even in an Islamic context, for instance, Africans can be likened to the Persians as described by Xenophon, their simplicity of education compared to the Persian ideal of riding, shooting and speaking the truth (Elliot 1945: 14). Crucially, the Report notes that the African can teach the European, specifically about the classical heritage of the latter. The Report notes the existence of West African rituals (1945: 18):

> which the rest of the world will never decipher, and whose lessons it will never read, without African tuition. Every now and then one comes on flashes that would light up much of our own forgotten history if they could but be made to last. Ancient European or Asiatic legends have counterparts, alive, and vigorous, governing the lives of many African people today.

If we allow that 'ancient European legends' are very likely to include classical narratives, Africans thus connect to the classical tradition via their own rituals and other cultural manifestations as well as by their linguistic skills. This connection to the ancient and the legendary does not disqualify Africans from humanity, but instead testifies to their participation in it, and in fact positions them to teach the rest of the world about itself. The Report can be seen here to construct a version of the 'Black Aegean', imagining the kinds of cross-cultural communication and cross-fertilization of traditions that might undermine imperial hierarchies.[34]

It is clear that the Elliot Report is motivated by very different considerations from those which drove Phelps-Stokes, and at one point, via a resonant rhetorical coup, it seems almost deliberately to distance itself from the earlier Commission. Although Phelps-Stokes is not mentioned by name, it is hard to avoid recognizing that body in the Elliot Report's vignette of a conversation with a young colonial subject about the role of classics in the education of Africans (1945: 16):

> A small boy in another part of Africa, discussing the question of classical education, said to a member of another educational commission, years ago, 'We desire to learn Latin because it is your secret language, from which you derive your power'.

Although this utterance is highlighted as the title of the present book, the attitude it represents has, in fact, been very rarely encountered in this study.[35] How West African opinion, as represented by the sources examined here, usually characterized Latin and the classics, was not as a mystical dimension of colonial power, and but as a route, difficult but not impossible, to temporal authority in the political and cultural spheres – and this is exactly why West African identification with Latin and the classics proved so troublesome to colonial overlords. The small boy, then, with his naive perception of the magical quality of Latin, would be almost too perfect a piece of evidence for Phelps-Stokes, confirming the opinion of the authors of that 1922 Report that classics is pernicious for Africans and their desire for it perverse. The Elliot Report of 1945, in turn, takes care to answer the small boy in terms that defuse the question of power. After quoting him, it continues: 'A free access to Horace may disabuse him of that belief [that Latin confers power]. Mere argument certainly will not' (16). The Report thus disavows Latin as a source of power, and indicates that once the small boy has learned Latin, he too will be able to see through any such claims. If Africans learn Latin just as Europeans do, they will know that there is no secret power in classics, and classics will thus no longer provide a bone of contention between the two peoples. Horace will not constitute a fount of authority for either Europeans or Africans, and they will to that extent be equal in the face of the classical authors.

The version of classics, and thus of the possible relations between Europeans and Africans, that is offered by this strand of the official discourse of 1945, is poised to usher in a different era from that characterized by anxiety over the 'educated African' and his stubborn refusal to embrace vocational training. It is not unprecedented, however, because some liberal European commentators had already theorized the contribution of the classical societies to European civilization in ways that included African cultures. In an important book on education in the colonial empire Arthur Mayhew, Joint Secretary to the British government's Advisory Committee on Education in the Colonies,[36] identified the West with an inspiration that derives from the Mediterranean, but that need not stop there (1938: 11–12):

> We of the West are mainly concerned with the ideas and values that first attained strength between 800 BC and AD 500 among the races that fringed the Mediterranean Sea. It is on the ideas of freedom of thought and unfettered search for truth, associated with the Greek race, of law, order, and justice, associated with the Roman race, and of a divinely ordered world progress, associated with the Jews, that our western civilisation is founded. It is these ideas that we are pledged to propagate.

Mayhew makes the transposition to Africa possible and desirable by modifying this initial notion of the ideas (1938: 12): 'That they are not dependent on any particular race is shown by their propagation among races that have very little in common with the Mediterranean races of the first century AD'. 'Western' civilization, derived from classical and Judaic antiquity, does not, it turns out, have to be identified exclusively with the West.

Earlier, in 1929, Victor Murray, famous for his *The School in the Bush*, had a lengthy section in which he discussed the claims of 'humanism' and literary studies (195–206), drawing on classical references to make his points, and moving towards the notion of a shared culture. He notes that carpentry can be 'humanistic' while Greek philosophy can be 'as inhuman as a table of statistics' (1929: 195), rejecting the easy categorizations dear to more conventional commentators. Emphasizing the speed of change in Africa, he again draws on a classical analogy: 'The important thing is not that he [the African] is where

Queen Boadicea was, but that while it has taken us 2000 years to advance from her type of civilization to our own, he can do the same distance in 20' (1929: 204). Murray here makes the same kinds of comparison between Britons and Africans as subjects of imperial powers as did the cultural nationalists of West Africa, like Horton, in the mid or late nineteenth century, and implies the same conclusion about the possibility of the Africans' advance. In a later section, he extends this inversion of expectations to the past: 'When we come to add up our indebtedness to the past, we shall find that the "barbarians" have brought their gifts as well as the Greeks' (1929: 224). The classical repertoire, conventionally thought of as the gift of Europe to Africa, nonetheless enables Murray to interrogate easy assumptions of European superiority.

Murray also anticipates Mayhew's point about the genesis and destination of ideas (1929: 215): 'In our own British art, as in our literature, the inspiration of Greece, Italy and Judaea has helped to stimulate modes of expression which are neither Greek, Italian, nor Semitic, but British'. The 'classical tradition', harking back to Greece and Rome, functions here to encourage expression independent of it, which could be British or, we are invited to conclude, African. On 326–7 Murray returns to the theme, pointing out that 'What we call "Western" or "European" or "modern" civilization is a blend of various elements not all of them Western or European or modern'. This civilization is emphatically not 'white', and in reference particularly to South Africa Murray goes on to point out that:

> it is obvious that the civilization of Greece and Rome, or Florence and Weimar, is much more likely to be in safe keeping with the educated Native students of Fort Hare than with the 'poor whites' of Orange Free State . . . we cannot say whether European civilization is safe or is not safe until the Bantu have come into it.

We might deduce that this 'civilization' must be shared across non-European cultures in order to thrive; 'European' civilization will be preserved precisely by not being European. We might even conclude that as African culture engages with modernity via classical education, so classical culture will attain a full role in modernity only by gearing to African requirements. Its strength is tested, and thus guaranteed, by its African location rather than its European.

The humanistic aspirations of earlier commentators such as Murray and Mayhew were brought into renewed focus by the political pressures of the mid-century post-war period, as legible in the Report of the Elliot Commission. Although not explicitly responding to the accounts of such as Horton and Blyden, the 'inclusive' versions of the classics can be understood as reactions to West Africans' independent formulations of African claims to the classical tradition. Within the new universities, the notion of classics as a heritage shared by European and African, and thus as a component of West African modernity, was prominent, but also troubled.

Classics in the new universities

The University Colleges of Ibadan and of the Gold Coast (at Legon near Accra) were both founded in 1948. They were in a 'special relationship' with the University of London, which meant that the degrees awarded were those of the University of London, but that teaching was provided in the colonies and examining was shared by London and colonial academics.[37] 'These relations made it clear that the products of the College were not to be regarded as holders of the external degrees of London but were to all intents and purposes on equal footing with the products from those other colleges of the university located in London – and some even outside London – at the time' (Banjo 2000: 24).[38] Within the relationship, the West African colleges were able to innovate and modify courses to be more relevant to local conditions, but the admissions criteria and the degree qualifications conformed to London policies. The 'special relationship' survived independence and the university colleges became autonomous universities only in the early 1960s.

At both Ibadan in Nigeria and Legon in Ghana the institutional status of Classics was represented as a sign of the decision to establish and maintain high standards from the outset.[39] Such commitment was over-determined in that the early staff members were usually European, and thus likely to be sold on the notion of classical education as a marker of quality, while the African administrators and politicians were equally determined to show that an African institution of higher education could earn genuine respect.[40] All were anxious to avoid 'another Yaba' (Ashby 1966: 236) where the qualifications had only local purchase and no international recognition, and subsequent historians of the universities, such as Ajayi and Tamuno 1973 and Agbodeka 1998, write as defenders of those initial choices. At Ibadan, candidates in Arts and

Humanities could study in only four departments – Classics, English, History and Geography – and were expected to choose at least one of English, Greek and Latin (Ajayi and Tamuno 1973: 175). As a consequence of this prominence, over 100 undergraduates were reading classical subjects at University College Ibadan in 1956, mostly in the context of a general degree with another Arts subject (Thompson 1966: 46). A table in Ajayi and Tamuno 1973: 282 shows clearly the dominance of the Arts faculty in the years before the mid-1960s. Although in 1948, Science students outnumber Arts (38 to 17), the ratios change so that in 1962–3, the year before many other Faculties opened, Arts students number 566 and Science, 400. By then there are also 292 Medical students and 116 in Agriculture, but the Arts faculty is neck and neck with Science for most of the early history, and has more students than Science (though not than Science, Medicine and Agriculture combined) throughout the late 1950s.

In the early years Classics was the only Honours degree offered at Ibadan, and even before the Special Relationship was fully in place, the department was the first to admit students to the external degree programme of the University of London (Ajayi et al. 1996: 58); the claim was again made that Classics alone among Humanities was not susceptible to any African adaptation and so its standards could not be compromised by local circumstances (Mabogunje 1973: 171).[41] The splendid isolation of the Classics degree was experienced as problematic, but when the students 'pleaded with the authorities to establish other honours courses', the authorities told them that honours courses would have to take six years rather than four, and 'we were unwilling to forfeit two whole years' (Segun 2000: 401).[42] That Classics remained seriously demanding is underlined by John Ferguson, the first Professor of Classics, who writes that the London examination board in Classics was much less indulgent when his department wanted to make changes to the syllabus than was, for instance, the History board (Ferguson 1981: 122).

At Legon, the new University College of the Gold Coast continued the Gold Coast tradition of excellence in classics even after independence. The 1958 report from the University of London notes that: 'In recent years students from Ghana have achieved some striking success in the BA Honours (Classics) Examination' (Agbodeka 1998: 115). At Legon, the first Principal, David Balme, was himself a classicist, but moreover, according to Agbodeka 'he believed in the fundamental equality of the races. That was why he brought the Oxbridge system of education with its high standards to the Gold Coast, believing that the African could rise to these same standards' (1998: 116). Fourah Bay College in Sierra Leone had, meanwhile, made its own adjustments to its predominantly classical offerings. While in the early period of affiliation it offered University of Durham degrees only in Classics and Theology, from 1918 it offered a BA Pass degree which was open to many more students than before, with a larger range of subjects that could be undertaken including English, Mathematics, Classical Greek, Latin, Philosophy, Education and Geography (Sawyerr 1977: 3). In 1946, after the war, another far-reaching change was enacted when it became possible for first-year students to take Greek and Roman Culture instead of the classical languages. Even if innocent of Latin or Greek, students could take Classical Culture and then read for a degree in Ancient History. In 1959 when Fourah Bay became the University College, a complete Honours course was introduced, and when it gained autonomy, as the University of Sierra Leone, it offered a degree in Greek and Roman History and Civilisation (Bradshaw 1977: 22).

Despite this position of status and regard, there was opposition to Classics in the new universities, and it came from two sides. Agbodeka's account of Balme continues: 'Some Europeans in Accra . . . disagreed with Balme and were outspoken among the early critics of Legon, wondering why anyone should establish an institution of that status and expense in the Gold Coast or indeed anywhere in the tropics' (1998: 116). Although this was a noticeable strand of reaction to the new West African universities, perhaps more common was the perception that these institutions were far too colonial (Agbodeka 1998: 124–5), with Classics as a signifier of exactly how colonial, or perhaps we should say neo-colonial, they were. Thus John Abiri, a lecturer in education at the University of Ibadan, notes that Greek and Latin were funded from 1948 whereas there was no money for a Linguistics degree until 1962, well after independence (1973: 57), and Nkrumah allegedly complained in 1957 that more university students were studying Latin and Greek than studied African languages (Mazrui 1978: 98). Legon was similarly criticized for teaching Classics while eschewing African philosophy or religion (Ajayi et al. 1996: 86). In 1956 the *Daily Times* of Nigeria asked 'Why do our boys and girls have to waste their time on Latin and Greek instead of studying something useful like the Theory of Relativity?' (Thompson 1966: 47–9). In this context the claims of African Studies, or of other demanding subjects such as Law, were neglected for years, even when their necessity was recognized by Europeans as well as Africans (Ajayi and Tamuno 1973: 41, Abiri 1973: 57). Commentators as diverse as the Nigerian nationalists Nnamdi Azikiwe and Tai Solarin, and the British educator Eric Ashby, concurred that the universities took too little account of how they should serve the specificities of the West African situation by providing new kinds of subject matter and even of degree structures (Ashby 1966: 245–6, Ogunsheye 2000: 374). Ashby even suggests that certain constituencies became suspicious if it were suggested that Arabic, as a language of the African continent, should replace Latin and Greek (1966: 241). As in earlier periods in colonial history, Latin and the classics help to form new identities, here of the first generation of people educated in West African universities, but controversy immediately arises over how productive these identities are.

The academic and political commentator Ali Mazrui summed up the conflicted situation by suggesting, in an essay of 1978,[43] that 'there is a crisis of identity confronting every modern African university – and the mystique of ancient Greece is at the heart of it' (1978: 82). His essay proceeds to argue that the situation is capable of solution, in that there are several different ways whereby Africans can 'concede to Europe the role of bearer of Greek culture without conceding her right to be Greece itself' (1978: 97). Africa can thus retain access to the classical heritage without the intellectual subjection of the colonial detour, exactly as Blyden proposed. In this context Mazrui quotes David Balme complaining about the careless use of the term 'European civilization' as the central preoccupation of a university (1978: 97–8). This passage is quoted in Ashby too (1966: 241):

> The whole issue has been bedevilled by our careless use of the phrase 'European civilisation'. It may be justifiable that the things which are studied at universities . . . are themselves the instruments of civilisation. If so, then it follows that there is only one modern civilisation. It happens to have started in Greece . . . and it spread first through Europe. But it is high time we stopped calling it European as though there were some other from which to distinguish it . . . I was astonished when I came here to find myself called a European. I had never thought of myself as one before, and I don't now.[44]

Balme's utterance points to the 'crisis' identified by Mazrui very precisely, because while he is anxious not to attribute all 'civilisation' to Europe, he seems to denigrate African civilization by supposing that there is no 'other'; his formulation has an uneasy relationship to the positions of Murray and Mayhew explored above.

The problem for the new universities, which we have encountered in various forms in this study, is thus how to lay hold of the classical inheritance as if it were, indeed, not connected to a colonial European history. To achieve this, Mazrui's article pursues two lines of enquiry, one investigating the African contribution to Greek culture, in terms familiar from the nineteenth-century nationalists, and the other suggesting the ways in which Greece is not necessarily European.[45] Mazrui concludes that Europe 'stole' Greece before going on to steal the rest of the world, and that 'The only mitigating factor in this blatant act of cultural impersonation is that Europeans did become the great carriers of the Graeco-Roman heritage in these later periods of world history' (1978: 95–6). Mazrui finally proclaims what the tradition of classics in the West African colonies endeavours to secure: 'The Greeks must at last be allowed to emerge as what they really are – the fathers not of a European civilisation but of a universal modernity' (1978: 97). For both African and European commentators in this period, modernity is tested by its ability to make the classics make sense on the African continent.

Within this overall context of struggle over the European identity of the classics, testimony from students who attended the university colleges before and just after independence suggests the range of ways in which Latin and the classics featured within and shaped their experience. 'Invention of tradition' was one noticeable development, such as Latin prayers at degree ceremonies and formal dinners (Ogunsheye 2000: 375),[46] but these were often experienced as deliberate tactics towards the self-respect of the institutions rather than the ideological sleight of hand often connoted by the phrase 'invention of tradition'.[47] One event in East Africa shows further constructive possibilities for invented traditions. School mottoes in West Africa had long been in Latin, as we have seen, but Mazrui notes that Makerere University in Uganda deliberately moved to a motto in Latin, abandoning Luganda, because Luganda only represented a fraction of the country's population (1978: 99). Latin thus offered a political resource rather than only a 'cultural cringe'. In a related move, the classicist

Alex Kwapong (who would later become the first Ghanaian Principal of the University) devised a Latin motto for the crest of the University College of the Gold Coast when it became, in 1963, the University of Ghana. The crest was redesigned to offer indigenous symbols, but Latin offered another, and complex, connection to local roots (Gibbs 2007: 60).[48]

Inventing tradition more informally, students speak of themselves and others in terms drawn from the classical repertoire, and to get a degree is often called going after the Golden Fleece, partly because of the fact that degrees used to involve compulsory overseas travel (Tucker 1977: 57, 58, Ajayi and Tamuno 1973: 15, Amissah 1980: 60). With some self-mockery, the first woman graduate from the University of Sierra Leone notes how students might regard themselves as 'gods partaking of ambrosia' (Hyde-Forster 1977: 56).[49] Another compares student meetings to Athenian democracy (Segun 2000: 407; cf. Tucker 1977: 58): 'Although we had a Students' Representative Council, at first ours was a sort of Athenian democracy. Most of the time we all deliberated together. And what deliberations – with three hundred students all trying to talk at the same time!'

Adetowun Ogunsheye notes that the largely expatriate staff were determined to make the students over in a certain image: 'to make us gentlemen and ladies, giving us what they had in their own culture, inviting us to their homes, organising literary and social events'. This last practice, incidentally, she claims 'prepared me for my subsequent sojourn in Cambridge'.[50] Elaborating on the theme, she describes dining in style with English table manners, treated throughout as 'future leaders who would take over from the colonialists. We did not mind being patronized and pampered by them. We must have become insufferable young students full of our own importance as future leaders, a role we accepted with a solemn sense of responsibility'. That these practices were also perceived as problematic she acknowledges with the words 'The Nigerian public was, however, not impressed'. Among the staff promoting these new dimensions of the university students' identity was Mr Cadle the Classics lecturer, insisting on 'knowledge of the classics and phonetically correctly spoken English' (2000: 371–2).

Although these 'inventions of tradition' were plainly motivated by colonial, or perhaps neo-colonial, assumptions about the nature of the university enterprise, for which the study of classics offered a metonymy, classical education was also experienced as part of a general widening of intellectual horizons which in itself might be a 'form of liberation' (Mazrui 1978: 81). Comfort Adedeji, a product of Queen's College where no Latin was taught, determined to read Latin for her degree (Segun 2000: 400); she and her colleagues were, among other things, breaking down the gender barriers that had attended classics in secondary schools for a long time. Other students undertook Greek in their own time, but with mixed success. Mabel Segun writes that (2000: 402):

> Our adventure into Greek fared no better [than classes in French]. We had asked the Greek lecturer, Mr E. A Cadle, to teach us Greek in his spare time. He was delighted. We found an empty classroom and the lessons began. I cannot remember how many we were but we were a sizable number. However, as our examinations drew nearer, some students began to stay away until only three of us were left.

A similar rate of attrition attended an extra-mural course for adult beginners in Ancient Greek in Ibadan in 1958; 20 enrolled but only 6 completed. Even these figures, Thompson states, were unthinkable ten years later (1966: 49).

The neo-colonial identity of the classics vied with the possibilities offered of intellectual experimentation, but Latin at least can also serve as a sign of the hard work and dedication required from this first generation of university students. Although novel, Latin is also represented as very effortful, and sometimes appears simply as an obstacle that must be overcome, even by studying while kneeling on the floor so as not to sleep, as did Comfort Adedeji in 'her Spartan approach' (Segun 2000: 401). In this connection, according to the volumes of reminiscences from foundation students, Latin elicits astonishing performances. Adetowun Ogunsheye decides to try to enter Cambridge University, but Latin stands as a familiar obstacle (2000: 375):

> I had one year to study and offer Latin in the Cambridge School Certificate! Mr Cadle, the lecturer in Classics was very doubtful that this could be done in a year, but was willing to help me from time to time. When the results came and I not only passed, but obtained the credit required he thought I had made history.

Isidore Okpewho, the academic and writer, went up to Ibadan with A level Latin but only a smattering of Greek, yet took a First in three years, which was a record (Ferguson 1981: 120).[51] As part of its role as gateway, as well as gatekeeper, Latin proves again useful for circumnavigating the obstacles to education that were routinely thrown in African students' paths. For instance, at the end of 1949, fully one-third of the first entering class of the University College of Ibadan was sent down as having failed the exams. African commentators attributed this to a desire to limit education even under the new post-war conditions, and John Ellah claims that the syllabuses of familiar subjects like English were suddenly changed, nominally in the name of 'adaptation', but perhaps with more sinister purposes (1981: 20–1).[52] Although the classicists were suspected along with other staff by the jaundiced students (Ellah 1981: 24), the classical languages nonetheless enabled some students to recover. Ellah notes that 'my friend, John Munonye, who was wise enough to drop English in good time and take up Greek in its place was, of course, able to retain his place' (1981: 22) and that 'One failed student was advised by a leaver of Kings College Lagos to sit Higher School Certificate in December 49, to obtain exemption from BA (Intermediate) of London University.' Although the subjects, Latin, History, and English, involved new texts and periods every year, so that the failed student had only three months in which to prepare for the exam, he nonetheless passed with honours (Ellah 1981: 23).

Despite these various connotations of dignity, novelty and practical use, some of the students who write accounts of the early days at the University of Ibadan lament the necessity of the classics. Ellah was forced into his University combination of subjects, which he resisted, because his Latin mark in the entrance examination had been very good (1981: 20). S. J. Okudu, later the University Registrar, was stuck, in 1953/4, with no chance to change course because the offerings were too few: 'I am therefore bogged down with reading History, Ancient History and English. How I wish I could be reading Law or something more exciting' (1981: 172).[53] After independence, secondary schools begin to phase out Latin (Thompson 1966: 54) and as noted above, the universities which were founded in the 1960s and subsequently did not feel the necessity to include classics in their offerings; the postcolonial conditions framed a very different place for Latin and the classics to occupy.

One of the contributors to the volume which celebrated the centenary of the University of Sierra Leone, Arnold Bradshaw, sums up the overall position and significance of Latin and the classics in the pre-independence context, making clear the various contradictions and compromises which attended it (1977: 21):

> Two main reasons for the astonishing dominance of Latin and Greek in school and university curricula were their traditional association with learning and their difficulty. Combining order with complexity, classical tongues demonstrated intelligence and industry ... Respect for wisdom is part of the fabric of African societies, and here was a new wisdom that could be attained in new ways. ... West Africans who wanted to draw on the Western tradition could only do so by going through the same exercises as Westerners, which ... involved the study of Latin ... Paradoxically the difficulty of Latin made it an ideal subject for West African students because it gave them a chance to demonstrate their intellectual competence [and to] rival colonists on their own terms ... people might be more impressed by a clergyman quoting Greek from the pulpit than by a medicine-man chanting in the vernacular.

Yet John Ferguson, who was the first Professor of Classics at Ibadan in 1956, offers a different approach to the predominance of the Classics, one which taps into the humanist discourse of the Elliot Report. Approaching the position with some reluctance, being 'as sceptical as, shall we say, another close and honoured friend, Jacob Ajayi, about the relevance of Greek and Latin to Nigeria' (1981: 109), Ferguson was persuaded by J. Saunders, Principal of Ibadan, that 'the Nigerian leaders had opted for European technology, and it was essential that they knew something of the springs from which that technology had come, that they were exposed to the underlying ideas'. While some might query the easy transition from technology to classics, or between Europe and the classical civilizations, Ferguson discovered once in place that the cultural transmission worked in two directions; he records that not only did Nigerians learn about European culture, but they could also contribute immensely to the understanding of the ancient world. 'Nigerian scholars plainly understand what it means to consult an oracle as Europeans can never do ... Nigerian scholars have a much deeper understanding of the nature of sacrifice' while mutual illumination results from the comparative study of classical and African proverbs, or Homeric and African epic (1981: 111).[54] Ferguson's work at the department included founding the Classical Association of Nigeria and publishing the proceedings of the annual conference for many years, while the student association of Hoi Phronistai (The Thinkers) published the Phrontisterion or Thinkery.[55] Within the published proceedings of the annual conference, Latin pedagogy is discussed in ways that could be recognizable in many other cultures, but the classics can also be described as having a particular relevance to the struggle for independence; the Roman empire's experience of different races, for instance, and of different religions, is seen to be especially thought-provoking in the context of the transition through which West Africa and the rest of the British empire is passing (Akabogu 1958: 56).[56] The Senior Education Officer at the Ministry of Education, Ibadan, goes even further in that he prescribes more classical education for Nigeria – even a reduction in other subjects – precisely because the country is at a crossroads, with the opportunity, he suggests, before settling down to a fixed way of life, of choosing the very best from all human heritage (Edgal 1959: 2–5).[57]

One of the more positive resonances of the classics in the new universities, perhaps in the inclusive, 'humanist' tradition proposed at the opening of this section, was the prevalence of student productions of classical dramas. Harold Preston, the University Bursar at Ibadan, notes that 'There was theatrical activity . . . right from the beginning. The first play I saw was the 1950 performance of *Oedipus Rex* by the students of the Teacher Training Course . . . superbly staged, acted and costumed' (1981: 45). Ferguson lists the attainments of his own students, which include play-readings in Greek and Latin, and productions during the conferences of the Classical Association such as Plautus' *Curculio* in Latin (Pathmanathan 1963: 29), Plautus' *Mostellaria* in Latin and Euripides's *Cyclops* in Greek and English (Ferguson 1981: 115). Ferguson's version of Aristophanes' *Birds* (1964), however, which he calls 'topicalized and tropicalized', was not well received, apparently because its contemporary political satire was too contemporary for the powers that be (1981: 115). However, *That Scoundrel Suberu*, a adaptation by Dapo Adelugba of Moliere's *Scapin*, which itself drew on the traditions of Greek and Roman comedy, was hugely successful as a touring production (1981: 114; see also Pathmanathan 1963: 32; July 1987: 65), and was revived to celebrate Adelugba's seventieth year (Burmah 2009).

Apart from the plays performed by classics students, the drama societies also produced Greek plays and adaptations, such as Sophocles' *Antigone*, Anouilh's *Antigone* and *Lysistrata* (Preston 1981: 50).[58] Legon, meanwhile, boasted an open-air Greek style theatre (Gibbs 2009: 186). Such activity drew not only on the culture of the expatriates who staffed the new universities, but also on the indigenous tradition of classical education, and with equal importance, on the indigenous traditions of drama. These two traditions had met earlier, in the schools, where dramatic activity was arguably a significant feature of the West African encounter with the classics. Bernth Lindfors (1980) lists Nigerian high school plays from 1950–72, among which are several that are either productions of Greek texts or adaptations from the classical repertoire more generally. Thus in 1951, Ibadan Grammar School put on 'The Sword of Theseus'; in 1958, Queens College Ede 'The Return of Odysseus'; in 1957, Ibadan Boys' High School 'Socrates'. In 1964 the Lutheran High School put on 'King Dyonisius' and 'Oddysius in the House of Cerce', but after that, the offerings are perhaps more conventional, including *Antigone* at St Andrews College Oyo in 1963, *Electra* at Ibadan Grammar School in 1964, Sophocles' *Oedipus Tyrannus* at the Hope Waddell Training Institute, Calabar in 1963, and Aristophanes' *Peace* and Anouilh's *Antigone* at the International School in Ibadan in 1969. James Gibbs (2007) has researched the corresponding history in Ghana, and notes in particular the productions at Adisadel, which we have already encountered as a school with a very strong classical tradition, abandoned in favour of Science only as late as the 1960s. While there is some confusion over the productions of the earliest date, an *Antigone* is recorded for 1932 and 1933,[59] which greatly moved the audience, an *Agamemnon* in 1936, and in 1944–5 an *Alcestis*, with narratives in English but choruses in Greek (Amissah 1980: 8–9). This last may have been witnessed by the dramatist Efua Sutherland, then a pupil at St Monica's School (Gibbs 2007: 62) (Figure 4.1). Certainly Sutherland went on, when teaching at a training college at Asante-Mampong, to produce *Medea*, *Antigone* and *Alcestis* (July 2007: 160). We have already seen the multilingual drama about Julius Caesar at Achimota, and at Mfantsipim, an *Antigone* was performed by the staff in 1956 (*Mfantsipim Magazine,* Bu Bir 1955, Adow Bir 1956: 27), and a *Medea* by visiting students from Florida in 1958 (*Mfantsipim Magazine,* Eso Bir and Bu Bir 1958: 29). The dramatic activity at the new universities, then, was perhaps driven by theatrical tradition in the schools as well as by the university students' desire to develop their own new cultural forms.

By the early 1980s, as reported by Mabel Segun, even Greek drama had been 'decolonized' at Ibadan, with dancing and drumming as part of the

A scene from "Alcestes" — a Greek play staged by the school in 1944/45.

Figure 4.1 'Alcestis' at Adisadel, Ghana, 1944. Reproduced with permission from G. Maclean Amissah, *Reminiscences of Adisadel* (Accra: Afram Publications, 1980).

performances (2000: 412).[60] Even before that, the interpenetration of African and classical traditions had produced the modern canon of West African adaptations of Greek drama, including *Song* of a *Goat* by John Pepper Clark, *Edufa* by Efua Sutherland (1962), *The Gods are Not to Blame* by Ola Rotimi (1968), *The Bacchae of Euripides* by Wole Soyinka (1973). More recently these have been joined by *Tegonni* and *The Women of Owu* by Femi Òsófisan.[61] In the twenty-first century this group of plays has generated considerable scholarly interest and theatrical activity; the dramas have become a recognized dimension of the 'classical tradition' themselves, testimony to the fructifying power of the African relationship to the classics. With an increasing scholarly awareness of the postcolonial context, too, the plays are understood to signify not only within the 'classical tradition' but also as part of the prolonged African response to European imperial culture and politics. Marked by the complexities of those relations, the plays also demonstrate the immense creativity unleashed by independence, perhaps even allowing Greece to play the non-colonial role that Mazrui suggests.

I have been privileged to write on these plays myself (Goff 2005, Goff and Simpson 2007), and the present project, growing out of those earlier writings, allows me to site them within yet another history, the long and difficult career of classics in the institutions of British West Africa. Despite the efflorescence of drama, however, it is hard to come to an entirely favourable judgement on that career. So many contradictions attended it, from the early nineteenth century through to independence, that it is hardly surprising if West African modernity should eventually turn its back on the classics, as witnessed by the offerings in most contemporary secondary schools and universities. Agbodeka concludes his study of the University of Ghana with the judgement that 'In most West African countries, Classics has lost the battle against modernity' (1998: 261). Greenwood 2010 (8–9, 108–11) and Lambert 2011: 125–32 remark a similar loss of ground for classical education in societies – the Caribbean and South Africa – which have emerged or are emerging into a very different kind of politics and political culture from the former white dominance.

Yet in fact, Agbodeka goes on to show that the Department of Classics at Legon took a strategic decision to teach the ancient world in translation, thereby 'adapting' to local conditions in exactly the same way as has enabled the discipline to negotiate modernity at so many other Anglophone institutions throughout the world. At the time of writing, in 2012, Departments of Classics or Philosophy and Classics persist at Ibadan, Cape Coast, Legon and Fourah Bay, maintaining a 'classical tradition' in the face of contemporary cultural, political and financial obstacles almost as pernicious as the history of European dominance.[62] Such persistence testifies to the unique history of classics in West Africa.

To have loved and lost: 'The Devil at Yolahun Bridge'

Joseph Appiah was visited by a ghost whose advice assisted him in parlaying his classical education into a nationalist career. I end this study with a very different apparition, the spirit which closes Abioseh Nicol's short story about a series of awkward colonial encounters. Written in 1951 while the author was a medical student, the story won a prize in the 1952 Margaret Wrong competition and was printed in *Blackwood's Magazine* in 1953, and it remains the most famous, as well as the first, of Nicol's stories. After publication in Blackwood's, it appeared again as one of *Two African Tales*, published by Cambridge University Press in 1965, and has since been anthologized.[63] Yet between 1953 and 1965, the story acquired an entirely new first half, which connects to the classical tradition in a number of different ways. The first, shorter version of the story included a discussion of Roman Britain, but the later includes a whole history of a particular classical text, plus discussion of the classical education of both Europeans and Africans. The new first half also contains several new encounters between Europeans and Africans, and one commentator suggests that the story was 'meant to be the opening chapter of a novel that was unfortunately never completed, as the writer has since been mainly engaged in medical and educational activities' (Palmer 1986: 849). Gérard elsewhere claims that the modifications were made without the consent of the author (1984: 169). In the absence of definitive information on these questions, I shall simply discuss the short story in its later, more classically inflected form. Quotations are drawn from Nicol 1972, which reprints the 1965 version.

Abioseh Nicol (1924–94) was the pen-name of Davidson Nicol, a Sierra Leonean who, as well as writing several well-known short stories, was a highly qualified doctor and served as first Sierra Leonean Principal of Fourah Bay College, Vice-Chancellor of the University of Sierra Leone, and Sierra Leonean Ambassador to the United Kingdom. He was also the first African to become a fellow of a Cambridge college (Palmer 1986: 847). Although he was not a classicist, he was well equipped to draw on the classical repertoire and deploy it to his own discursive ends, but none of his subsequent stories, to my knowledge, uses any classical references. 'The Devil at Yolahun Bridge' is fulsomely praised in many sources for its penetration and wit; as late as 1971 Nicol was being acclaimed as 'in the very forefront of African short story writers' (Palmer 1986: 849). Critics all recognize the skill with which the story exposes 'the overlapping spheres of understanding and misunderstanding' among European and African members of the colonial administration (Palmer 1986: 849). To date, however, most criticism has concentrated on the second half, and the classical references in the first half have drawn no attention.

The second half of the story, 180–94, concerns only three characters: two Europeans, Sanderson and Hounslow, and the African engineer Olayemi Jones (called Hughes in the 1953 version). Sanderson is the Acting District Officer in a region of Kissiland, Sierra Leone, and Hounslow the son of a Kenya settler who is now the agent of a large firm (181). But the first half of the story, while organized around Sanderson, is populated by a large cast of Europeans and

Africans, and although Sanderson remains the main character, the narrative is focalized by a series of different figures, each motivated by his or her own fears and desires. An array of different subjectivities is thus unfolded for the reader, and the ease with which the reader gains access to their private thoughts contrasts to the awkward, halting contacts that characterize the various colonial encounters themselves. The narrative thus lays claim to a generous understanding of and even a compassion for its numerous characters, while demonstrating that they have little or none for each other.

How the classical references work within this overall scheme is by providing a paradigm of misunderstanding, via texts which cannot be read or understood, or conversely texts which are so well known and familiar that they dictate behaviour which is unthinking. The classical references thus serve as an indictment of British imperialism, yet at moments they also evoke a sense of loss and nostalgia which works to counter any easy triumphalism about African independence.

The classical references of the story form a persistent backdrop or counterpoint to the other events of the first half, which is ostensibly made up of a series of vignettes in the life of the Acting DO. An actual classical text features early on, found by Sanderson in his trunk when he is searching for a different book, and never precisely identified. Why Sanderson is looking for a book is because he thinks it will help him compile his annual report, which is proving troublesome; Sanderson has already spent some time wondering whether to write a new kind of report or to follow the practice of his predecessor, Macpherson. He has even wondered if he could simply send in blank sheets or reports from 1923 (164)[64] – would anyone notice? The classical text thus potentially takes its place among other predictable and meaningless narratives, and the colonial civil service is already seen to be something of a game, an autotelic exercise with arcane rules that govern white as well as black.

The classical text also exposes the lack of integrity in relations between white and black, because Sanderson is on the point of throwing the book at a cockroach when he is surprised by the entry of his servant Ahmed, and quickly pretends to be reading it instead (165). The gesture of pretending to read is perhaps symptomatic of all the characters, who repeatedly either face texts that they cannot negotiate, or else manipulate texts to deceive others; the story's characters are rarely honest with each other or themselves, and conversely they often read from texts rather than speaking naturally. After the encounter with Ahmed, when Sanderson does turn properly to read the book he had picked up, he discovers that it is an 'old classical text' and furthermore that it bears the flyleaf inscription, 'Balliol, Michaelmas 1938'. The text then becomes a portal to a series of memories of pre-war Oxford and his own very desultory career there. He had read Classics even though it seemed 'faintly absurd' (166), and his choice had been dictated by his uncle, because Sanderson could not make up his mind to a career, and Classics would not 'commit' him to anything. Having done very little work, although always promising himself that he would soon get started on it, he scraped through his degree only because of his previous sixth form training. Yet he had noticed that the classics subsequently gave him an 'aura' of being 'well-educated', which was emphatically 'undeserved' (166). Sanderson's university career had thus been founded on various forms of blindness and self-deception, from which he was rescued by the war. The evocative power of the classical text, conjuring up Oxford, is contrasted with the implicit indictment of the system that produces the colonial administrators.

Yet Sanderson becomes a not entirely unsympathetic figure, as we learn about how he was orphaned at a young age, and about how socially awkward he was at tea with his Tutor's family in Oxford. He is, moreover, aware that this life at Oxford could be cast as 'wasted' and 'useless' (167), and only during the war, in North Africa, does he connect with it. With a fellow-officer, Higgins, he had gone to visit some ruined Roman fortifications, which cast 'strange shadows' across the 'lovely desert' (167). Sanderson is able to explain that these are 'part of the line of fortifications built by the Emperor Severus in the third century Anno Domini' (167), and to comment, appropriately if predictably, 'sic transit' (168). While Sanderson has some specific knowledge, Higgins has a more general view that takes in most kinds of antiquity; he simply wishes for a postcard to add to his girlfriend's collection of Stonehenge, Fountains Abbey, the British Museum, etc. (168). The men look at the ruin silently, 'each with his own private thoughts', (167) which in this case the narrative voice does not divulge. Like Joe Appiah, Sanderson has the opportunity to meditate on the fall of empires in Africa, but in the context of the war in the desert, with a retreating army in front and large numbers surrendering (167), he is perhaps more likely to think of the fall of the Reich. The 'Ozymandias' quality of the 'crumbling bastions' in the sand makes them available for numerous reflections on loss and change.

The desert scene is the last of the memories prompted by the accidental encounter with the classical text, but the book itself next moves to the African officials in Sanderson's office. Here, John Momoh, the junior clerk, and Mr Alfred Thomas, the older clerk, are locked in a secret drama whereby Thomas resents Sanderson's acting appointment, since he feels he could have acted in Macpherson's place – not realizing, perhaps, the extent of colonial racial prejudice – and Momoh enjoys acting as 'agent provocateur'. Momoh shows Mr Thomas the 'Catholic prayer book', expressing wonder that Mr Sanderson is 'Roman', but Thomas recognizes it properly (169):

> 'This is Latin; this is what they call the classics. Amo, amavi, amatum, amare; first conjugation, 'to love', I love, I have loved, to have loved and lost, that sort of thing'. He looked through the pages with the hopeless air of a connoisseur examining an objet d'art which he had first rejected then returned to buy and found it sold. 'I could have gone to college if I had wanted to, but I wanted to get on. I was young then' he added reminiscently. His manner changed. 'Classics indeed, with those annual reports six weeks overdue. Some people have no idea of Her Majesty's time'.

The classics here seem to be aligned with loss and exclusion, with regret for a past not taken. Hence, perhaps, the mistake whereby 'to have loved and lost' becomes an element of the recitation of principal parts, where it does not usually belong; the dead language is made live by its sudden connection to Thomas's apparent regret for the lost 'objet d'art'.[65] The text also draws attention to the barrier between black and white whereby Sanderson has gone to college to get on, with mixed results, and Thomas has tried to get on by not going to college. The end of this scene repeats and inverts that between Sanderson and his servant, since Momoh is replacing the book when Sanderson comes in unexpectedly. Momoh pretends to have been looking for a file and grabs the nearest one in his confusion. The classical book is again posed against the texts of the colonial administration, as when Mr Thomas, at the end of his speech, contrasted the 'classics indeed' with the 'annual reports six weeks overdue'. Despite the classical text's evocative connections to the entire pre-war world of Oxford, then, and indeed to world history, African history and the personal history of Sanderson and Thomas, it is also part of the random relay of texts generated by the characters' tactical mendacity.

The following scene pairs the Acting DO with Father Horgan, in quest of an improved grant for his secondary school. At this school, Latin cannot be taught because of lack of funds (170), so the Father is pleased by the classical book on Sanderson's desk, as it seems to promise a generous attitude towards education. He pretends to engage Sanderson in a discussion about 'the benefits of teaching the ancient tongues to the African' inviting 'the advice of a lay, unprejudiced mind' (170), but he leaves no room for responses, instead answering his own question in terms of 'knowledge itself' and the origins of English, and finally turning the conversation round to the issue of subsidy. When Sanderson carries out the annual inspection, it turns into a hideous parody, in which the boys are seen to learn pointless facts by rote and then to misunderstand and misremember them. Sanderson's predecessor had always asked them a silly question to which the answer was 'a mathematical coincidence', and when Sanderson departs from tradition and 'wickedly' (172) asks about the meaning of Empire Day, he causes a 'cataclysm' (173) among unprepared boys and teachers alike. Only one boy can be found to 'faithfully repeat his lesson' (174) and it is telling that this boy is the only one who has not put his hand up to offer the erroneous answer of 'mathematical coincidence', and who instead looks down with 'a veiled look of mystery and a slight smile of superior knowledge' (173). He is clearly recognized as the 'best pupil in the class', well able to deliver himself of the rote-learned platitudes about Empire Day, but he maintains an attitude of ironic detachment about the whole proceedings – the conclusion offers itself that he is on the way to becoming that most dangerous of adversaries, the educated African. While the classics have been offered to us as an index of empire's ineptitude, in terms of Sanderson's Oxford education and the fall of Rome, the education at Father Horgan's non-classical school does not represent much of an advance; useless and outworn texts dominate and colonialism comes across as a corrupt game which traps the participants in collusion.

The final part of Sanderson's day is when he visits a market. Although there is no classical reference here, the story is still focused on issues of language, translation and text. Thus Sanderson is trying to practise his African language but is thwarted by his messenger, who speaks English in a bid to be promoted to interpreter (174). A woman talks about Sanderson to her child, not realizing that Sanderson can understand her (175), and the final encounter, between Sanderson and a market trader, is framed by the trader's grandiloquent hand-painted sign and the list of government control prices which he hides from his few literate customers. Within this relay of texts hidden or half-understood, the African characters each try to extract something from Sanderson, as representative of the empire, and he conversely tries to maintain his dignity and that of the colonial system. But all characters continue to conspire with the system's pretences, as when the trader presents himself as 'ex-serviceman' and Sanderson responds 'At ease', 'entering into the spirit of the thing . . . savouring the atmosphere of the British Legion, the regimental dinner, the reunion of good fellows' (176–7).

'The months wore on' (177) and Sanderson does not depart from tradition in the writing of his annual report, but instead, embraces 'continuity' in its formulations (178), and correspondingly addresses the local African Club on the topic of Roman Britain. Chosen to be uncontroversial, his talk, like much of the other writing and reading in this story, is a rehash of another talk given to an army educational course (178), but it nonetheless provokes a nationalist journalist, who accuses Sanderson of implying that Sierra Leone is as primitive as was Roman Britain (178). Even without the presence of the journalist at the Club, the topic would have afforded plenty of material for controversy, because of its regular invocation by nationalist intellectuals like Horton and De Graft Johnson. As it is, the journalist opens 'a folded piece of paper in his hand and harangued the meeting for five minutes on British Imperialism' (179). Sanderson is also put on the spot by another African, a 'retired schoolmaster' who argues about the dates of the Roman landings and questions whether Roman remains in Britain will be returned to their rightful owners, the Italians (178–9). When the meeting ends, the vote of thanks is moved by the 'young wife of a junior clerk', who, unlike almost everybody else in the story, speaks impromptu, and suggests that while some are interested in politics, the majority of the society focuses on 'more lasting matters' (179). The classics are called upon here to signify the transcendence of mundane matters like politics, but they have already been seen to be implicated in too many banal and undistinguished struggles. In fact the schoolmaster seconds the vote of thanks by reading out Latin quotations which he has 'copied out in his pocket notebook', so that the classical reference reverts to the type of the uselessly predictable text.

The second half of the story ostensibly abandons classics in favour of engineering and bridge-building, activities more practical than literary, and also endeavours to allow its three characters to extemporize their relationships rather than be bound by ancient scripts. While Sanderson has a momentary 'absurd desire' (180) to ask the members of the African Club back to his bungalow for a beer, he does indeed invite to dinner the African engineer Jones, who built the bridge at Yolahun, along with Hounslow the Kenya-born British agent. Part of the reason for this hospitality, however, is that Sanderson cannot bring himself to invite Jones to the European club. The ensuing scenes among the three ill-assorted men, brought together by the various needs of the imperial colony, are painful with suppressed resentments, anxieties and misjudgements, even though the men do also try to communicate and to negotiate ways through the minefields of race and official position. Since the narrative again focalizes each in turn, the reader is given ample access to their private fears and suspicions of each other, even as they try to overcome them.

The theme of the fall of empires resurfaces insofar as the two Europeans ask Jones about how Africans see their prospects, and talk themselves about their role in the future of Africa. Hounslow, the commercial agent, is already suffering the loss of his sense of belonging in Africa, but knows also that London is no longer his home; there he was pushed out of the way by a 'common' fellow when he was standing for the National Anthem at the end of a cinema show (188). Conversely, Jones was impressed by London when he studied there, and evokes the scene of the capital in a way that obviously pleases the other two (189). At the other end of the cultural spectrum from London is the bridge at Yolahun, which Jones himself built, complete with the tradition of an offering to placate the 'devil' alleged to preside there. The Europeans cannot bring themselves to tell him that the locals are still too apprehensive to use it.

Once the evening finishes, however, Jones and Hounslow separately make their way to Yolahun Bridge, Hounslow to test if it is indeed properly made, Jones to admire his own handiwork, and incidentally to prove to himself that he is not afraid of the 'water-spirit'. While they pursue their secret inspections, they are both startled by an impala which leaps into the middle of the road and is picked out by Hounslow's headlights. Concluding, as readers are invited to, that this is the source of the legendary devil, Hounslow drives away and Jones starts his walk back to the rest-house. But he must run, because it is raining; in the last line of the story, 'the rain had begun to fall in single heavy drops like the slow, quiet weeping of a woman proud, proud to distraction for an only son, yet vaguely afraid' (194). Even though one mystery has apparently been solved, the melancholy foreboding of the ending suggests that greater challenges remain. If the 'only son' is Jones, perhaps the 'woman' is a version of Mother Africa, and her fear for her son perhaps involves the difficulties of independence; yet if she is Mother Africa, is it not possible that many other sons both white and black will claim her? The ending precipitates the cosmic out of the quotidian, in the manner that often marks the rhythm of the short story, and after all the criss-crossing fields of force in the multiple subjectivities that the story has canvassed, it is not clear how the reader should grasp the final mystery. Although there are no specific classical references in the second half of the story, the notions of tradition and misreading persist, and Alfred Thomas's sense of nostalgia and loss seems to mark the ending.

'The Devil at Yolahun Bridge' seems an apposite text with which to conclude this study of the cultural politics of classics in the British colonies of West Africa. The story assembles various versions of the classics, including classics as part of subject-formation for English colonial administrators, classics within the context of missionary education, classics as part of the equipment of the educated African, and classics as bone of contention between colonizers and nationalists. It glancingly suggests classics as a humanist enterprise that might help to unify, and it also suggests classics as a discourse of obliteration and loss. When it leaves classics behind, as in the second half of the story, it finds no ready solution to hand.

Notes

1 On Lloyd Thompson see Ige 2007: 163–4.

2 For the statistics on numbers of secondary schools and secondary school students, see the Introduction. Ogunkoya 1979: 79–80 claims that alumni of St Andrews College, Oyo, founded nine secondary schools in the 1940s. We may judge of demand by the fact that over 2,000 boys applied for 30 places at the new Government College, Umuahuia, in 1948 (Taylor 1996: 206).

3 Cf. Moore-Gilbert 2009: 118 on the 'many postcolonial writings' which 'plot the formation of the individual protagonist in allegorical relation to the emergence of collective national aspirations to an independent identity'.

4 We can perhaps compare the experience of Austin Clarke entering the 'fourth form', as quoted in Greenwood 2010: 91.

5 We might compare the antics of Chinua Achebe's contemporaries at Government College Umuahuia, who apparently used to entice the Principal to repeat 'amabunt' so they could see his belly jiggle (Ezenwa-Ohaeto 1997: 25).

6 This is the title of Miescher 2005. Although there is a chapter on education, it does not extend to exposure to classics.

7 I have come across no explicit reference to homosexual or homoerotic activity in the sources consulted, although reference to 'immorality' might be imagined to include this as well as heterosexual transgressions. Aluko 1979 has a scene of boys getting up during the night to re-live the nocturnal gatherings of their villages. This is at first misinterpreted as 'immorality' but is eventually understood and condoned.

8 'puella' means 'girl', and the sentences are 'I love the girl' 'O good girl! Give me a rose'.

9 Latin is envisaged for girls by Gold Coast Methodists in 1943 (*Secondary Education for Girls* 1943: 11), Report of the Commission appointed by the Synod of the Methodist church of the Gold Coast.

10 When the nationalist Nnamdi Azikiwe's father gives him his life-savings so that he can go to the United States for his education, he invokes the myth of Jason and the Argonauts in quest of the Golden Fleece, which he read in school, and Zik answers in kind with his own classical knowledge. See Azikiwe 1970: 72–3. Zik also compares himself, yielding to his mother's entreaties not to go, to Coriolanus (1970: 61). Zik went on to study Latin among other subjects at Storer College, and to teach Ancient Philosophy and History, as well as other philosophies and histories including African, at Lincoln University.

11 Much comment on *Kossoh Town Boy* has concentrated on its representation of a particular social formation, often in rather dismissive terms. An early reviewer opined that 'it does not seem typical of the highly sophisticated and cultured urbanity that one usually associates with intellectual Krios' (S. Akanji, *Black Orpheus* 9 (1961) 66, quoted by Palmer 1986: 848). Its main significance has been held to be sociological, because of its 'unaffected picture of Freetown society in the early twenties' and its representation of the narrator's family as 'almost unbelievably Victorian' (Palmer 1986: 848). More recently, there have been proper assessments of its contribution to a discourse of cultural and linguistic hybridity (Dixon-Fyle and Cole 2006: 239).

12 We may recall the article in *Mfantsipim Magazine* about kinship between Latin and African languages.

13 My colleague Dr Matthew Nicholls points out that these verbs, 'I seize' and 'I drive or beat', are a coincidence, if not a joke.

14 Compare the ultimatum at Wesley College Ibadan, discussed in Chapter 3.

15 The son, known often as Anthony Appiah, has of course turned out to be a philosopher.

16 Appiah 1990: 15–18 discusses, from the other side of the linguistic divide, the consequences of the youthful Appiah writing the sentence 'The chief commissioner has no follicles on the cutaneous apex of his cranial structure' instead of 'The

chief commissioner is bald'. When in the course of subsequent proceedings he is called upon to recite a Psalm, he offers 'Deity is my pastor; I shall not be indigent; Yea, though I perambulate the abyss of the sepulchral dormitories, I shall not be perturbed by any appalling catastrophe ...' While his teachers are dismayed by this display, his classmates are delighted that his English has 'defied even the whiteman'. We might compare this incident with Blyden's encounter with 'Johnsonian' English; see on the Appiah passage also Newell 2002: 205.

17 See e.g. 1990: 259–655 and 311–13. In the interests of full disclosure I should note that Appiah took the Bible and a volume of Shakespeare, not any classical text, on his first spell in prison. When he asked for his Shakespeare, however, 'the officer replied that in the first place reading was not allowed; in the second place, even if it were allowed, Shakespeare would not be permitted as he was a known writer of seditious literature and was, in fact, a wanted man by the British government'. When Appiah protested that he died in 1616, the guard replied 'Ah, you see, you no know what is happen for outside' (1990: 258–9).

18 Compare 233, 'Was this honor [the necessity to continue as President of WASU] the reward for excellence assigned to the good as propounded by Aristotle? Hmmm!'

19 On Appiah's cosmopolitanism, and on other important dimensions of this text, see Caine 2010.

20 See further Gates 1990 on the audience of the text.

21 Greenwood 2010: 101 suggests that C. L. R. James too combines a rebellion against colonial authority, aided by his use of classical antiquity, with an identification with the 'masses'.

22 Bartels 2003: 68–72 queries much of Appiah's account of the strike, but agrees that its impetus derived partly from anti-colonial sentiment.

23 As we shall see below, the proper authorities also include the inhabitants of the Ghanaian spirit world.

24 Lockhart does indeed come over, in his writings and the writings of others, as thoroughly anti-British, even though he was apparently serving the empire as head of a colonial school.

25 Cf. Greenwood 2010: 94 on the Barbadian writer Austin Clarke's youthful love of Hannibal, even though he was not aware that Hannibal was African.

26 In *Aeneid* Book 2, for instance, the dead Hector appears to Aeneas and helps to motivate him towards his own destiny. I am indebted to Stephen Harrison for this observation.

27 Commentators like Ayandele 1974: 2, Tibenderana 2003: 120–1 and Lulat 2005: 17 concur in viewing this development as a largely cynical plan to extend colonial power into the neo-colonial era.

28 See e.g. Johnson 1998 and Banham et al. 2002. On the roles of English literature in colonial India, see Viswanathan 1989 and Seth 2007.

29 For a detailed account of the negotiations prior to and consequent on the two Elliot Reports, especially the pressure from African sources, see Nwauwa 1997.

30 Later on, R. J. Mason compared the military education of the Spartans to that of the Zulu Chaka (1959: 2).

31 See also the preliminary discussion in Goff and Simpson 2007: 46.

32 Despite the three African members, the use of 'we' here suggests that the Report's voice is largely European.

33 I would not press it, but I suspect that the wobble in the tenses, between 'would be' and 'will find', might speak to the cultural difficulty of the identifications that the Elliot Report is here drawing.

34 On the 'Black Aegean' see Goff and Simpson 2007.

35 See also on this quotation the Introduction.

36 On Mayhew, see Whitehead 2003: 149–71.

37 On the role of London University exams in West African education, see Omolewa 1979 and 1980.

38 Professor Banjo is Emeritus Professor of English and former Vice-Chancellor of the University of Ibadan.

39 Osinulu 2001 gives further insights into the context of classics in his autobiography. He narrates that at Yaba he was enrolled by an Education Officer, Randolph Hogarth, in a course for secondary school teachers, but decided to do a degree in Classics instead, causing Hogarth to try to block his career; his degree was funded by a Classics scholarship awarded by Chief Obafemi Awolowo's organization Egbe Omo Oduduwa (2001: 105–6). The publisher's blurb attributes the author's fine English to his classical training. I am indebted to Kunbi Olasope for this reference; the Education Officer is the Randolph Hogarth of Hogarth 1944 in the bibliography.

40 By contrast, the University College of the West Indies did not offer a Classics degree, even though it included a department of Classics. See Greenwood 2010: 79. Classics in the Caribbean secondary schools was well established, as Greenwood shows.

41 Mabogunje was Professor and Head of Geography at the University of Ibadan. In reference to Classics, Ashby 1966: 239 notes that one welcome adaptation was to offer a course in 'Roman North Africa 146 BC to 337 AD'. He further points out that some claim that African studies can be diffused throughout the curriculum, because even Latin and Greek can be taught with an African bias. He is not necessarily advocating the radical moves of Mazrui et al. noticed in the Introduction.

42 Mabel Segun worked at the institute for African Studies and at UNESCO.

43 The essay, 'Ancient Greece in African Thought', collected in *Political Values and the Educated Class in Africa*, is based on an inaugural lecture given in 1966.

44 'Inaugural address to the first ordinary convocation, 2 December, 1950', University College of the Gold Coast, Notices (1950–1) no. 5.

45 On this point, coordinating historical with geographical definitions, see now Young 2011: 183–4.

46 Mills 2006 discusses the ambivalence of some similar developments at Makerere under the heading of 'mimesis'.

47 Murray had earlier identified the importance of a 'historical feeling' in generating a 'university feeling' (1929: 117). Kwame Nkrumah abolished Latin graces as well as other colonial practices when he founded the Nkrumah University of Science and Technology (Ajayi et al. 1996: 88).

48 In 1973 an African educator remarks, from the opposite side of the debate, that it is 'ludicrous to see African universities adorned by foreign coasts of arms under Latin adages as if the continent is devoid of folk sayings' (Ki-Zerba 1973: 25). He also notes that a decision was taken in the 1970s explicitly to downgrade Latin and Greek (1973: 24).

49 Lati Hyde-Forster went on to become the first African woman Principal of the Annie Walsh School in Freetown.

50 Adetowun Ogunsheye is retired Professor of Library Science.

51 Thompson 1966: 54 claims that his success was published in 1964 without specification of his subject, because official sources no longer wanted to encourage the study of classics.

52 John Ellah became a diplomat and politician.

53 We might compare the testimony of a student at the University College of the West Indies, in the 1950s, who demanded of her professor 'Look, I have got to change. I don't know how you are going to do it, sir, but I have to do [West Indian] history and I want to drop Latin' (quoted in Greenwood 2010: 79).

54 Eruvbetine et al. praise the way in which the department 'related classical issues to indigenous cultures', and the stress on critical thought which (perhaps paradoxically) promoted Christian values as well as classical (2003: 23–3). I am again indebted to Kunbi Olasope for this reference.

55 The publication of the Classical Association of Nigeria was *Nigeria and the Classics* up until 1971, when it became *Museum Africum*.

56 George Akabogu was Senior Latin Master at Government College Umuahuia. See further Ige 2007: 165. On these comparative relations between empires see also Vasunia 2005.

57 The specificity of this prescription for Nigeria might remind us of Blyden's analysis of classical literature as a resource particularly positive for Africans.

58 July 1987: 64 suggests that the two *Antigones* were put on in one evening, but he gives no source. Arnold Bradshaw had some criticisms of the productions; see the Appendix to Ferguson ed. 1958: 75.

59 See Gibbs 2007: 61 on the contradictory information about dates in the sources. The Gold Coast Education Report for 1933 agrees with Gibbs' conclusion. Amissah (1980: 8–9, 39) claims that the *Antigone* was produced on the occasion of the school's Silver Jubilee, in 1934–5, and that it later toured to Sekondi and Kumasi.

60 Segun finds that African audiences do not always distinguish between tragedy and comedy; cf. Nwoga 2002: 41 on how 'A group of Nigerian students watching a production of Antigone laughed in the last scene when the grief-stricken Creon came on stage weeping over his dear son'. Nwoga considers that the laughter 'has to do with the irony of fate, with the sense of relief at the re-establishment of order, with the bringing into line of one who had dared to claim a new morality to himself' and thus can trace further connections between Greek and West African theatrical priorities. Evans 1996: 71 notes Nigerians laughing at *Hamlet* too.

61 On these and related adaptations see Wetmore 2002 and 2003, Budelmann 2005, Goff 2005, Hardwick 2007, 2006, 2005, and 2004, Goff and Simpson 2007, van Weyenberg 2010. I omit here the Greek tragedies of South Africa, on which see Lambert 2011, with bibliography.

62 See Ige 2007 for accounts of classicists trained at Ibadan in the 1960s.

63 See e.g. Edris Makward and Leslie Lacy ed. *Contemporary African Literature* (New York: Random House, 1972).

64 In the 1953 version, the date of the imaginary report was 1936.

65 Greenwood 2010: Chapter Three examines a series of classical 'mistranslations' in Caribbean literature, which she construes as deliberate reinterpretations, with particular resonances within the colonial context. Chapter Two, on classical education, ends with a sense of regret for its loss that might be relevant to Mr Thomas's scene.

Bibliography

Abarry, Abu Shardow (1991) 'The Significance of Names in Ghanaian Drama', *Journal of Black Studies* 22: 157–67.

Abiri, John O. O. (1973) 'The Making of the University of Ibadan 1957–62', 49–68 in Ajayi and Tamuno (eds).

Achebe, Chinua (1989) 'Politics and Politicians of Language in African Literature', in Doug Killam (ed.), *FILLM Proceedings* (Ontario: University of Guelph).

Achimota College (1932) *Report of the Committee Appointed in 1932 by the Governor of the Gold Coast Colony to Inspect the Prince of Wales College and School, Achimota* (London: Government of the Gold Coast).

— (1938) *Report of the Committee Appointed in 1938 by the Governor of the Gold Coast Colony to Inspect the Prince of Wales College and School, Achimota* (London: Government of the Gold Coast).

Addae, Stephen (2004) *The Gold Coast and Achimota in the Second World War* (Accra, Ghana: Sedco).

Adderley, Charles (1865) *Report from the Select Committee on Africa* (Western Coast) (London: HMSO).

Adebiyi, Bayo (1969) *The Beloved Bishop: the life of Bishop A. B. Akinyele* (Ibadan: Daystar Press).

Agbeti, J. Kofi (1980) *West African Church History* (Leiden: E. J. Brill).

Agbodeka, Francis (1977) *Achimota in the National Setting: a unique educational experiment in West Africa* (Accra: Afram Publications).

— (1998) *A History of University of Ghana: half a century of higher education (1948–1998)* (Accra: Woeli Publishing Service).

Ajayi, J. F. Ade (1961) 'Nineteenth Century Origins of Nigerian Nationalism', *Journal of the Historical Society of Nigeria* 2: 196–211.

— (1965) *Christian Missions in Nigeria 1841–1890: the making of a new elite* (London: Longmans).

— (1970) 'Introduction' to Crowther 1970.

— (1998) *Africa in the Nineteenth Century until the 1880s* (London: James Currey).

— (2001) *A Patriot to the Core: Bishop Ajayi Crowther* (Ibadan: Spectrum Books).

Ajayi, J. F. Ade and Tekena N. Tamuno (1973) *The University of Ibadan 1948–73* (Ibadan: Ibadan University Press).

Ajayi, J. F. Ade, Lameck K. H. Goma and G. Ampah Johnson (1996) *The African Experience of Higher Education* (Accra: The Association of African Universities).

Ajibola, J. O. (1985) 'Life at Wesley College', 67–73 in Wesley College Old Students' Association (ed.).

Akabogu, George (1958) 'The Teaching of Latin in Nigerian Schools', 56–64 in Ferguson (ed.).

Allman, Jean (2004) *Fashioning Africa: power and the politics of dress* (Bloomington, IN: Indiana University Press).

Aluko, T. M. (1979) *Built on the Rock: Government College, Ibadan* (Ibadan: Heinemann Educational Books).

Amissah, George Maclean (1980) *Reminiscences of Adisadel* (Accra: Afram Publications).

Anderson, Sir G. W. (1853) 'Ceylon' 299–326 in The reports made for the year 1852 to the Secretary of State having the Department of the Colonies; in continuation of the reports annually made by the governors of the British colonies, with a view to exhibit generally the past and present state of Her Majesty's colonial possessions. Transmitted with the blue books for the year 1852 (1693) (London: HMSO).

Andrews-Ayeh, E. F. (1937) *Tete hellafo anansesem*. A Twi translation of Kingsley's 'Heroes'. Contents: Perseus – Argonautfo – Teseus. Ill. by H. J. Ford. By E. F. Andrews-Ayeh, house master and Twi master at Adisadel College. With a foreword by the headmaster of Adisadel. Published with the approval of the Education Department of the Gold Coast (London: Longmans, Green and Co., and Accra: Scottish Mission Book Depot).

Appiah, Joseph (1990) *Joe Appiah: autobiography of an African patriot* (New York: Praeger).

Arnold, David (2004) 'Deathscapes', *Nineteenth Century Contexts* 26:4.

Ashby, Eric (1966) *Universities: British, Indian, African: a study in the ecology of higher education* (London: Weidenfeld and Nicolson).

Awolowo, Obafemi (1960) *Awo: the autobiography of Chief Obafemi Awolowo* (Cambridge: Cambridge University Press).

Ayandele, E. A. (1966) *The Missionary Impact on Modern Nigeria, 1842–1914* (New York: Humanities Press).

— (1970) *Holy Johnson: pioneer of African nationalism, 1836–1917* (London: Frank Cass).

— (1971) 'James Africanus Beale Horton, 1835–1883: Prophet of Modernization in West Africa', Review of *West African Countries and Peoples. African Historical Studies* 4.3: 691–707.

— (1974) *The Educated Elite in the Nigerian Society* (Ibadan: Ibadan University Press).

— (1979a) *African Historical Studies* (London: Frank Cass).

— (1979b) 'The Coming of Western Education to Africa', 75–106 in Ayandele 1979a.

— (1979c) 'Edward Wilmot Blyden 1832–1912: The Myth and the Man', 196–210 in Ayandele 1979a.

Azikiwe, Nnamdi (1934) 'How Shall We Educate the African?' *Journal of the Royal African Society* 33: 143–51.

— (1970) *My Odyssey* (London: C. Hurst and Co.).

Bacchus, M. Kazim (1994) *Education as and for Legitimacy: developments in West Indian Education between 1846 and 1895* (Waterloo, ON: Wilfrid Laurier University Press).

Baku, Kofi (1991) 'Kobina Sekyi of Ghana: An Annotated Bibliography of His Writings', *The International Journal of African Historical Studies* 24.2: 369–81.

Banham, Martin, Roshni Mooneeram and Jane Plastow (2002) 'Shakespeare and Africa', in Stanley Wells and Sarah Stanton (eds), *The Cambridge Companion to Shakespeare on Stage* (Cambridge: Cambridge University Press).

Banjo, Ayo (2000) 'Fifty Years of the Humanities', 23–34 in Mojuetan (ed.).

Barber, Karin (ed.) (2006) *Africa's Hidden Histories: everyday literacy and making the self* (Bloomington, IN: Indiana University Press).

— (2006a) 'Writing, Genre, and a Schoolmaster's Inventions in the Yoruba Provinces', 383–415 in Barber (ed.).

Bartels, F. L. (1965) *The Roots of Ghana Methodism* (Cambridge: Cambridge University Press).

— (2003) *The Persistence of Paradox* (Accra: Ghana Universities Press).

Bassey, Magnus O. (1991) 'Missionary Rivalry and Educational Expansion in Southern Nigeria, 1885–1932', *The Journal of Negro Education*, 60.1: 36–46.

— (1999a) *Missionary Rivalry and Educational Expansion in Nigeria, 1885–1945* (Lewiston, NY; Lampeter: Edwin Mellen Press).

— (1999b) *Western Education and Political Domination in Africa* (Westport, CT: Bergin and Garvey).

Berman, Edward H. (1971) 'American Influence on African Education: The Role of the Phelps-Stokes Fund's Education Commissions', *Comparative Education Review* 15.2: 132–45.

— (1974) 'African Responses to Christian Mission Education', *African Studies Review* 17.3: 527–40.

Bernal, Martin (1987) *Black Athena: Afro-Asiatic Roots of Classical Civilisation. Volume 1: the fabrication of Ancient Greece 1785–1985* (Rutgers: Rutgers University Press).

Bhabha, Homi (2004) [1994] *The Location of Culture* (London: Routledge).

Bishop of North Victoria Nyanza (1905) 'Education in Uganda' 183–99 in *Special Reports on Educational Subjects. Volume 13.* Educational systems of the chief Crown colonies and possessions of the British Empire, including reports on the training of native races. Part II. West Africa: Basutoland: Southern Rhodesia: East Africa Protectorate: Uganda: Mauritius: Seychelles (London: HMSO).

Bishop, Alan (2006) 'Western Mathematics: The Secret Weapon of Cultural Imperialism', 80–88 in Bill Ashcroft, Gareth Griffiths and Helen Tiffin (eds), *The Postcolonial Studies Reader*. 2nd edn (Abingdon: Routledge).

Blyden, Edward Wilmot (1865) 'Our Origin, Dangers, and Duties', *The Annual Address to the Mayor and Common Council of the City of Monrovia* (New York: John A. Gray and Green).

— (1969) [1908] *African Life and Customs* (London: African Publication Society).

— (1978) *Selected Letters of Edward Wilmot Blyden*. Edited and with introductions by Hollis R. Lynch (Millwood, NY: KTO Press).

— (1994) [1887] *Christianity, Islam and the Negro Race* (Baltimore, MD: Black Classic Press).

Boahen, A. Adu (1996) *Mfantsipim and the Making of Ghana* (Accra: Sandkof Education Publishers).

Bouche, Denise (1975) *L'enseignement dans les territoires francais de l'Afrique occidentale de 1817 a 1920* (Lille: Atelier Reproduction des Thèses).

Bourdieu, Pierre (1986) *Distinction: a social critique of the judgement of taste.* Tr. Richard Nice (London and New York: Routledge and Kegan Paul). First published Paris 1979, Les editions de minuit.

Bowlby, Rachel (2007) *Freudian Mythologies: Greek Tragedy and modern identities* (Oxford: Oxford University Press).

Bradshaw, Arnold (1977) 'The Development of the Humanities – Classics', 21–3 in Celebrations Committee (ed.).

Brown, G. N. (1964) 'British Educational Policy in West and Central Africa', *The Journal of Modern African Studies* 2: 365–77.

Brown, Judith M. and Wm Roger Louis (1999) *The Oxford History of the British Empire*. Vol IV. The Twentieth Century (Oxford: Oxford University Press).

Budelmann, Felix (2005) 'Greek Tragedies in West African Adaptations', 118–46 in Goff (ed.).

Burmah, Juliet (2009) 'That Scoundrel Suberu Takes the Stage for Adelugba'. *Punch* Friday 27 November.

Burroughs, Peter (1999) 'Imperial Institutions and the Government of Empire', 170–97 in Porter (ed.).

Buxton, Thomas Fowell (1840) *The African Slave Trade and its Remedy* (London: John Murray).

Caine, Barbara (2010) 'Writing Cosmopolitan Lives: Joseph and Kwame Anthony Appiah', *History Workshop Journal* 70: 153–71.

Campbell, Carl C. (1996) *The Young Colonials: a social history of education in Trinidad and Tobago, 1834–1939* (Kingston, Jamaica: University of the West Indies Press).

Carr, Henry (1905) 'The System of Education in Lagos', 31–72 in *Special Reports on Educational Subjects. Volume 13*. Educational systems of the chief Crown colonies and possessions of the British Empire, including reports on the training of native races. Part II. West Africa: Basutoland: Southern Rhodesia: East Africa Protectorate: Uganda: Mauritius: Seychelles. Cd. 2378 (London: HMSO).

Carretta, Vincent and Ty M. Reese (2010) *The Life and Letters of Philip Quaque, the First African Anglican Missionary* (Athens, GA: University of Georgia Press).

Carson Ryan, W. Jr. (1923) 'The Phelps-Stokes Fund and Educational Adaptation', *Journal of Social Forces* 1.3: 279–81.

Casely Hayford, Joseph Ephraim (1969) (1911) *Ethiopia Unbound: studies in race emancipation* (London: Frank Cass).

Castle, E. B. (1972) *Education for self-help: new strategies for developing countries* (London: Oxford University Press).

Celebrations Committee (ed.) (1977) *100 Years of University Education in Sierra Leone 1876–1976*. Celebrations Committee, Centenary of University Education 1876–1976 and Sesquicentennial of Fourah Bay College. 1827–1977 (Freetown: Government Printing).

Cell, John W. (1999) 'Colonial Rule', 232–54 in Brown and Louis (ed.).

Chafer, Tony (2002) *The End of Empire in French West Africa: France's successful decolonization?* (London: Berg Publishers).

Chanaiwa, David (1996) 'Colonial Education in Southern Africa', in Collins (ed.).

Churchill, Winston (1960) *My Early Life* (London: Oldhams).

Cole, Robert Wellesley (1960) *Kossoh Town Boy* (Cambridge: Cambridge University Press).

— (1988) *An Innocent in Britain* (London: Campbell Matthews).

Collins, Robert O. (1996) *Historical Problems of Imperial Africa* (Princeton: Markus Wiener Publishers).

Comaroff, Jean and John Lionel Comaroff (1991) *Of Revelation and Revolution: Christianity, colonialism and consciousness in South Africa* (Chicago: University of Chicago Press).

Conklin, Alice (1997) *A Mission to Civilize: the republican idea of empire in France and West Africa, 1895–1930* (Stanford, CA: Stanford University Press).

Cook, William and James Tatum (2010) *African American Writers and Classical Tradition* (Chicago: University of Chicago Press).

Cookey, S. J. S. (1980) 'Sir Hugh Clifford as Governor of Nigeria: An Evaluation', *African Affairs* 79: 531–47.

Corby, Richard A. (1981) 'Bo School and Its Graduates in Colonial Sierra Leone', *Canadian Journal of African Studies / Revue Canadienne des Études Africaines*, 15.2: 323–33.

— (1990) 'Educating Africans for Inferiority under British Rule: Bo School in Sierra Leone', *Comparative Education Review* 34.3: 314–49.

Crowder, Michael (1968) *West Africa under Colonial Rule* (London: Hutchinson).

Crowther, Samuel (1970) Journals of the Rev. James Frederick Schön and Mr. Samuel Crowther who, with the sanction of Her Majesty's Government, accompanied the expedition up the Niger in 1841 on behalf of the Church Missionary Society. With an Introduction by J. F. Ade Ajayi. Reprint of the 1842 edition (London: Frank Cass).

Curtis, Kenneth (1996) 'Indirect Rule', 569–70 in James Olson and Robert Shadle (eds), *Historical Dictionary of the British Empire* (Westport, CT: Greenwood Publishing).

Dalton, R. H. F. (1984) *Papers at Rhodes House, MSS. Afr. s. 1755 (7) (Box I).* The University of Oxford Development Records Project.

De Graft Johnson, Joseph William (1971) (1928) *Towards Nationhood in West Africa.* London: Frank Cass.

Desai, Gaurav (2001) *Subject to Colonialism: African self-fashioning and the colonial library* (Durham, NC: Duke University Press).

Dixon-Fyle, Mac and Gibril Raschid Cole (2006) *New Perspectives on the Sierra Leone Krio* (New York: Peter Lang).

Djangmah, J. S. (2008) 'Seventy Years of Excellent Secondary Education: The Success Story of Presbyterian Boys' Secondary School'. Odadee Class of 1975. Adapted for download from an article appearing in the June 2008 edition of the Daily Graphic. www.odadee75.org/downloads/70years.pdf

Dolphin, L. M. (1961) 'A foretaste of Latin Poetry', in Ferguson (ed.).

Driver, Felix (2001) *Geography Militant: cultures of exploration and empire* (Oxford and Cambridge, MA: Blackwell).

Echeruo, Michael (1974) 'Nnamdi Azikiwe and Nineteenth-century Nigerian Thought', *The Journal of Modern African Studies* 12.2: 245–63.

— (1977) *Victorian Lagos: aspects of nineteenth century Lagos life* (London: Macmillan).

— (1998) *Igbo-English Dictionary* (New Haven and London: Yale University Press).

Edgal, S. G. (1959) 'Why and How the Classics Should be Taught in West Africa', 1–13 in Ferguson (ed.).

Egerton, Walter (1908) *Colonial Reports – Annual. No. 583. Southern Nigeria.* Cmd. 3729–47 (London: HMSO).

Ellah, F. J. (1981) 'My Era at Ibadan', 12–56 in Tamuno (ed.).

Elliot, Walter (1945) *Report of the Commission on Higher Education in West Africa.* Session 1944–45. Cmd 6655 (London: HMSO).

Eruvbetine, A. E. Udu Yakubu and Harry Olufunwa (2003) *Gamaliel Onosode: a biography* (Lagos: CIBN Press).

Evans, Jean (1996) *Not Bad for a Foreigner* (London and Ibadan: Safari Books).

Ezenwa-Ohaeto (1997) *Chinua Achebe, a biography* (Oxford: James Murray).

Fafunwa, A. Babs (1974) *A History of Education in Nigeria* (London: George Allen & Unwin).

Fage, J. D., A. D. Roberts and Roland Oliver (1986) *The Cambridge History of Africa: from 1905 to 1940* (Cambridge: Cambridge University Press).

Fagunwa, D. O. (1939) 'Discipline', *Nigeria Magazine* 303–4.

Falade, S. Ade (1985) 'Wesley College: A Springboard to Greatness', 45–8 in Wesley College Old Students Association (ed.).

Falola, Toyin and A. D. Roberts (1999) 'West Africa', 515–29 in Brown and Louis (ed.).

Ferguson, John (ed.) (1958–66) *Nigeria and the Classics* (Ibadan: Ibadan University Press).

Ferguson, John (1981) 'Ibadan 1956–60', 109–26 in Tamuno (ed.).

Foreign Missionary, The, containing particular accounts of the foreign missions of the Presbyterian church, and selected articles from the missionary publications of other Protestant churches (1854) (New York: Mission House).

Foster, Philip (1965) *Education and Social Change in Ghana* (Chicago: University of Chicago Press).

Fradinger, Moira (2011) 'An Argentine Tradition', in Erin Mee and Helene P. Foley (eds), *Antigone on the Contemporary World Stage* (Oxford: Oxford University Press).

Fraser, Donald (1927) *The New Africa* (London: The Livingstone Press).

Fyfe, Christopher (1962) *A History of Sierra Leone* (London: Oxford University Press).

— (1972) *Africanus Horton 1835–1883, West African Scientist and Patriot* (New York: Oxford University Press).

Gandah, S. W. D. K. (2004) *The Silent Rebel* (Accra: Institute of African Studies, University of Ghana).

Gates, Henry (1990) 'Foreword', ix–xx in Appiah.

Gérard, Albert (1984) *Essais d'histoire littéraire africaine* (Paris: Agence de Coopération Culturelle et Technique).

— (1986) (ed.) *European Language Writing in Sub-Saharan Africa. Vol 2 of A Comparative History of Literatures in European Languages* (Akadémiai Kiadō Budapest: John Benjamins Publishing Company).

Gibbs, James (2007) 'Antigone and Her African Sisters', 54–71 in Hardwick and Gillespie.

— (2009) *Nkyin-Kyin: essays on the Ghanaian theatre* (Amsterdam: Rodopi).

Gikandi, Simon (1996) *Maps of Englishness: writing identity in the culture of colonialism* (New York, NY: Columbia University Press).

Gilroy, Paul (1993) *The Black Atlantic: modernity and double consciousness* (London: Verso).

Ginio, Ruth (2006) *French Colonialism Unmasked: the Vichy years in French West Africa* (Lincoln: University of Nebraska Press).

Goff, Barbara (2005) 'Dionysiac Triangles: The Politics of Culture in Wole Soyinka's *The Bacchae of Euripides*', in Victoria Pedrick and Steven Oberhelman (eds), *The Soul of Tragedy: essays on Ancient Athenian Drama and its contexts* (Chicago: University of Chicago Press).

— (ed.) (2005) *Classics and Colonialism* (London: Duckworth).

— (ed.) (2007) *Classical Subjects and Modern Subjectivities.* Special edition of *Helios* 34.2.

Goff, Barbara and Michael Simpson (2007) *Crossroads in the Black Aegean: Oedipus, Antigone, and dramas of the African Diaspora* (Oxford: Oxford University Press).

Goings, Kenneth W. and Eugene O'Connor (2011) 'Black Athena before *Black Athena*: The Teaching of Greek and Latin at Black Colleges and Universities during the Nineteenth Century', 90–105 in Orrells et al.

Graham, C. K. (1971) *The History of Education in Ghana: from the earliest times to the declaration of Independence* (London: Frank Cass).

Graham, Sonia (1966) *Government and Mission Education in Northern Nigeria 1900–1991, with Special Reference to the Work of Hanns Vischer* (Ibadan: Ibadan University Press).

Gramsci, Antonio (1998) *A Selection from the Prison Notebooks* (New York: Lawrence and Wishart).

Gray, Richard (1986) 'Christianity: Trusteeship and Education', 182–190 in Fage et al.

Greenwood, Emily (2005) '"We speak Latin in Trinidad": Uses of Classics in Caribbean Literature', 65–91 in Goff (ed.).

— (2009) 'Re-rooting the Classical Tradition: New Directions in Black Classicism', *Classical Receptions Journal* 1.1: 87–103.

— (2010) *Afro-Greeks: dialogues between Anglophone Caribbean literature and classics in the twentieth century* (Oxford: Oxford University Press).

Hair, P. E. H. (1967) 'Review of *Blyden of Liberia* by Edith Holden', *The Journal of Modern African Studies* 5.3: 433–5.

Haley, Shelley (1993) 'Black Feminist Thought', 23–44 in Nancy Rabinowitz and Amy Richlin (eds), *Feminist Theory and the Classics* (New York and London: Routledge).

Hall, Edith (2007) 'Subjects, Selves, Survivors', 125–59 in Goff (ed.).

— (ed.) (forthcoming) *Classics and Class* (London: Institute for Classical Studies).

Hall, Edith and Phiroze Vasunia (2010) *India, Greece, and Rome, 1757–2007* (London: Institute for Classical Studies).

Hall, Edith, F. Macintosh and A. Wrigley (eds) (2004) *Dionysus since '69: tragedy at the dawn of the millennium* (Oxford: Oxford University Press).

Hardwick, Lorna (2004) 'Greek Drama and Anti-colonialism: De-colonising Classics', 219–44 in Hall et al.

— (2005) 'Refiguring Classical Texts: Aspects of the Post-colonial Condition', 107–17 in Goff (ed.).

— (2006) 'Staging Sophocles in Post-colonial Contexts', 75–94 (Greek) and 258–76 (English) in N. Shiafkalis (ed.), *The Influence of Sophocles on Contemporary Theatre* (Nicosia: International Theatre Institute).

— (2007) 'Contests and Continuities in Classical Traditions: African Migrations in Greek Drama', 43–72 in Hilton and Gosling (eds).

Hardwick, Lorna and Carol Gillespie (eds) (2007) *Classics in Post-colonial Worlds* (Oxford: Oxford University Press).

Hargreaves, John (1985) 'British Policy and African Universities: Sierra Leone Revisited', *African Affairs* 84: 323–30.

Harloe, Katherine (2013) *Winckelmann and the Invention of Antiquity: history and aesthetics in the age of Altertumswissenschaft* (Oxford: Oxford University Press).

Harrison, Stephen (2007) 'Horace and the Construction of the English Victorian Gentleman', 207–22 in Goff (ed.).

Hegel, G. W. F. (1956) *The Philosophy of History*. Tr. J. Jibree (New York: Dover).

Hilton, John and Anne Gosling (eds) (2007) *Alma Parens Originalis?: the receptions of classical literature and thought in Africa, Europe, the United States, and Cuba* (Bern: Peter Lang).

Hogarth, Randal F. (1944) *Information Requested by the Elliott Commission. Mss. Brit. Emp. S. 351*. Rhodes House Papers. The University of Oxford Development Records Project.

Holden, Philip (2008) *Autobiography and Decolonization: modernity, masculinity, and the nation-state* (Madison, WI: University of Wisconsin Press).

Horton, James Africanus Beale (1969) (1868) *West African Countries and Peoples*. With an introduction by George Shepperson (Edinburgh: Edinburgh University Press).

— (1970) (1870) *Letters on the Political Condition of the Gold Coast* (London: Frank Cass).

Hunt, James (1864) 'On the Negro's Place in Nature', *Journal of the Anthropological Society of London* 2: xv–lvi.

Hyde-Forster, Lati (1977) 'Women at Fourah Bay College', 53–6 in Celebrations Committee (ed.).

Ige, Johnson O. (2007) 'Chief Bola Ige: The Making of a Classical Orator in Nigeria', 159–76 in Hilton and Gosling (eds).

Ijere, Dr Martin O. (ed.) (1965) *Essays in Honour of St Charles' College, Onitsha* (University of Nigeria Nsukka: University of Nigeria Press).

Jacobs, Sylvia (1996) 'James Emman Kwegyir Aggrey: An African Intellectual in the United States', 'Vindicating the Race: Contributions to African-American Intellectual History', *The Journal of Negro History* 81. 1/4: 47–61.

Jenkins, Ray (1994) 'William Ofori Atta, Nnamdi Azikiwe, J.B. Danquah and the "Grilling" of W.E.F. Ward of Achimota in 1935', *History in Africa* 21: 171–89.

Johnson, David (1998) 'From the Colonial to the Post-colonial: Shakespeare and Education in Africa', 218–34 in Ania Loomba and Martin Orkin (eds), *Post-colonial Shakespeares* (London: Routledge).

Johnson, Samuel (1921) *The History of the Yorubas: from the earliest times to the beginning of the British Protectorate* (London: George Routledge and Sons).

Jones, Revd Thomas Jesse Jones (1922) *Education in Africa: a study of West, South, and Equatorial Africa by the African Education Commission under the auspices of the Phelps-Stokes Fund and the Foreign Mission Societies of North American and Europe* (New York: Phelps-Stokes Fund).

— (1925) *Education in East Africa: a study of East, Central and South African by the second African Education Commission under the auspices of the Phelps-Stokes Fund, in cooperation with the International Education Board* (New York and London: Phelps-Stokes Fund).

Jones, Thomas Jesse (1917) *Negro Education* (Washington, DC: Government Printing Office).

July, Robert (1987) *An African Voice: the role of the humanities in African independence* (Durham, NC: Duke University Press).

— (2007) 'Interview with Efua Sutherland', in Anne V. Adams and Esi Sutherland-Addy (eds), *The Legacy of Efua Sutherland: pan-African cultural activism* (Banbury: Ayebia Clarke).

Keita, Maghan (2011) 'Believing in Ethiopians', 19–39 in Orrells et al.

Kelly, Gail Paradise (2000) *French Colonial Education: essays on Vietnam and West Africa* (New York: AMS).

Kemp, Dennis (1898) *Nine Years at the Gold Coast* (London: Macmillan and Co.).

Kendall, Diana (2008) *Sociology in our Times* (Belmont, CA: Cengage).

King, Kenneth (1969) 'James E. K. Aggrey: Collaborator, Nationalist, Pan-African', *Canadian Journal of African Studies / Revue Canadienne des Études Africaines* 3.3: 511–30.

Ki-Zerba, J. (1973) 'Africanization of the Higher Education Curriculum', 20–26 in T. M. Yesufu (ed.), *Creating the African University* (Oxford: Oxford University Press).

Know, Ronald (1939) *Let Dons Delight: being variations on a theme in an Oxford common room* (London: Sheed and Ward).

Koehl, Robert (1971) 'The Uses of the University: Past and Present in Nigerian Educational Culture, Part I', *Comparative Education Review* 15.2: 116–31 (*Colonialism and Education*).

Laird, Andrew (2006) *The Epic of America: an introduction to Rafael Landívar and the Rusticatio Mexicana* (London: Duckworth).

Lambert, Michael (2011) *The Classics and South African Identities* (London: Bristol Classical Press).

Lang, George (1986) 'Ghana and Nigeria' 108–115 in Gérard (ed.).

Langley, J. Ayo (1974) 'Introduction' to *Kobina Sekyi: The Blinkards* (London: Heinemann Educational).

Leonard, Miriam (2005) *Athens in Paris* (Oxford: Oxford University Press).

— (2010) *Derrida and Antiquity* (Oxford: Oxford University Press).

Lindfors, Bernth (1980) 'Nigerian High School Plays 1950–1972', *Kiabara* 3.1: 47–93.

Lugard, Frederick Lord (1926) *The Dual Mandate in British Tropical Africa* (Edinburgh: Blackwood).

— (1970) (1919) *Political Memoranda, Revision of Instructions to Political Officers on Subjects Chiefly Political and Administrative 1913–1918* (London: Frank Cass).

Lulat, Y. G-M. (2005) *A History of African Higher Education from Antiquity to the Present: a critical synthesis* (Westport, CT: Praeger).

Lynch, Hollis R. (1967) *Edward Wilmot Blyden: pan-Negro patriot 1832–1912* (Oxford: Oxford University Press).

Mabogunje, A. C. (1973) 'The Humanities and the Social Sciences', 186–90 in Ajayi and Tamuno (eds).

Macartney, W. M. (1949) *Dr Aggrey, Ambassador for Africa* (London: SCM Press).

Macaulay, Herbert (1924) *British West Africa: transfer or retirement Henry Carr must go* (Lagos: Kirsten Hall).

Macdonald, Norman (Governor of Sierra Leone) (1851) [1421] The reports made for the year 1850 to the Secretary of State having the Department of the Colonies; in continuation of the reports annually made by the governors of the British colonies, with a view to exhibit generally the past and present state of Her Majesty's colonial possessions. Transmitted with the blue books for the year 1850. Sierra Leone, 157–97 (London: HMSO).

— (1852) [1539] The reports made for the year 1851 to the Secretary of State having the Department of the Colonies; in continuation of the reports annually made by the governors of the British colonies, with a view to exhibit generally the past and present state of Her Majesty's colonial possessions. Transmitted with the blue books for the year 1851. Sierra Leone, 172–84 (London: HMSO).

MacMillan, W. M. (1934) 'The Importance of the Educated African', *Journal of the Royal African Society* 33: 137–42.

Malamud, Margaret (2011) 'Black Minerva: Antiquity in Antebellum African American History', 71–89 in Orrells et al.

Malouf, David (2009) *Ransom* (London: Abacus).

Manela, Erez (2007) *The Wilsonian Moment: self-determination and the international origins of anticolonial nationalism* (Oxford: Oxford University Press).

Manning, Patrick (1998) *Francophone Sub-Saharan Africa, 1880–1995* (Cambridge: Cambridge University Press).

Marshall, J. R. (1981) Papers at Rhodes House, *MSS Afr.x.1755 (20) Box IV*. The University of Oxford Development Records Project.

Martindale, C. C. (1949) 'Are Missions a Menace?, *Journal of the Royal African Society* 48: 128.

Mason, R. J. (1959) *British Education in Africa* (London: Oxford University Press).

Mayhew, A. (1938) *Education in the Colonial Empire* (London: Longmans, Green and Co).

Mazrui, Ali (1978) *Political Values and the Educated Class in Africa* (London: Heinemann).

McCaskie, T. C. (1999) 'Cultural Encounters: Britain and Africa in the Nineteenth Century', 665–89 in Porter (ed.).

Miescher, Stephan F. (2005) *Making Men in Ghana* (Bloomington, IN: Indiana University Press).

Miller, Madeleine (2011) *The Song of Achilles* (London: Bloomsbury).

Miller, Paul Allen (2007) *Postmodern Spiritual Practices: the reception of Plato and the construction of the subject in Lacan, Derrida, and Foucault* (Columbus, OH: Ohio State University Press).

Mills, David (2006) 'Life on the Hill: Students and the Social History of Makerere', *Africa* 76: 247–66.

Milverton, Lord (1956) 'The Realities of African Civilisation', *African Affairs* 55.220: 178–87.

Missionary Magazine, The (various dates) (Boston: American Baptist Missionary Union).

Missionary Register, The (1854) (London: Seeley, Jackson and Halliday, for the Church Missionary Society).

Mojuetan, B. A. (2000) *Ibadan at Fifty, 1948–1998: Nigeria's premier university in perspective* (Ibadan: Ibadan University Press).

Moore-Gilbert, Bart (2009) *Postcolonial Life-writing: culture, politics and self-representation* (London: Routledge).

Morley, Neville (2008) *Antiquity and Modernity* (New York: Wiley-Blackwell).

Moumouni, Abdou (1996) 'Education in Africa', 214–16 in Collins (ed.).
Mudimbe, V. Y. (1988) *The Invention of Africa* (Bloomington, IN: Indiana University Press).
— (1994) *The Idea of Africa* (Bloomington, IN and London: Indiana University Press and James Currey).
Mumford, W. Bryant and B. N. Parker (1937) 'Education in British African Dependencies', *Journal of the Royal African Society* 36.142: 17–32.
Murray, A. Victor (1929) *The School in the Bush: a critical study of the theory and practice of native education in Africa* (London: Longmans, Green and Co.).
— (1935) 'Education under Indirect Rule', *Journal of the Royal African Society* 34: 227–68.
Musgrove, F. (1952) 'What Sort of Facts?' *African Affairs* 51: 313–18.
Newbury, Colin (1999) 'Great Britain and the Partition of Africa 1870–1914', 625–50 in Porter (ed.).
Newell, Stephanie (2002) *Literary Culture in Colonial Ghana* (Manchester: Manchester University Press).
— (ed.) (2002) *Readings in African Popular Fiction* (Bloomington, IN and London: Indiana University Press and James Currey).
— (2006) *West African Literatures: ways of reading*. Oxford Studies in Postcolonial Literatures (Oxford: Oxford University Press).
— (2006a) 'Entering the Territory of Elites: Literary Activity in Colonial Ghana', 211–35 in Barber (ed.).
Nicol, Abioseh (1972) 'The Devil at Yolahun Bridge', 164–94 in Edris Makward and Leslie Lacy (eds), *Contemporary African Literatures* (New York: Random House).
Njoku, Scholastica Ibari (1969) *The Development of the British System of Education in Nigeria*, 1882–1929. PhD thesis, University of Oregon.
Nkrumah, Kwame (1973) *The Autobiography* (London: Panaf).
Nnadozie, Martin (1965) 'The Peculiarity of Our Times', 62–65 in Ijere (ed.).
Nuffield Foundation and the Colonial Office, The (1953) *African Education: a study of educational policy and practice in British tropical Africa* (London: Oxford University Press).
Nwauwa, Apollos O. (1997) *Imperialism, Academe and Nationalism: Britain and university education for Africans 1860–1960* (London: Frank Cass).
— (1999) 'Far Ahead of His Time: James Africanus Horton's Initiatives for a West African University and His Frustrations, 1862–1871' (James Africanus Horton: un précurseur malheureux du projet de création d'une université ouest-africaine, 1862–1871). *Cahiers d'Études Africaines*, 39. 153: 107–21.
Nwoga, Donatus (2002) 'Onitsha Market Literature', 37–50 in Newell (ed.).

Oduyoye, Modupe (1982) *The Planting of Christianity in Yorubaland 1842–88* (Ibadan: Daystar Press).

Ofusu-Appiah, L. H. (1975) *Joseph Ephraim Casely Hayford: the man of vision and faith.* The J. B. Danquah Memorial Lectures series 8 (Accra: Ghana Academy of Arts and Sciences).

Ogado, Donatus Emeka Onyemaobi (1988) *The Catholic Missionaries and the Liturgical Movement in Nigeria.* Vol. 1 (Rome: Verlag Bonifatius-Druckerei Paderborn).

Ogunbowale, P. O. (1970) *The Essentials of the Yoruba Language* (London: University of London Press).

Ogunkoya, T. O. (1979) *St Andrew's College Oyo 1896–1978* (Ibadan: Ibadan University Press).

Ogunlade, F. O. (1974) 'Education and Politics in Colonial Nigeria: The Case of King's College, Lagos (1906–1911)', *Journal of the Historical Society of Nigeria* 7.2: 325–44.

Ogunsheye, Adetowun (Banjo) (2000) 'Reminiscences of a Foundation Student/ Foundation Staff of a Department', 368–89 in Mojuetan (ed.).

Ohaegbulam, F. Ugboaja (2002) *West African Responses to European Imperialism in the Nineteenth and Twentieth Centuries* (Lanham, MD: University Press of America).

Oke, D. Olatunbosun (1968) *A Grammatical Study of the Yoruba Verb System.* PhD thesis, University of York.

Okudu, S. J. (1981) 'Diary of an Alumnus Registrar', 169–98 in Tamuno (ed.).

Olubummọ, Adegoke (1980) *In a Christian College* (Ibadan: Ibadan University Press).

Omolewa, Michael (1979) 'London University's Earliest Examinations in Nigeria, 1887–1931', *West African Journal of Education* 20: 2.

— (1980) 'The Promotion of London University Examinations in Nigeria, 1887–1951', *International Journal of African Historical Studies* 13.4: 651–71.

— (2006) 'Educating the "Native": A Study of the Education Adaptation Strategy in British Colonial Africa, 1910–1936', *The Journal of African-American History* 91.3: 267–87.

Orrells, Daniel, Gurminder K. Bhambra and Tessa Roynon (2011) *African Athena: new agendas* (Oxford: Oxford University Press).

Osei-Nyame, Kwadwo (1999) 'Pan-Africanist Ideology and the African Historical Novel of Self-Discovery: The Examples of Kobina Sekyi and J. E. Casely Hayford', *Journal of African Cultural Studies* 12.2: 137–53.

Osinulu, Samuel Adeoye (2001) *My First Eighty Years: a celebration of his graces* (Lagos: CSS Press).

Osuntokun, Akinjide (1984) *Chief S. Ladoke Akintola: his life and times* (London: Frank Cass).

Oswald, Alice (2011) *Memorial* (London: Faber and Faber).

Otegbeye, Tunji (1995) *A Humble Beginning* (Ibadan: Statics).

Owen, H. Burnard (1865) 'Missionary Successes and Negro Converts', *Journal of the Anthropological Society of London* 3: clxxxiv–ccxlvi.

Oxford, Lord Bishop (1850) (53) Report from the Select Committee of the House of Lords, appointed to consider the best means which Great Britain can adopt for the final extinction of the African slave trade; and to report thereon to the House; together with the minutes of evidence, and an appendix and index thereto. Session 1849 (London: HMSO).

Palmer, Eustace (1986) 'Sierra Leone and the Gambia', 844–62 in Albert Gérard (ed.) *European Language Writing in Sub-Saharan Africa*. Vol. 2 of *A Comparative History of Literatures in European Languages* (Akadémiai Kiadō Budapest: John Benjamins Publishing Company).

Paracka, Daniel (2003) *The Athens of West Africa* (London: Routledge).

Parkinson, Sonia (1998) 'Sir Hanns Vischer, Champion of African Cultures: a portrait'. *Education Research and Perspectives* 25.1: 1–45.

Parsons, Robert T. (1963) *The Churches and Ghana Society 1918–1955* (Leiden: Brill).

Pathmanathan, R. S. (1963) 'Producing a Latin Play in School', 29–37 in Ferguson (ed.).

Patton, Adell (1996) *Physicians, Colonial Racism, and Diaspora in West Africa* (Gainesville: University Press of Florida).

Peel, J. D. Y. (2000) *Religious Encounter and the Making of the Yoruba* (Bloomington, IN: Indiana University Press).

Perham, Margery (1960) *Lugard: the years of authority, 1898–1945* (London: Collins).

Pickard-Cambridge, A. W. (1940) 'The Place of Achimota in West African Education', *Journal of the Royal African Society* 39.155: 143–53.

Pine, Richard (1848) [1005] The reports made for the year 1847 to the Secretary of State having the Department of the Colonies: in continuation of the reports annually made by the governors of the British colonies, with a view to exhibit generally the past and present state of Her Majesty's colonial possessions, and of the United States of the Ionian Islands. Transmitted with the blue books for the year 1847 (London: HMSO).

Pormann, Peter (2006–7) 'The Arab "Cultural Awakening (Naha)", 1870–1950, and the Classical Tradition', *International Journal of the Classical Tradition* 13: 3–20.

— (2009) 'Classics and Islam: From Homer to al-Qā'ida', *International Journal of the Classical Tradition* 16: 197–233.

Porter, Andrew (1999) 'Introduction: Britain and the Empire in the Nineteenth Century', 1–30 in Porter (ed.).

— (ed.) (1999) *The Oxford History of the British Empire. Vol III The Nineteenth Century* (Oxford: Oxford University Press).

Pratt, Rev. Dr. W. E. Akinumi (1973) *Autobiography* (Sierra Leone: Government Printing Department).

Preston, H. (1981) 'My Era at Ibadan', 33–56 in Mojuetan (ed.).

Ranger, T. O. (1983) 'The Invention of Tradition in Colonial Africa', 211–62 in E. Hobsbawm and T. O. Ranger (eds), *The Invention of Tradition* (Cambridge: Cambridge University Press).

Rankine, Patrice (2006) *Ulysses in Black: Ralph Ellison, Classicism, and African American Literature* (Madison: University of Wisconsin Press).

Reade, Winwood (1865) 'Efforts of Missionaries among Savages', *Journal of the Anthropological Society* 3: clxiii–clxviii.

Report of the Education Department of the Government of the Gold Coast (various dates) (Accra: Government Printing Office).

Roberts, Andrew (1990) *The Colonial Moment in Africa* (Cambridge: Cambridge University Press).

Ronnick, Michele (1994) 'The Latin Quotations in the Correspondence of Edward Wilmot Blyden', *The Negro Educational Review* 46: 101–6.

— (2004) '12 Black Classicists', *Arion* 11: 85–102.

— (2004a) 'Early African-American Scholars in the Classics: A Photographic Essay', *Journal of Blacks in Higher Education* 43: 101–5.

— (2005) *William Sanders Scarborough, The Autobiography of William Sanders Scarborough: an American journey from slavery to scholarship* (Detroit: Wayne State University Press).

— (2006) *The Works of William Sanders Scarborough: Black classicist and race leader* (Oxford: Oxford University Press).

Ross, Robert (2008) *Clothing: a global history: or, The Imperialists' new clothes* (London: Polity).

Rowan, James and Henry Wellington (1827) *Report of the Commissioners of Inquiry into the State of the Colony of Sierra Leone*. 1826–27 (312) Sierra Leone (London: HMSO).

Roynon, Tessa (2011) 'The Africanness of Classicism in the Work of Toni Morrison' 381–97 in Orrells et al.

— (2013) *Toni Morrison and the Classical Tradition: transforming American culture* (Oxford: Oxford University Press).

Sandon, Viscount (1842) *Report from the Select Committee on the West Coast of Africa*. 551 (London: HMSO).

Sarbah, John Mensah (1968) [1897] *Fanti Customary Laws*. 3rd edn. With a new introduction by Hollis R. Lynch (London: Frank Cass).

— (1968a) (1906) *Fanti National Constitution*. 2nd edn. With a new introduction by Hollis R. Lynch (London: Frank Cass).

Sawyerr, Canon Harry (1977) 'The Development of Theology at Fourah Bay College', 1–7 in Celebrations Committee (ed.).

Schenk, Walter (1983) *Henry Venn, Missionary Statesman* (Maryknoll, NY: Orbis Books).

Scott, James (1990) *Domination and the Arts of Resistance: hidden transcripts* (New Haven: Yale University Press).

Secondary Education for Girls (1943) *Report of the Commission Appointed by the Synod of the Methodist Church of the Gold Coast in January 1943* (Accra: Methodist Church).

Segun, Mabel (2000) 'Reminiscences about Ibadan University', 398–416 in Mojuetan (ed.).

Sekyi, Kobina (1974) *The Blinkards* (London: Heinemann Educational).

— (1997) *The Blinkards and the Anglo-Fanti* (Accra, Ghana: Heinemann).

Selden, Daniel (1998) 'Aithiopika and Ethiopianism', 182–218 in R. Hunter (ed.), *Studies in Heliodorus* (Cambridge: Cambridge Philological Association).

Seth, Sanjay (2007) *Subject Lessons: the western education of colonial India* (Durham, NC: Duke University Press).

Shaloff, Stanley (1974) 'The Cape Coast Asafo Company Riot of 1932', *The International Journal of African Historical Studies* 7.4: 591–607.

Shepperson, George (1969) 'Introduction' to Horton 1969.

Shilliam, Robbie (2011) '"Ethiopia shall stretch forth her hands unto God": Garveyism, Rastafari, and Antiquity', 106–21 in Orrells et al.

Sibthorpe, A. B. C. (1970) (1906) *The History of Sierra Leone* (London: Frank Cass).

Simpson, Donald (1995) 'Aggrey and Fraser: A Unique Photograph', *African Affairs* 94.374: 87–9.

Sivonen, Seppo (1995) *White Collar or Hoe Handle? African Education under British Colonial Policy 1920–1945* (Helsinki: Suomen Historiallinen Seura).

Smith, Edwin (1932) *Aggrey of Africa* (London: Student Christian Movement Press).

Smith, Noel (1966) *The Presbyterian Church of Ghana, 1835–1960: a younger church in a changing society* (Accra: Ghana Universities Press).

Stephens, Susan A. and Phiroze Vasunia (eds) (2010) *Classics and National Cultures* (Oxford: Oxford University Press).

Stray, Christopher (1998) *Classics Transformed: schools, universities and society in England, 1830–1960* (Oxford: Oxford University Press).

— (forthcoming) 'Classics and Social Closure', in Edith Hall (ed.).

Sumner, D. L. (1963) *Education in Sierra Leone* (Freetown: The Government of Sierra Leone).

Taiwo, C. O. (1975) *Henry Carr: an African contribution to education* (Ibadan: Oxford University Press).

Tamumo T. H. (ed.) (1981) *Ibadan Voices* (Ibadan: Ibadan University Press).

Taylor, William H. (1996) *Mission to Educate: a history of the educational work of the Scottish Presbyterian mission in east Nigeria, 1846–1960* (Leiden: E.J. Brill).

Temple, Sir Charles (1968) (1918) *Native Races and their Rulers* (London: Frank Cass).

Thiong'o, Ngugi Wa (1986) *Decolonising the Mind: the politics of language in African literature* (London: James Currey).

Thompson, L. A. (1966) 'The Classics in Nigeria 1956–66', in Ferguson (ed.).

Tibenderana, Peter K. (2003) *Education and Cultural Change in Northern Nigeria 1906–1966: a study in the creation of a dependent culture* (Kampala: Fountain Publishers).

Tucker, Peter (1977) 'Students' Activities at Fourah Bay College', 57–9 in Celebrations Committee (ed.).

Ukeje, B. O. (1979) *Foundations of Education* (Benin City: Ethiopia Publishing).

Unsworth, Barry (2002) *The Songs of the Kings* (Harmondsworth: Penguin).

Van Weyenberg, Astrid (2010) 'Revolutionary Muse: Femi Osofisan's *Tegonni: An African Antigone*', in S. E. Wilmer and Audrone Zukauskaite (eds), *Interrogating Antigone in Postmodern Philosophy and Criticism* (Oxford: Oxford University Press).

Vasunia, Phiroze (2005) 'Greater Rome and Greater Britain', 38–64 in Goff (ed.).

— (2013) *Classics and Colonial India* (Oxford: Oxford University Press).

Viswanathan, Gauri (1989) *Masks of Conquest: literary study and British rule in India* (New York: Columbia University Press).

Wadley, W. J. D. (1938) *Tetefo anansesem abiesa bi*. Longman's Twi Series. With illustrations by E. A. Shearlock. Contents: Venetia guadini bi ho asem [after Shakespeare's Merchant of Venice] – Sindbad hyeng muni no [after Arabian nights] – Sika afurum no [after Apuleius's Golden ass] (London: Longmans, Green and Co. and Accra: Scottish Mission Book Depot).

Walker, Samuel Abraham (1847) *The Church of England Mission in Sierra Leone: including an introductory account of that colony, and a comprehensive sketch of the Niger expedition in the year 1841* (London: Seeley, Burnside and Seeley).

Wallbank, T. Walter (1934) 'The Educational Renaissance in British Tropical Africa', *The Journal of Negro Education* 3.1: 105–22.

— (1935) 'Achimota College and Educational Objectives in Africa', *The Journal of Negro Education* 4.2: 230–45.

Walters, Tracy L. (2007) *African American Literature and the Classicist Tradition: Black women writers from Wheatley to Morrison* (Basingstoke: Palgrave Macmillan).

Walton, M. B. na F. A. Acquaah kyeree ase (1946) *Romefo anansesem mu bi*. Contents: Ovid mu anansesem – Aeneid mu anansesem. Translation based on 'Stories from the Latin poets', arr. M.R. Pease. Published with the approval of the Education Department of the Gold Coast (Cape Coast, Ghana: Methodist Book Depot).

Waquet, Françoise (2001) *Latin or the Empire of a Sign* (London: Verso).

Ward, W. E. F. (1965) *Fraser of Trinity and Achimota* (Accra: Ghana Universities Press).

Wehrs, Donald (2008) *Pre-Colonial African in Colonial African Narratives: from Ethiopia Unbound to Things Fall Apart, 1911–1958* (Hampshire and Burlington, VT: Ashgate).

Wesley College Old Students' Association (ed.) (1985) *Wesley College Ibadan: 80th Anniversary Publication 1905–1985* (Ibadan: Ibadan University Press).

Wetmore, Kevin J. (2002) *The Athenian Sun in an African Sky* (Jefferson, NC: McFarland).

— (2003) *Black Dionysus* (Jefferson, NC: McFarland).

Whitehead, Clive (2003) *Colonial Educators: the British Indian and colonial education service 1858–1983* (New York: I.B .Tauris).

Wiles, Revd C. E. (1955) *Oron Boys' High School Fifty Years 1905–1955*. n.p.

Williams, C. Kingsley (1962) *Achimota : the early years, 1924–1948* (Accra: Longmans of Ghana).

Willis, Ika (2011) *Now and Rome* (London: Continuum).

Wilson, John (1996) 'Problems in Applying the Phelps-Stokes Report', 205–8 in Collins (ed.).

Wyse, Akintola J. G. (1989) *The Krio of Sierra Leone: an interpretive history* (London: C. Hurst and Co.).

— (1990) *H. C. Bankole-Bright and Politics in Colonial Sierra Leone, 1919–1958* (Cambridge: Cambridge University Press).

Yankah, Kwesi (1995) *Speaking for the Chief: ökyeame and the politics of Akan royal oratory* (Bloomington, IN: Indiana University Press).

Young, Robert J. C. (2011) 'The Afterlives of *Black Athena*', 174–88 in Orrells et al.

Zachernuk, Philip (1998) 'African History and Imperial Culture in Colonial Nigerian Schools', *Africa: Journal of the International African Institute*, 68.4: 484–505.

— (2000) *Colonial Subjects: an African intelligentsia and Atlantic ideas* (Charlottesville: University Press of Virginia).

Index